CAPTURING JONATHAN
POLLARD

CAPTURING JONATHAN POLLARD

How One of the
Most Notorious Spies
in American History Was
Brought to Justice

RONALD J. OLIVE
SPECIAL AGENT, NCIS (RET.)

The latest edition of this work has been brought to publication with the generous assistance of Marguerite and Gerry Lenfest.

Naval Institute Press
291 Wood Road
Annapolis, MD 21402

First Naval Institute Press paperback edition 2009.

ISBN 978-1-59114-647-6 (paperback)
ISBN 978-1-61251-454-3 (eBook)

The Library of Congress has cataloged the hardcover edition as follows:
Olive, Ronald J.
  Capturing Jonathan Pollard : how one of the most notorious spies in American history was brought to justice / Ronald J. Olive.
    p. cm.
  Includes bibliographical references and index.
  ISBN 1-59114-652-6 (alk. paper)
  1. Pollard, Jonathan Jay, 1954– 2. Spies—Israel—Biography. 3. Spies—United States—Biography. 4. Espionage, Israeli—United States—History—20th century. I. Title.
  UB271.I82O45 2006
  364.1'31—dc22

                                                                                    2006015639

♾ Print editions meet the requirements of ANSI/NISO z39.48-1992 (Permanence of Paper).
Printed in the United States of America.

18 17 16 15 14   6 5 4 3 2

Jacket and chapter opening images include unclassified surveillance photos extracted from the NIS evidence video of 15 and 18 November 1985. —PETER BURCHERT

To my wife, Gail,
my best friend and the most loving person
I have ever met and for
my dear mother and father and
our entire family.

CONTENTS

PREFACE

Over the course of eighteen months, between June 1984 and November 1985, Jonathan Jay Pollard, an intelligence analyst working in the U.S. Naval Investigative Service's Anti-Terrorist Alert Center (ATAC), illegally took highly sensitive national security secrets from almost every major intelligence-gathering agency in the United States for the purpose of providing them to a foreign government. What he took, and subsequently sold to Israel—more than one million pages of classified material—would fill a six-by-ten-foot room with the stacks rising six feet high. No other spy in the history of the United States has sold so highly classified documents, in such a short period of time, as Jonathan Jay Pollard. Tragically, long before he started spying, the Navy had many opportunities to fire him but didn't. As a result, his espionage activity did irreparable damage to the national defense of the United States.

I was the assistant special agent in charge of foreign counter-intelligence at the Naval Investigative Service's Washington, D.C., field office when the Pollard case broke wide open in November 1985. The account that follows tells the inside story of Jonathan Pollard, untold until now, and held closely by the government for the past twenty years. I interrogated Pollard and garnered the confession that helped lead to his arrest and subsequent conviction and life sentence.

Since 4 March 1987, controversy has swirled around the life sentence Pollard received. A handful of books and thousands of articles have been written, the majority of which denounce his sentence as unjust. What the public doesn't realize is that Pollard was a master of deceit and manipulation who repeatedly beat the system. Nor does the public realize the extent of the damage he inflicted.

Because his case never went to trial, and so much of the information surrounding it is still classified, over the years many unanswered questions have arisen. Uncertainty has fueled speculation, rumor, and lies, all fanned by the far-fetched stories Pollard himself makes up in his prison cell.

My goal in the following pages is to set the record straight. What bizarre behavior did Pollard exhibit that might have served as a red flag for espionage? How did security break down? What mistaken assumptions and leadership failures enabled him to continue ransacking America's defense intelligence? How was he really caught, and what went on inside the investigation? What did Pollard confess to immediately following his arrest and in debriefing sessions following his guilty plea? What other countries was he illegally involved with before and during his spying activities with Israel? What are the significant events of his life, while in prison, that keep him in the media today? What role did the so-called Weinberger memorandum play in Pollard's sentencing? These questions and many more will be answered for the first time.

The true Pollard story is a textbook case of a disastrous counter-intelligence failure. To this day, it haunts the people who held top management positions in the Department of the Navy when Pollard was active there. But out of tragedy come lessons. In addition to presenting a behind-the-scenes account, my hope is to provide vital insight into how Pollard's espionage activities could have been prevented. I will consider my effort in writing this book worthwhile if it raises awareness about the need for vigilance on the part of those entrusted with protecting the national defense secrets of the United States.

It was after five years in the U.S. Marine Corps and eight years in city law enforcement—working undercover operations and then working on organized crime in the intelligence unit—that I joined the Naval Investigative Service (NIS) as a civilian special agent. (Although in the mid-1980s, during the Pollard investigation, the NIS was renamed the Naval Security and Investigative Command [and today is known as the Naval Criminal Investigative Service], to prevent confusion I will stick to the acronym NIS throughout this book.)

After joining the NIS, I was assigned to the naval base in Charleston, South Carolina. I found myself increasingly interested in the world of counterintelligence and counterespionage operations many times called double-agent operations. Foreign governments committing or attempting to commit espionage against the United States have always been a major problem. Double-agent operations are conducted and designated to identify hostile agents recruiting military personnel or civilians and/or handling walk-in, wanna-be spies; take up the hostile foreign country's personnel time by providing them with a supposed provocateur, who pretends to be a legitimate spy; and identify what are called essential elements of information that every hostile country targeting the United States is trying to acquire through volunteers or recruiting American spies and other means. Following some training I took my first stab at recruiting a double agent. His name was William Tanner, a civilian engineer working on submarine communications at the Naval Electronics Engineering Command in Charleston. Tanner convinced an East German intelligence officer that he was a spy who was willing to sell his nation's secrets for money. The officer, Alfred Zehe, was arrested, and a subsequent trial in Boston culminated in his incarceration. He was later released in the largest spy swap in history.

In 1981, three years before Pollard met his Israeli spy handlers, I was assigned to the NIS field office in Naples, Italy, to work criminal cases. From this base I worked counter-narcotic operations during several U.S. Navy ship port calls. Both the NIS confidential source and the host country's police source would attempt to buy narcotics from drug dealers, and the local or federal police would make the arrest. I had the opportunity to go to Israel with Special Agent Steve Einsel to work one of these operations, and while there we took the time to sightsee, traveling to the border at the Golan Heights, visiting Bethlehem and the Garden of Olives, and eating lunch in the community kitchen of a kibbutz on Israel's remote northern border. It was the trip of a lifetime. Little did I know there would come a time when I would draw on my experiences in Israel to coax a confession from a person who would become one of the most notorious spies in U.S. history.

Eventually, back in Naples, I was assigned as the squad leader for foreign counterintelligence. My squad and I recruited and trained a double agent for an operation we initiated against the Soviet Intourist Bureau in Rome. Operation Sackett Land was launched some two years before Pollard's arrest. Ultimately this operation would lead to the defection of a Soviet KGB officer to the United States. The information he provided to the Central Intelligence Agency (CIA) and the Federal Bureau of Investigation (FBI) about American spies working for the Soviets was invaluable. In an incredible twist of fate, what he told them indirectly caused Jonathan Pollard's wife to panic while trying to dispose of Pollard's stacks of classified information. This set off a chain of events that led to the arrest of both husband and wife.

The information presented in the pages that follow is an accumulation of facts taken strictly from unclassified sources: extensive personal interviews with NIS and FBI agents and navy brass who were personally involved with the Pollard case; public court records; unclassified reports of the navy judge advocate general (JAG) administrative investigation; NIS reports; debriefing reports following Pollard's guilty plea, all retrieved under the Freedom of Information Act (FOIA); and my personal recollections of Pollard before and during the investigation. The information contained in this book was submitted to the Department of the Navy's Office of the Chief of Naval Operations, Information and Personnel Security Section, for a pre-publication security review. The content was authorized for public release and officially stamped on 15 June 2005 indicating there were "No security objections to open publication."

In writing this book, my goal is not to demonize Israel and its intelligence agents, regardless of the strain in diplomatic relations the Pollard case caused between that country and the United States. This is a sad story of how a close ally made a terrible mistake and was caught. Nor is my goal to demonize Pollard. I have tried to present the information about this highly publicized spy without bias, based on the facts of the case. I hold no personal grudge against him. He continues to fight for his freedom with great determination and wide exposure, and that is his right. But the fact remains that he lost his way because of a misguided notion that it was okay to sell his nation's secrets. He took the law into his own hands to "help" an ally, believing that, when the time came, Israel would save him from capture. This was a fatal miscalculation. When it was too late, he found no one to turn to, and in a panicked last-minute decision, made in the heart of the U.S. capital, he drove through the gates of the Israeli embassy only to discover it offered no asylum.

ACRONYMS

AIPAC	American Israel Public Affairs Committee
ATAC	Anti-Terrorist Alert Center
CAF	Central Adjudication Facility
CIA	Central Intelligence Agency
Code 22B	NIS Special Operations Division (Counterespionage)
DCID	Director of Central Intelligence Directive
DCII	Defense Central Index of Investigations
DIA	Defense Intelligence Agency
DIS	Defense Investigative Service
DNI	Director of Naval Intelligence
FBI	Federal Bureau of Investigation
FOIA	Freedom of Information Act
HPSCI	House Permanent Select Committee on Intelligence
JAG	Judge Advocate General
KGB	Committee for State Security (Soviet Union)
LAKAM	Lishka Lekisherey Mada (Israel Bureau of Scientific Relations)
MENAS	Middle East and North Africa Summary
NCIC	National Crime Information Center
NCIS	Naval Criminal Investigative Service
NFOIO	Navy Field Operational Intelligence Office
NIC	Naval Intelligence Command
NIS	Naval Investigative Service
NISC	Naval Intelligence Support Center
NOFORN	No Foreign Dissemination
NOSIC	Naval Ocean Surveillance Information Center
NPIC	National Photographic Interpretations Center

NSA	National Security Agency
ONI	Office of Naval Intelligence
PLO	Palestinian Liberation Organization
PRC	People's Republic of China
RAN	Royal Australian Navy
RASIN	Radio Signal Notations
SA	Special Agent
SCI	Sensitive Compartmented Information
SPINTCOM	Special Intelligence Communications
TF 168	Task Force (TF 168 conducted human intelligence positive military collection operations)
TS	Top Secret
WNINTEL	Warning Notice: Intelligence Sources and Methods Involved

CAPTURING JONATHAN
POLLARD

Chapter 1

A DREAM COME TRUE

In early June 1984, a bespectacled nearly thirty-year-old man with a dimpled chin, chubby cheeks, and wavy, receding hair left his modest apartment in Washington, D.C., and walked two blocks to the fashionable Hilton Hotel, spread across seven manicured acres at 1919 Connecticut Avenue. In the lobby, a sumptuous space lit up by a massive crystal chandelier, he glanced around and located the person he had come to meet for lunch, a stranger to him until now. After a quick consultation, the two decided to eat in the Hilton's refurbished coffee shop, at a corner table where no one would overhear their conversation.

It was a watershed moment in the life of this man—the first step in the culmination of a lifelong dream. For the guardians of America's national security, it was a disaster in the making. Jonathan Jay Pollard, a naval intelligence analyst, had

Hilton Hotel, Washington, D.C. —SHANNON OLIVE

recently been temporarily assigned to the ATAC, a newly established division of the NIS. As a watch stander, he was responsible for answering phones, interpreting classified information about potential terrorist activity, and writing draft reports for review before they were disseminated to the fleet. His position gave him access to the most highly classified material the defense intelligence community possessed.

His lunch partner, Israeli air force colonel Aviem Sella, was a striking, articulate man with a slightly pointed chin and a lean, trim build. A famed fighter jock and an Israeli national hero, he was the exact opposite of the bookish, baby-faced Pollard, who had been a social outcast for much of his life. Some said that Pollard was a wise guy and a troublemaker, a flamboyant, loose-lipped person who invited insults and basked in attention, whether positive or negative. The analyst claimed he was harassed because he was Jewish. Whatever the case, he had spent much of his life on the sidelines, and like many a sidelined youth, over the years he developed an active fantasy life. During his undergraduate years at Stanford University he told a lot of far-fetched tales, most notably, bragging to acquaintances about working for the Israeli foreign-intelligence agency Mossad and being a colonel in an elite Israeli army outfit. He dreamed of someday becoming a real spy. Now, after years of longing for it, his opportunity had arrived.

In the annals of spy lore, the encounter at the Hilton would have been laughable had it not led to such a disastrous result. Both the analyst and the air force colonel were wet behind the ears. Though, in the past, Pollard had tried to pass classified information off to various people, his attempts had been bungled. Despite all the big talk about working for Mossad, there is no indication that up to this point he had ever given someone classified information for money. As for Sella, he was a pilot and a student, not an intelligence operative. Currently he was attending New York University, working on his doctorate in computer science and raising money for Israeli bonds by lecturing about his combat missions. Sella was an excellent speaker, well known throughout the New York Jewish community for the riveting accounts he gave of his legendary exploits. But he knew little about the art of recruiting a spy.

When the two men met for lunch, both were nervous. Colonel Sella didn't know what to expect from the figure sitting across the table from him. Sure, someone had sung Pollard's praises, saying that he was a brilliant man and an ardent Zionist, but the person who made this claim was just a passing acquaintance. Was the colonel doing the right thing? Sella made up his mind not to say much of anything other than impressing the analyst with his background. He would just listen to what Pollard had to say and report it to his superior at the Israeli consulate in New York City, Yosef Yagur.

Although Pollard had his own reasons for being cautious, by nature he was less inclined to hold back. No sooner had they met than he pegged his lunch companion as the Chuck Yeager type, and his nerves began to settle. Before long, Sella was telling Pollard that he had shot down Soviet-piloted MiG aircraft over the Suez in 1969, and Pollard was addressing Sella as Avi. Anyone with Russian blood on his hands is all right with me, Pollard thought, and he began giving Sella a detailed description of the high-level access he had working for the ATAC.[1]

Israeli Air Force Colonel
Aviem Sella —AP/WWP

Pollard cited specific examples of what he could get his hands on, including documents classified TS for top secret and SCI for sensitive compartmented information, the U.S. government's highest classification level.[2] He had access to classified materials housed at the Defense Intelligence Agency (DIA), the CIA, the National Security Agency (NSA), the Naval Intelligence Command (NIC), the Naval Intelligence Support Center (NISC), and the National Photographic Interpretations Center (NPIC), among others, and he knew how to exploit security "chasms."[3] The analyst was blunt: he wanted to work as an undercover agent for Israel. His ultimate goal, he admitted, was to immigrate to Israel, but for now he was willing to stick with his job and exploit holes in the U.S. intelligence system on behalf of the Jewish homeland.

Sella was stunned. What this fellow was telling him was so incredible and so bold that, thinking it must be a setup, the Israeli glanced around the room to see if anyone was watching. "I can't believe that security is so lax in the U.S. government," he said with a skeptical look.

Pollard, a nonstop talker, kept chattering away about his access, claiming that he could get signal intelligence in addition to technical information. His manner was so convincing that Sella in turn began to relax. No one could be this bold and sincere at the same time. Pollard must be telling the truth.

The colonel had already been authorized by Yagur to set up another meeting as well as a clandestine communications plan, but only if he believed Pollard to be sincere. By now, Sella was sold. This was a golden opportunity, one that he couldn't let slip through his fingers.

Leaning forward on his elbows, Sella said they were going to set up a communications link using pay phones near Pollard's apartment. The analyst should locate several phones and write down their numbers. Not wasting a second, Pollard catapulted out of his seat and told his companion to wait right there, he would be back soon. About twenty minutes later, he returned to the coffee shop with the numbers scribbled on a piece of paper and handed it over. Sella assigned each phone number a one-letter code from the Hebrew alphabet.[4]

The plan was that the colonel would ring Pollard up at his residence at a specific time and give him the code letter that corresponded to a given pay phone. As soon as Pollard heard the Hebrew letter, he was to hang up, go to the appropriate phone, and wait for Sella to call with further instructions.

The colonel told him to bring to their next meeting anything he could get his hands on about Saudi Arabia and Soviet air defense systems. He needed several samples of the types of classified material to which Pollard had access. Then Sella began pushing the button to test his companion. In June 1981 the colonel had led a raid on a nuclear reactor facility in Tuwaitha, Iraq. He had been only verbally briefed following the mission and was dying to see the damage inflicted. Could Pollard produce satellite photos of the outcome?[5] Sella figured that if there were any such photographs being held by the United States, they were probably coded top secret. That would be a good test of Pollard's claims.

When lunch was finished, the two men parted ways with a warm handshake. Sella promised he would soon be in touch.

If the meeting had started with nervousness on both sides, it ended with joint elation. The colonel was under the impression that he would be Pollard's operational case officer. This was far different from downing Soviet MiGs, but it was thrilling just the same. As for Pollard, he was in his glory. Although the issue of pay had not been mentioned, for years he had been dreaming about espionage, and now here he was, exiting the Hilton with a secret code already established, an Israeli war hero as his handler, and a virtual warehouse of highly sensitive defense material to disclose. And this was only his first meeting. . . .

Barely keeping his joy in check, he hurried home. Pollard had a girlfriend, Anne Henderson, with whom he shared everything. Before his encounter with Sella he had told her about it, saying this was his big chance to help Israel, and she had encouraged him to go forward with the meeting. Now, as soon as he walked through the door of his apartment, he spilled everything to Anne. His dream was coming true. Not only was he about to become a spy for Israel but also, he was convinced—though no promises had been made—Israel was going to pay him. He and Anne were on their way to a better life.

> *"Insider betrayal is the most dangerous threat to our national security and national economy."*
>
> RON OLIVE
> Special Agent, NCIS

Chapter 2

POLLARD LAUNCHES HIS CAREER

J onathan Jay Pollard was born 7 August 1954, in Galveston, Texas, the youngest of three siblings in a close-knit, accomplished Jewish family whose patriarch, Dr. Morris Pollard, was a well-known research microbiologist. Before Jonathan reached his eighth birthday, Morris was offered a prestigious position as head of the Lobund Laboratory at Notre Dame University, and the family relocated to South Bend, Indiana.

A slender child with an inquisitive mind, Jonathan consumed books. He had a dimpled chin, thick brown hair always neatly combed from left to right, and full cheeks that were partially covered by owlish black-framed eyeglasses. Considered a sissy, he was an easy target at school. Bullies taunted him, chased him home, picked fights with him. As a result of the constant turmoil, his family decided to enroll Jonathan in a private Jewish school. There he flourished, playing the cello and reading every book he could lay his hands on.

His father traveled overseas extensively and often took the family along. While Jonathan was still in his early teens, they went to Germany and visited the concentration camp at Dachau. The experience shocked him, kindling a deep, enduring loyalty to Israel and the Jewish people. In 1970 Jonathan was accepted into the summer science school at the world-renowned Weizmann Institute in Israel. It was the most exhilarating time of his life, despite the trouble he had getting along with other students. One of his instructors alleged he was a troublemaker.

After finishing high school with honors, Pollard attended Stanford University, where he started using drugs and bragging about working as a secret agent for Mossad. Some of his classmates wrote him off as a kook, but others believed his crazy stories.

Naval Intelligence Support Center —NIS PHOTO

Pollard graduated with a degree in political science and was accepted into the Fletcher School of Law and Diplomacy at Tufts University in Boston. After attending Fletcher for two years, he failed to complete final papers in several courses and dropped out. This didn't matter to Pollard. The young man, whose only exposure to espionage at this point was likely to have been a John Le Carré novel or a James Bond movie, was eager to jump-start his career as a secret agent.

While looking for a job, Pollard came across an opening for a graduate fellowship with the CIA, headquartered in Langley, Virginia. The CIA called Pollard for an interview. At the time, the CIA was one of the few government agencies that required a polygraph examination of prospective employees. The polygraph questions were designed to uncover any circumstances that might make an employee susceptible to compromise or blackmail.

Pollard easily skated through the security questions. No, he had never had access to classified information. Yes, he had used Thai sticks and hashish one time, and had smoked marijuana—not on just a few occasions, but about six hundred times, between July 1974 and March 1978.[1] Needless to say, he was turned down for the job.

During the summer of 1979 Congress approved a grant for the navy to hire thirty intelligence analysts. Pollard applied for a position with the Navy Field Operational Intelligence Office (NFOIO) located in Suitland, Maryland, which was part of the NISC. Rear Admiral Thomas A. Brooks, U.S. Navy (Ret.), who was a captain at the time, informed me that he hired

Pollard in September of that year as an intelligence research specialist to work on Soviet issues. Pollard, like most young analysts hired right out of college, had to be trained from the ground up.

His position required a security clearance for top secret (TS) and sensitive compartmented information (SCI) classifications. SCI clearances, which allow access to some of the United States' most closely guarded defense secrets, are given only to military and civilian personnel with a "need to know" for their specific area of concentration. Pollard also had to undergo a special background investigation ensuring that he was trustworthy and stable enough to handle such highly sensitive information.

In those days the Defense Investigative Service, or DIS (now called the Defense Security Service), had the responsibility of conducting background investigations for personnel requiring special clearances. Background investigations took an enormous amount of time, and by mid-November 1979, the DIS wasn't close to finishing Pollard's. His first assignment was to get a feel for how the Soviets were thinking by studying Soviet history, culture, and publications. He spent a lot of time at the Library of Congress conducting research while waiting for the clearance to come through. At the end of the month, Pollard was granted an interim TS clearance after a national agency check revealed no criminal background and no incriminating information from any of the agencies consulted, including the CIA, the FBI's National Crime Information Center and identification fingerprint division, and the Department of State's passport office.

On 7 December the navy special security officer who authorized SCI clearances provided Pollard's command with an interim waiver giving him temporary access to SCI as well. It is common practice to issue waivers; without them, commands could not immediately place hired personnel in the specific sensitive jobs they were initially hired for. In essence, however, this creates a "Catch 22" situation. The waiver would expire in August 1980, at which point, Pollard hoped, the background investigation would be complete. Immediately after being indoctrinated into several SCI programs, he was assigned as a watch stander in the Naval Ocean Surveillance Information Center (NOSIC), a component of the NFOIO.[2]

At one point during the background investigation, the DIS asked the CIA for any information it might have on Pollard. The CIA claimed—

mistakenly, it turns out—that Pollard's right to privacy prevented it from releasing information on him.[3] Thus the DIS never learned that Pollard's application for a position with the CIA had been outright rejected.

This job was his first exposure to extremely sensitive national security information. With it, Pollard entered the rarefied world of which he had only dreamed as a child, a world where he could physically lay his hands on defense secrets that just a select few in the United States, the most powerful nation on earth, ever had the occasion to share.

Admiral Brooks remembered Pollard at this time as being an impressive, smart, knowledgeable young man. Nothing had showed up in the background investigation that caused concern about his employment. "The CIA," Brooks lamented, "didn't tell the navy they had kicked him out."[4]

At the time, Mr. Richard Haver was technical director of the NFOIO and the special assistant to then-Captain Brooks. Haver was the first person at the center to sense that Pollard was a potential danger.

One afternoon in the late fall of 1979, Pollard approached Haver outside the NFOIO and informed him that he had contacts with the South African government. He expressed concern that the navy was having problems keeping track of merchant vessels and gunrunners operating out of the South Atlantic. Pollard offered to solve the problem; all he needed was permission to run a back-channel collection operation against the South Africans. His father had been the CIA station chief at the American embassy in South Africa, Pollard claimed. As a renowned microbiologist, Morris Pollard traveled extensively overseas giving lectures and attending conferences, and he was on the board of several government agencies, including the Defense Department. What his son told Haver was patently false—Morris did not work for the CIA, nor was he ever assigned to the U.S. embassy in South Africa. Jonathan also told Haver that he knew a South African intelligence officer from college, which was true.

Haver was taken aback, not least because Pollard's comment about his father was probably a downright lie. How could an analyst who was still wet behind the ears make such an absurd, brazen proposal?[5] Haver had heard many stories about Pollard during the time he was waiting for his clearance to come through. Apparently, he had impressed some people with his intellectual capabilities; others just thought he was an oddball.

Haver listened politely to Pollard's proposal, made some non-committal answer, and promptly went to Captain Brooks, saying that he thought the analyst had the makings of a troublemaker and should be terminated. Brooks heard Haver out and told him he would look into the matter. Haver repeated his recommendation: Pollard should be fired, right then. After all, the analyst had been on the job for merely a couple of months. He was still on probation. All Brooks had to do was tell him his services weren't needed and that would be the end of it.

Captain Brooks had a background in military human intelligence. Rather than heeding Haver's warning about firing the analyst, Brooks decided that Pollard, because he had claimed to have a connection with South African intelligence, might be useful to Task Force 168 (TF 168), a secret outfit that ran operations to collect human intelligence for the navy. It operated under tight constraints and focused solely on collecting military intelligence from certain designated countries. The CIA coordinated its efforts and monitored it closely. TF 168, as I understand it, dealt strictly with positive intelligence collection, that is, using human sources to collect information.

In February 1980 Captain Brooks, apparently believing Pollard not to be a threat, turned him over to TF 168 as a possible recruit. Pollard was vetted by the outfit as a potential collection source while retaining his analyst position under Brooks. In vetting Pollard, TF 168 did a background interview instead of a background check. During the interview, Pollard claimed to have applied for a commission to become an officer in the Naval Reserve. This was false. He also misrepresented his educational accomplishments, overstated his language ability, failed to mention his history of drug use, and, again, lied about his father's relationship with the CIA.[6] TF 168 hired Pollard on.

A month later a position opened at the NISC's surface ships systems division in Suitland, Maryland. Looking for a pay increase, Pollard applied for the position. Since his business with TF 168 was conducted on the side, he was able to work for both outfits simultaneously. He told TF 168 the story of his connection with a South African naval intelligence officer whom he had befriended in graduate school. Later the officer returned to South Africa, but not before introducing Pollard to the naval attaché at the South African embassy in Washington D.C.

In the late 1970s and early 1980s, the United States and most of the free world shut off South Africa from intelligence sharing because of that country's official policy of apartheid and the atrocities associated with it. The one democratic country that allegedly refused to do so was Israel. Intelligence information and media reports claimed that the South Africans were getting ready to test Jericho missiles capable of carrying a nuclear device, and that Israel was very much interested in the results.

TF 168, the super-sleuth command of the navy, insisted that Pollard not tell anyone about their association. Pollard turned right around and told no less than four supervisors in the surface ships division. Moreover, he could not resist bragging to his coworkers about his personal encounters with official representatives of South Africa.[7] Why, one might ask, did the man draw attention to himself with such reckless abandon? For, as it turns out, Pollard was engaging in more than just braggadocio. In fact, it was at this stage of his career that he first passed highly classified information to someone who had no need to know.

During his debrief session in July 1986 following his arrest and guilty plea, Pollard "said he approached the South Africans on his own initiative (1979/80) in order to obtain information on a Soviet ship transiting the South Atlantic that was of interest to the U.S. Navy. Pollard was given a photograph of the ship in question by the South African, and Pollard later gave the South African a photograph of a Soviet submarine stationed at Luanda (Pollard obtained the photograph from work). Pollard said he reported this contact to his Navy supervisor and was later put in contact with TF 168, which wanted to collect information on South Africa through Pollard."[8]

Pollard hoped to convince the navy of his established relationship and therefore be given permission to mount an operation against the South Africans. It was after these contacts with South Africa that he approached his supervisor. Pollard never revealed to the Israelis his prior involvement with the South African embassy.

Pollard later contended in court records that he had never passed classified information to South African government officials without authorization from his handlers at TF 168. He was trying to cover himself. In an unclassified portion of an NIS briefing report, however, he did admit to disclosing classified information, without authorization, to a South African representative. The information concerned foreign ship and troop movements, and equipment and shipment of aircraft involving three separate countries.[9] Pollard did this, he claimed, to curry favor with the South Africans.

In Pollard's sentencing motion before the court, his comments relating to his association with South Africa—with the exception of one sentence—were redacted. In reply to Pollard's motion, close to eight pages of the government's response were also redacted and classified secret because they provided specific details about involvement with the South Africans.

No evidence has ever shown that Pollard took money from any South Africans, and the U.S. government never charged him with passing classified information to South Africa. He seemed to possess a sense of inflated importance and a keen desire for recognition—traits the CIA's polygraph test hadn't detected. It was just a matter of time before his ego burst any remaining constraints and took to the skies.

In March 1980 Rear Admiral Sumner Shapiro, then-director of naval intelligence (DNI), met Pollard for the first time at a party commemorating the anniversary of the Office of Naval Intelligence (ONI). The affair was held at the plush Naval Officers Club in Bethesda, Maryland. Admiral Shapiro and his wife were fulfilling their duty in the receiving line, greeting people as they arrived, when along came Jonathan Pollard, accompanied by a young civilian friend. Planting himself in front of the admiral, Pollard began talking nonstop. Shapiro smiled and rattled off a few pleasantries, then turned to the next person in line. But Pollard would not stop talking. This kid is strange, Shapiro thought. Pollard almost had to be pried away from the receiving line. Later, the analyst and his companion approached the admiral again and rambled on for about half an hour.

It was obvious to Shapiro that Pollard was trying to suck up to the boss and impress his friend by talking with the DNI. He was "a young kid desperately seeking attention, very immature and loose with the truth," the admiral told me.[10] Though mildly annoyed, Shapiro didn't give the incident much more thought.

Around the time of that anniversary party, Pollard was growing increasingly distressed. He had laid out his plans to initiate a collection operation against the South Africans, and TF 168 wasn't listening. Pollard then demanded a meeting with the DNI to explain his plan of action. (Pollard evidently told the people at TF 168 that he personally knew the DNI, and if they didn't listen to him, surely Admiral Shapiro would.) TF 168 caved in to the pressure, and on 16 April 1980, Pollard showed up at Shapiro's door for a meeting.[11]

Somebody in the admiral's chain of command had decided this meeting was important enough to schedule. Word had filtered up to Shapiro that there was a young civilian analyst claiming to have had contact with a South African attaché. Because relations with South Africa were strained, South African operatives might be trying to penetrate the ONI. The last thing the admiral needed was some young kid playing James Bond.[12]

Present at the meeting were Admiral Shapiro's executive assistant, Commander Francis Carden, two representatives from TF 168, and two CIA representatives.[13] As soon as Pollard walked into the office, Shapiro recognized him as the guy from the party in Bethesda who had made a pest of himself.

Pollard launched into a detailed account of how he had visited South Africa while his father worked there, presumably under the auspices of the CIA—the same old tale he had reeled off to Rich Haver and Captain Brooks. "We've got a kook on our hands!" the admiral exclaimed after Pollard had finished his presentation and left the office.[14] At their first encounter Pollard had merely been a blip on the admiral's radar. Now Shapiro was worried. Had South Africa recruited this fellow? He would have to check Pollard out and get him under control.

The admiral ordered Pollard moved to a job that didn't require access to TS/SCI material.[15] Captain Brooks, informed of Shapiro's decision, immediately set the process in motion, informing the commander in charge of the NOSIC and the operations officer that he wanted Pollard moved out of the SCI environment.

According to the JAG manual investigation, arrangements were made to move Pollard within the same complex, to the Soviet/free world merchant ship division at the NISC, where he would be required to have only a secret clearance. During the same time period, however, Pollard was hired for the new GS-7 position in NISC-33 he had applied for previously. The problem the command faced was that in his new position, Pollard still needed an SCI clearance. He worked in the merchant ship division for merely two weeks before he formally changed jobs on 4 May 1980. He moved from his first position at NFOIO, a command dealing with operational intelligence, to NISC, where the focus was on scientific and technical intelligence.[16] Pollard was right back in the middle of access to SCI information. The ball was dropped somewhere along the line, and Pollard managed to beat the system—if only temporarily.

Meanwhile, in response to a request from Admiral Shapiro's office, TF 168 arranged to have the CIA assess Pollard's operational trustworthiness. The CIA evaluators spoke with Pollard and listened to his story, trying to determine the potential for problems were he to conduct operational activities. Afterwards they informed Admiral Shapiro that in their opinion Pollard was a risk and shouldn't be used in any collection operation. Precisely what they said is unknown because the full CIA assessment remains classified.

Admirals grow accustomed to people trying to butter them up. Sycophants pop up out of nowhere, and if an admiral is lucky, they vanish. Little did Admiral Shapiro know that the eccentric man who had tried to make a good impression on him in the receiving line at the Bethesda Naval Officers Club wasn't going away any time soon. The name Jonathan Pollard would come to haunt him for decades.

Chapter 3

THE DOUBLE-AGENT RUSE

■■■

fter Pollard became an analyst in the NISC's scientific and intelligence division (NISC-33), unbeknownst to anyone at his command, he began whisking TS/SCI material out of the office and taking it home. He would read the material and bring it back to work the next morning—but not all of it. Some remained in his apartment.[1]

Meanwhile, Admiral Shapiro, still struggling to find out what Pollard was up to, if anything, put in a call to Special Agent Sherman Bliss, deputy director of the NIS as well as Shapiro's special assistant for counterintelligence and investigations. Shapiro told Agent Bliss about the growing suspicion that Pollard had made overtures to the South Africans without the navy's knowledge. Could Bliss help clarify the analyst's activities? Bliss had an idea: the NIS could tell Pollard that it was considering using him in a double-agent role. Blindly ambitious, the analyst seemed keen on being a double agent. Whether he liked it or not, he would have to agree to undergo the assessment required of any candidate for the job. It was a promising ploy, and Admiral Shapiro promptly gave his authorization.[2]

Code 22B, the NIS's special operations division, was responsible for conducting counterespionage double-agent operations. Special Agent Kenneth Anthony, Code 22B's supervisor, had recently received orders to take over an NIS office in Japan, and because he was leaving in a few weeks, he assigned Special Agent John Odom, an operations desk officer with a lot of Code 22B experience, to be Pollard's case control agent. In an allusion to his impending departure, Anthony named the scheme Operation Swan Song and, for reporting purposes, assigned Pollard the code name Sy O Nara.[3]

TF 168 informed Pollard that the NIS was thinking of using him as a double agent. Pollard was ecstatic, no doubt under the impression that his talk with the DNI had borne fruit. When some eighteen years later I asked Bliss for his take on Pollard, he replied, "In my opinion, Pollard was a wanting spy with a budding 007 complex."[4] The NIS had to make this look good so as not to raise any suspicions that it was a sham. First, Pollard was officially transferred from TF 168 to Code 22B. Then, on 16 July 1980, he was introduced to his new case handler, Special Agent Odom.[5]

Getting Pollard on the polygraph was the only reason this scheme had been undertaken in the first place. Oddly, as it turned out, he didn't know that potential double agents had to submit to a lie detector test. Caught unawares, and having already committed serious security violations, the analyst wasn't prepared for the trauma that lay ahead.

The person chosen to administer the examination was Special Agent Milt Addison, the very man who had developed the NIS's counterintelligence polygraph program. He had a pleasant personality, but at six feet five inches tall, his imposing figure could intimidate someone answering questions with sensors attached to his chest, fingers, and arm. Before the encounter, Agent Anthony gave Addison a limited briefing, deliberately omitting the fact that Operation Swan Song was a ruse so that he wouldn't go into the examination with a biased opinion.

Hilton Hotel, Springfield, Virginia —RON OLIVE

Addison needed to have an open mind, unclouded by anything Anthony or Odom might tell him about the subject.

In recruiting double agents, it was standard NIS operating procedure to meet in a secure, relaxing, quiet environment where a polygraph test and interviews could be con-ducted without interruption and without producing anxiety in the candidate. Odom contacted Pollard and arranged to meet him on 23 July at the Hilton Hotel, where I-395 crosses Old Keene Mill Road in

Springfield, Virginia. Though he didn't want to scare Pollard, Odom did want to catch him off guard, and for that reason the analyst wasn't told beforehand that Agent Addison would be present to administer a polygraph.

Agents Addison and Odom were waiting for Pollard in separate adjoining rooms. Pollard arrived, entered Odom's room, and was informed of the procedure to recruit him as a double agent. Odom handed him a declaration of cooperation, which he would have to sign before going any further. The document read:

> I, Jonathan Jay Pollard, voluntarily agree to assist the Naval Investigative Service in a counterintelligence matter in the interest of the United States and to maintain absolute secrecy concerning this relationship. I understand that all information, equipment, funds, or other material obtained from a hostile service as a result of this operation are the property of the U.S. Government. Further, I understand and agree that I may be administered periodic polygraph examinations (lie detector tests) as a matter of operational security. This relationship may be terminated at any time by either me or the Naval Investigative Service. After termination, I will not disclose this relationship or any information acquired by me during it without the express consent of the Naval Investigative Service.[6]

Although the declaration said that he might have to undergo a polygraph, it didn't say that an agent was sitting in the very next room ready to administer one. Pollard signed the declaration with boyish zeal. No sooner was the ink dry than he was ushered into the adjoining room and introduced to Agent Addison. It would be a long ordeal for all, starting around six thirty in the evening and not ending until three thirty the following morning.

"It was the hardest polygraph I ever did," Agent Addison later recalled, adding that after the first series of questions, "Pollard went bonkers." That is, he began shouting and shaking and making gagging sounds as if he were about to vomit. Pollard repeatedly staggered into the bathroom. Although he may have had an upset stomach owing to stress, Addison believed that he was faking his sickness.[7] Addison assured him that he was free to stop the test at any time. Pollard agreed to continue, but he reacted negatively to every question.

The first set of questions concerned possible security violations: Have you given us any false or misleading information about your background? Have you ever had contact with a foreign intelligence agent? Have you ever provided classified material to an unauthorized person? Have you ever associated with a dissident or subversive organization? Have you told anyone about your contact with NIS?

The second set of questions involved lifestyle: Have you ever committed a serious crime for which you were not caught? Have you ever been involved with illegal drugs or narcotics?[8]

One of the strongest negative readings on Pollard's polygraph had to do with unauthorized contact with a foreign intelligence agent and providing classified information to an unauthorized person. He also fared poorly on counterintelligence questions asking whether he had given false or misleading information about his background. According to Addision, his reactions produced "very ragged" polygraph charts. Whatever lies he was telling, Pollard did admit, however, to prior drug use, making false statements, and making unauthorized contacts with the representatives of a foreign government.[9]

Addison tried everything conceivable to calm the analyst down, giving him soda, numerous breaks, anything he wanted, but no matter what he tried, it was fruitless. The agent explained that it was important to verify or refute certain information in the answers, but because of Pollard's emotional reactions, Addison couldn't get him completely through any question. In the end, Addison judged the entire exam "inconclusive," meaning Pollard had been unable to clarify the gray areas. He would have to retake the test at another time. Alas, that time never arrived.

Following the test, Addison filled out a technical data sheet documenting the results. Never before in his eighteen years of conducting polygraph exams, he commented, had he formed such a strong opinion about someone's need to seek professional medical help. Pollard should never be used as a double agent, Addison stated emphatically, nor should he be granted access to highly sensitive information.[10]

Pollard appeared to have developed an aversion to the NIS, and I believe it was this polygraph exam that precipitated it.[11]

On 24 July, Agent Addison briefed Agent Bliss and the NIS's assistant director for counterintelligence, Special Agent Ronald Ruesch, about the polygraph session. The two agents immediately contacted Admiral Shapiro, informing him of the polygraph results and recommending possible courses of action. These included removing Pollard's security clearances, firing him if it were administratively and operationally feasible, and getting him an emotional evaluation. The navy contacted Dr. Neil Hibler, a clinical psychologist with the U.S. Air Force Office of Special Investigations. He was the first psychologist to also become a trained investigator in the federal government. Dr. Hibler consulted with law enforcement agencies to help them determine candidates' fitness for duty and counterintelligence. Based on his interview with Pollard, Dr. Hibler recommended that Pollard not be employed in an operational capacity. He further recommended that Pollard's work-related access be temporarily suspended and he be assigned nonsensitive administrative duties.[12] Hibler provided Pollard's command with the names of four mental health professionals in the Washington, D.C., area who had high security clearances. Any of them could perform a mental fitness-for-duty evaluation of Pollard.

Less than two weeks later, detailed polygraph reports—probably written by Agent Odom—were turned over to the NISC's outgoing commanding officer, Captain Jean Sheets, who in turn briefed Captain Chauncey Hoffman, prospective commanding officer of the NISC. The JAG manual administrative investigation* stated that neither man requested additional assistance from the NIS regarding Pollard's admissions about drugs, false statements, and unauthorized contact with the representatives of a foreign country. Nor did NIS director Captain Jerry Soriano look further into the matter.[13]

Later, after he'd retired as an admiral, Hoffman told me that initially he believed Pollard should be given the ax. Evidently Rear Admiral John Butts, commander of the NIC, informed Hoffman that this wasn't an option. I never discovered why the navy command was so reluctant to get

---

*A JAG manual investigation is an administrative investigation based on chapters II through VI of the Manual of the Judge Advocate General. The command having custodial responsibility for the material compromised convenes the investigation. The purpose of a JAG manual investigation is to answer, in detail, questions about the who, what, where, when, and why of the security violation. The JAG manual investigation gives the command an opportunity to make a critical review of its security posture. The terms JAG manual investigation, JAG manual administrative investigation, JAG's administrative investigation, and JAG investigation will be used interchangeably in the text.

rid of Pollard. It should be pointed out, however, that terminating civilian employees in the 1980s was perceived to be all but impossible. Most officers considered it a highly risky business, because if the employee sued and won, it was the officer who would pay the price. No officer wanted a lawsuit hanging over him on his watch. The fact that a lot of time and effort went into grooming new analysts might also help explain their reluctance.

At any rate, according to the JAG investigation, "The decision to allow Pollard continued access to secret material was based on the fact that while there were serious misgivings about his judgment, it was not clear that he represented a security risk of sufficient degree to warrant termination of all his access to classified information, which for all practical purposes, [would mean] his termination. It was the view of both Admiral Butts and Admiral Shapiro that Mr. Pollard was worth attempting to salvage, but only if the risks were kept to a minimum by reducing his access and keeping him under close monitoring."[14] Admiral Shapiro obviously didn't know that Pollard was in a new job that required TS and SCI clearances.

On 6 August, Agent Odom and NIS Special Agent Michael Barrett met with Pollard. According to the report they wrote up afterwards, he was "in good spirits. . . . At first he appeared to be somewhat on guard, but he soon relaxed and became quite talkative."[15] At this meeting Pollard was terminated as a double agent.

Toward the end of the month, Pollard's commanding officer informed him he was being reassigned to less sensitive duties, and he transferred from NISC-33, Soviet surface combatants, back to NISC-34, Soviet merchant ships. Pollard inquired if his new assignment was permanent. If not, could he return to his previous position? The command told him that was a possibility, but they made no promises.[16] On 28 August the analyst was formally debriefed from all his TS/SCI code-word programs and his clearance was reduced to secret.

In mid-September 1980, while the navy was trying to figure out what to do with Pollard, his one-year probationary period ended. For a non-veteran excepted civil service employee, it was a significant milestone. "Had he been fired for cause during that probation period, Mr. Pollard would not have had recourse to the remedies available to career employees under the civilian personnel system,"[17] Captain Laurence Schuetz later wrote in his report for the JAG's administrative investigation. Two months later, Pollard was promoted to GS-9 and was earning more than eighteen thousand a year.

Pollard should have been fired or relieved of his duties for any one of the admissions he made during the NIS polygraph. It would have been within the navy's rights to terminate the analyst without giving him a reason, though the people in charge of his case, admirals Butts and Shapiro and captains Hoffman and Brooks, might not have realized this. Certainly the decision not to lay him off didn't arise out of stupidity or incompetence, for these were highly intelligent, accomplished officers. Perhaps in the end their decision was based on a sincere desire to give a brilliant young man who had the potential to be a great analyst a second chance. Unfortunately, not firing Pollard when they had the opportunity would be the worst personnel decision they ever made.

The reluctance of navy leaders to fire Pollard proved fatal for the national defense of the United States. It was a counterintelligence failure of catastrophic proportions, yet the signs of trouble were obvious from the very beginning.

Chapter 4

POLLARD'S BATTLE WITH THE NAVY

ollard could have continued to work for the navy with a secret
clearance and nothing more would have been said, but because he
wanted his TS/SCI clearance back at all costs, it was imperative
that he obtain an evaluation of his mental health. According to Mark
Shaw in his book *Miscarriage of Justice*, Pollard approached his father
for advice on which psychiatrist to choose. This, despite the fact that
Pollard had the names of four security-cleared psychologists. Morris
Pollard got in touch with an acquaintance who recommended Dr. Neil
Pauker, based at Johns Hopkins. Pauker "saw Jay several times and
pronounced him fit," Morris told Shaw.[1] (Pollard preferred for people
to call him Jay.)

With this clean bill of health, Pollard was positive he would get his
SCI clearance back. In October 1980 he provided Captain Hoffman,
commander of the NISC, with a copy of Pauker's evaluation and
informed him that he wanted his clearance restored immediately. Not so
fast, Pollard was told. Because this was a navy matter involving fitness
for duty, he would first have to receive an evaluation from one of the
four previously mentioned security-cleared psychologists.

Not pleased with Captain Hoffman's response, Pollard filed a
grievance against him on 3 February 1981, and addressed it to Admiral
Butts, commander of the NIC. Though the navy redacted sections of the
grievance, this is the gist of it:

> During the spring and summer of 1980 I was employed as an
> analyst by NISC-33, working on Soviet surface combatants. At
> this time I was also involved in a rather sensitive collection effort
> outside NISC that eventually resulted in my being turned over

to the Naval Investigative Service (NIS) for reasons of personal safety. Due to the severe mental and physical mistreatment I experienced at the hands of NIS (they had apparently forgotten on whose side I was), I asked my branch head for help in extracting myself from what was fast becoming an intolerable situation.[2]

Pollard went on to complain about his transfer from NISC-33 to NISC-34. In failing to inform him that the transfer would be permanent, Captain Hoffman had not been forthright: "[H]is actions have . . . prevented me from advancing in my career, humiliated me in the eyes of my coworkers, caused me extreme financial hardship, and produced a degree of mental trauma in my life that I find unbearable."

Pollard claimed that because he had "agreed to this set of humiliating conditions under protest," he "should have received written orders explaining the actions expected" of him.

Whether this latter oversight was committed unconsciously or not I have no way of determining, but it was a significant omission by the command and is the root cause of this grievance.

Even though I was physically moved to NISC-34, organizationally I was still considered as filling a NISC-33 billet by the relevant branch/division heads seeing to the firsthand observations of my mental competency and the consequent expectation that I would be coming back to my old position in short order. In the meantime, however, another complication arose that affected a promotion I was due for in September. Both my former and then current supervisors had approved a grade jump from GS-7 to GS-9 as part of my career ladder advancement. I was not officially informed of this promotion until December due to the indirect intimidation of the responsible branch chief. . . .[3]

On 16 March Pollard received a memorandum from the NIC commander with his findings. "Based on a thorough review and investigation" of Pollard's grievance, Butts stated, "it has been determined the relief you seek cannot be granted." The actions taken by the NISC's commanding officer were in accordance with navy regulations and the policy of the

Office of Personnel Management. The command, moreover, had the right to reassign an employee to a position of equal grade. "This decision is final and there is no additional right of appeal," Butts concluded.[4]

Pollard conceded, and in March and April had several appointments with an approved navy doctor. "Pollard is thoroughly capable of handling the duties of his job and does not represent a risk to security," the doctor concluded. He added, however, that "Mr. Pollard needed additional mental health therapy."[5]

After receiving the psychologist's evaluation of Pollard in late April, Captain Hoffman sent a memo to the navy special security officer, Captain Earl DeWispelaere, who handled all requests for SCI clearances, inquiring whether Pollard's adjudication process was still pending because there had been no response since December 1980. He wanted to be notified in writing concerning Pollard's current eligibility for an SCI clearance.[6] In early May Captain DeWispelaere sent Admiral Butts a summary of Pollard's history, and Butts in turn wrote to Captain Hoffman with DeWispelaere's comments:

[S]ubject was given access to Sensitive Compartmented Information (SCI) based on a waiver granted on December 7, 1979. He was debriefed by the NISC Command Security Officer (CSO) on June 9, 1980, for [SCI compartments] GG/CY/CL/MA/DN . . . and on August 28, 1980, he was debriefed for [SCI compartments] SI/GG/TK/ES and placed in a non-SI [special intelligence] billet. His debrief occurred prior to . . . eligibility being granted. Accordingly, his case was closed and [is] not pending. An eligibility determination is not appropriate since the subject was not at the time of adjudication in an SI billet nor is he occupying one now.

Commander, Naval Intelligence Command, makes eligibility determinations for access to SCI on all "suitable" nominees. Procedures for nominating personnel are contained in paragraph 1133 of the Navy Department. . . .[7]

In mid-May Captain Hoffman requested that Captain DeWispelaere make yet another determination about Pollard's eligibility. DeWispelaere responded once again, making his point as clear as possible: "He is not a suitable candidate for SCI access . . . accordingly, request submission of another individual to occupy SCI billet. . . ."[8] There were inconsistencies in the dates of employment entered on Pollard's personal qualification statement and on his official personnel file, but DeWispelaere didn't discover these.

Frustrated by all the hurdles, Pollard informed his supervisor that he had a lawyer, and if his clearance was not restored he would pursue legal action to regain his SCI access should it prove necessary.[9] That message apparently reached the higher echelon.

On 21 July, Pollard wrote a memorandum to Admiral Butts requesting that Captain Hoffman "be advised that I am a suitable nominee for access to SCI. . . ."[10] The next day Captain Hoffman conceded to Pollard's demands. In a memorandum to Admiral Butts, Hoffman wrote that Pollard was highly intelligent and doing a great job in his position with the merchant ships division: "Mr. Pollard has steered a straight course. . . . In fact, his former supervisors in the Surface Ship Division at NISC strongly desire that he return to his old position because of his excellent analytical abilities. . . . It would be my recommendation that Mr. Pollard's access to SCI be reinstated."[11]

This memo was forwarded to the new navy special security officer, Captain Milton Lloyd McCutcheon, with a request for yet another opinion on Pollard's eligibility for SCI access. On 4 August Captain McCutcheon informed Admiral Butts, "Given the history to date, I cannot recommend that Mr. Pollard be given access to SCI." His report included extracts from various reports, one of them the NIS assessment from the previous year.[12]

That fall Captain Hoffman sent yet another memo to Admiral Butts recommending that Pollard's access to SCI be reinstated and asking for a status report on his clearance.[13] It may be that Hoffman was concerned about mounting threats from Pollard to sue the U.S. Navy and everyone involved.

In October 1981, after receiving outstanding evaluations saying that he had performed his duties above and beyond expectation, Pollard was promoted from a GS-9 step 2 to a GS-11 step 1. He was now making more than twenty-four thousand dollars a year. So far, the lack of SCI clearance wasn't curtailing his career advancement, but that didn't stop the analyst from aggressively pursuing his dream. He wanted to be somebody again. Having once tasted the thrill of reading highly sensitive documents, and having enjoyed the prestige that came with it, he desperately wanted his clearance back.

And that's just what Jonathan Pollard got. In the report of the investigation conducted by the JAG years later, Admiral Butts was said to have ordered the reinstatement of the analyst's TS/SCI access in mid-January 1982. Before reportedly making this decision, Butts consulted with the DNI, Admiral Shapiro. He concurred, the clearance should be restored; nevertheless, Pollard would still have to be watched closely. Shapiro gave specific instructions about this, asking for quarterly reports on Pollard's progress.[14]

In an interview I had with Butts years later, in his retirement, he admitted that he was the person responsible for keeping Pollard on. He emphatically stated that contrary to what Captain Schuetz had written in his JAG investigation report, he, Butts, did not authorize or restore the TS/SCI clearance. According to Butts, he decided that Pollard could retain his *secret* clearance only. His work would have to be monitored, and eventually, *if* he kept up his work, he could be reinstated and briefed back into SCI programs.

Whatever the case may be, Pollard's SCI access was restored on 19 January 1982.

No one in the office of the DNI, NIC, or NISC asked the NIS for assistance in monitoring Pollard's activities. He was reassigned to his old position as an analyst with NISC-33, reporting to Captain Hoffman. On 20 April, after carefully monitoring him for three months, Hoffman submitted his first quarterly report to Admiral Shapiro. Pollard's performance and behavior, he informed the DNI, had been outstanding. Among other accomplishments, the analyst had authored nearly a dozen NISC weekly wires, briefed a naval sea technology advisory group on the Falklands crisis, and increased production from his fellow analysts. His supervisor had received complimentary remarks after a briefing Pollard gave to another command on the Indian Ocean navies. "Pollard applies himself with great dedication," Hoffman pointed out, adding with rather naive sincerity, "He routinely works a ten-hour day and at times on weekends."[15]

To the seasoned Admiral Shapiro, working long hours and weekends was a red flag for possible espionage, especially considering Pollard's

DEPARTMENT OF THE NAV
NAVAL INTELLIGENCE SUPPORT CE
4301 Suitland Road
Washington, DC. 20390

MEMORANDUM FOR THE DIRECTOR OF NAVAL INTELLIGENC

Via: Deputy Director of Naval Intelligence

Subj: Quarterly Update on Mr. Jonathan Pollard

1. I have carefully monitored the performance a
Mr. Jonathan Pollard since the decision was made
SCI access. During the past three months Mr. Po
and behavior in NISC-33 have been outstanding.

2. Mr. Pollard received an Outstanding Basic Pe
for the period 1 October 1981 to 31 January 1982,
NISC-33, he has:

    - Authored nearly a dozen NISC Weekly Wires,
rate of two per week.

    - Written four major STIR articles.

    - Briefed   *BC*   (NIC-OOB)\ on Indian Ocean Navies.
BC   Mr. Pollard's immediate supervisor, received complimentary remarks from   *BC*   regarding the content and presentation of the briefing.

    - Briefed the NAVSEA Foreign Surface Technology Advisory Group
on British and Argentine Naval capabilities in regard to the Falkland
Island crisis.

    - Applied himself with great dedication; he routinely works a
ten hour day and at times on weekends.

    - Stimulated, by example, increased production from other NISC-33
analysts.

3. I continue to have confidence that Mr. Pollard will maintain his
stable and effective performance.

U R

BC

Enclosure (30)

*OOB_*
As I know you will
need to continue to
monitor this one very
closely. The case
litigation have been
known to do a
to.

BC

Admiral Shapiro's handwritten note (on top right hand corner) attached to memorandum enclosure to JAG manual investigation.

checkered history. But it was only a red flag, not a firm indication that something was wrong. He forwarded the report to Admiral Butts and the deputy director of naval intelligence with a short note: "We need to continue to monitor this one very closely. Cases like this have been known to do a . . ." he wrote, then added a turnaround symbol.[16] In other words, cases like this have been known to come back and bite you in the ass.

On 20 July, right on schedule, Captain Hoffman sent his second quarterly update to the DNI. "Pollard has made significant and valuable contributions to NISC's mission and his performance has been exemplary," he wrote. In addition to displaying a potential for leadership, "Mr. Pollard continues to demonstrate stability, resourcefulness, and maturity in the performance of his job." And, again, the analyst was working "long hours voluntarily to complete assigned tasks."[17]

Time moves on, people are transferred or retire. By October 1982 Hoffman had become commander of the NIC. Following Admiral Shapiro's retirement, Admiral Butts moved up to the position of DNI. The NISC reports on Pollard had indicated that he was still performing stellar work. Captain Hoffman wrote a note to Admiral Butts and attached it to the October 1982 report that crossed his desk: "I recommend we secure these reports."[18] In response, Admiral Butts promptly authorized the request to stop them.[19] Hoffman then wrote an informal note to Captain David Cooper, who was taking over as commanding officer of the NISC: "Give me a verbal as needed on subject's status/progress only if downward."[20]

No updated reports on Jonathan Pollard, either written or verbal, were ever delivered again. The analyst had won his battle with the navy, and the navy didn't even realize it was in a fight—at least not until 21 November 1985, when it was too late.

Chapter 5

RED FLAGS

![divider]

I n 1981, while Pollard was waging his battle to secure an SCI clearance, he met Anne Henderson. The analyst was smitten. Anne was an intelligent, attractive redhead with large blue eyes and a magnetic smile. She became infatuated with Pollard because of his keen mind, articulate conversation, and gentle manner. In the summer of 1982 she moved into his apartment in Arlington, Virginia. Now Pollard had everything he wanted—his job back, a promotion, his SCI clearance, additional responsibilities, and a beautiful woman. Just when everything seemed to be on the right track, however, problems began to surface.

Although Pollard had been receiving outstanding performance reports, he was showing more signs of instability. His coworkers often wrote off his odd behavior as harmless, the reflection of a brilliant mind. Not everyone was so ready to overlook it.

In the previous year, around the summer of 1981, Lieutenant Commander David G. Muller Jr. was assigned to the NFOIO, the part of the ONI responsible for analysis of foreign naval operations and tactics. He formed a world navies branch that dealt with the Soviet Union, China, Cuba, North Korea, and various Middle Eastern countries. Pollard, whose office was upstairs, often came down to talk with Muller and his staff about what they were working on. He impressed Muller, who thought "he was bright, very positive, and had good information."

An opening came up for an analyst in Commander Muller's branch, in 1982, and when Pollard expressed interest in the position, a pleased Muller promptly scheduled a formal interview. Based on Pollard's past interactions with the commander, he was a shoo-in for the job.

When the analyst came in for his interview, Commander Muller almost did a double take. "He was bedraggled, he looked physically exhausted and stressed, and his clothes were all askew," Muller later told me, adding that Pollard must not have taken a shower in a couple of days. The first thing Pollard said when he walked in was, "I'm sorry I'm late. You won't believe what I've been up against this weekend." When Muller asked what was wrong, Pollard told him that some members of the Irish Republican Army had kidnapped Anne. Muller sensed it was a blatant lie, yet Pollard seemed genuinely upset. He had spent the entire weekend without sleep, he claimed, chasing the terrorist thugs around the greater Washington area and engaging them in quick negotiations by phone. He had just rescued Anne a few hours earlier and barely made it to the job interview.

Astonished, Muller glanced at Pollard's dirty wrinkled shirt. No doubt there was something terribly wrong, but it had nothing to do with the IRA or Anne being kidnapped. This guy is really strange and I don't want him in my branch, Muller thought. He cordially thanked the interviewee for coming in, hastily putting an end to Pollard's bid for the job. Muller didn't remember Pollard coming around his branch anymore after that.[1] In retrospect, Muller told me, he could kick himself for not taking it a step further and going to security.

In the winter of 1982–83 Pollard and Anne moved to the Dupont Circle area of Washington, D.C., into apartment 304 on 1733 20th Street. Later, after his arrest, Pollard admitted that he and Anne had smoked marijuana and used cocaine on several occasions at Washington-area parties.[2] Pollard was living on the edge. Drug use is a red flag for security and counterintelligence investigators, and if the analyst's supervisors had found out, his SCI clearance could have been revoked. Fortunately for Pollard, if not for the United States, no one reported him during this period.

At least, no one with a name. In late 1983 an anonymous caller did telephone the NISC's Consolidated Security Office alleging that he had witnessed an altercation involving Pollard at a Georgetown bar. The caller claimed that Pollard had identified himself as an intelligence analyst. Pollard's department head at the time counseled him regarding the episode and reported it up the chain of command, but it never reached Captain William Charles Horn, the navy's new special security officer for SCI clearances, and nothing ever came of the incident.

The Nelson, Pollard's apartment in the Dupont Circle area of Washington, D.C.
—MONICA JENNINGS

In the meantime, although he had been promoted to a GS-12 step 1 and now made thirty-plus thousand dollars a year, Pollard was starting to have problems managing his money. It was common knowledge that he had credit card debts, loan debts, debts on rent and incidental items. He missed his rent payment on 1 December 1983, paid it at the end of the month, then missed subsequent payments due on 1 March and 1 April 1984. The landlord initiated legal action to have Pollard and Anne evicted. At the end of April they paid up again and the landlord stopped the eviction process. Some of Pollard's coworkers were aware he was having financial difficulties, but no one informed his supervisors.[3]

To help him out of his financial mess, the analyst borrowed money from a coworker. After several months of not paying the money back, Pollard began writing checks to the coworker to cover the loan, but all the checks came back from the bank marked "insufficient funds." Then the lender told Anne Henderson about the situation. Within hours, Anne had repaid the entire loan in cash.[4]

Pollard was growing reckless. Highly intelligent, he nevertheless apparently didn't possess enough sense to realize that this sort of behavior could invite suspicion and spell the end of his SCI clearance.

None of these red-flag incidents was reported to Pollard's supervisors or any security or counterintelligence professionals, however. Now that Pollard wasn't being closely monitored, the only way his activity could be uncovered was through a special background investigation. These were undertaken just once every five years for people holding TS and SCI clearances.

Perhaps more significant, the analyst who had previously received so many outstanding performance reports began to slack off on the job. His demeanor and attitude changed, and a number of coworkers and supervisors started regarding him as a problem employee. He paid no attention to his assigned work, instead concentrating on projects that he found personally interesting. He failed to meet deadlines. He ignored administrative paperwork. He complained about his work being excessively edited. He even questioned the professional competence of his immediate supervisors, expressing his dissatisfaction to his peers and those above his supervisors in the chain of command.[5] Oddly, he continued to receive excellent performance reports.

During all this turmoil, Pollard continued to put in long hours and work weekends. On many occasions he was alone in the NISC's SCI facility. The facility was under twenty-four-hour security protection, and strict guidelines had to be followed for handling documents. For example, no copied, printed, or written material could be removed without the permission of a supervisor or destroyed without two people present. Despite the security wall, all the extra time Pollard spent alone in the SCI facility should have been cause for concern. The truth is, no one was paying attention, and certainly no one was reporting suspicious behavior.

As Pollard continued his downward spiral in 1983 (and into the spring of 1984), world events were reshaping the way the Department of the Navy collected intelligence. Who could have predicted that as the department streamlined and improved its efforts, the result would help Pollard fulfill his wildest dream?

On 18 April 1983, a suicide bomber drove a van filled with two thousand pounds of explosives into the U.S. embassy in Beirut, Lebanon, ripping open the façade of the seven-story building and killing sixty-three people, including seventeen Americans. Exactly six months after the attack on the U.S. embassy, a terrorist bomb destroyed the U.S. Marine Amphibious Unit Compound at Beirut International Airport on 23 October. A lone Hezbollah terrorist driving a Mercedes Benz stake-bed truck accelerated through a public parking lot south of the battalion headquarters, barreled over barbed- and concertina-wire obstacles, and passed between two Marine guard posts without being engaged by fire. Entering through an open gate, the truck bypassed one sewer pipe barrier and moved between two others, flattened the sergeant of the guard's booth, penetrated the lobby of the building, and blew up while the majority of the occupants inside were sleeping. The TNT packed an explosive force of more than twelve thousand pounds as it ripped the building from its foundation. Two hundred twenty Marines and twenty-one other service members died as a result, and more than one hundred were injured.

The assault on the Marine barracks was one of the largest foreign terrorist attacks against the United States in history, and the DNI lost no time calling a meeting in response. Although at first it wasn't clear how intelligence collection should be overhauled, the Navy Department came to the conclusion that it needed a means of accessing, analyzing, and getting "all source" information to fleet and navy installations—

that is, a central repository of intelligence that could give advanced warning to U.S. Navy and Marine Corps commands about pending terrorist attacks.

It was a tremendous undertaking, one that should have been done long before. The NIS took on the task. Along with the ONI, it began working feverishly to set up a center with computers that had secure links to all military intelligence collection commands. The new NIS unit was called the Anti-Terrorist Alert Center (ATAC).

Start-up personnel were being drawn from various NIC components. In May 1984 Captain Duane Feuerhelm, the NISC's executive officer, discussed the possibility with Pollard of his being assigned, at least temporarily, to one of the analytical positions in the ATAC. Frustrated in his current position, Pollard thought it might be a good idea to try something new, so he expressed an interest.[6] This was good news for the NISC. Though Pollard was still receiving positive evaluations from the supervisors about whom he was so bitterly complaining, the analyst had been a thorn in their side for a long time.

NIS Seal belonging to author.

Over the next six to eight weeks, a group consisting of five officers and five enlisted personnel began working in the ATAC's research and development division. Rich Perkins from the DNI's office was put in charge of the unit. NIS Special Agent Richard Sullivan reported to Perkins, and Perkins reported to Special Agent George Bedway and Bill Worochock, the NIS's deputy assistant director of counterintelligence. Secure computers and teletypes were set up along with terminals giving direct access to highly classified information coming in from the navy's Special Intelligence System. The first "watch standers" for this new makeshift analysis division were Sullivan and Lieutenant Ron Brunson, who worked twelve-hour shifts reading operational intelligence reports and intelligence information reports coming in from all over the world, including naval attaché message traffic from the Middle East. The U.S. Navy did not want to be caught off guard again.

With TS/SCI coming in on the secure networks, access to the area was highly restricted, the ATAC was turned into an SCI storage facility, and security procedures were implemented.

After several months the officers and enlisted personnel were scheduled to return to their original commands unless strings could be pulled to keep them at the ATAC longer. In June 1984 Pollard transferred to the ATAC for a six-month tour as a watch stander; officially, he still worked for the NISC. His watch-standing duties consisted of answering phones and reading intelligence traffic, intelligence information reports, and attaché reports coming in from everywhere. This information would be summarized in an ATAC report, turned over to a regional analyst for evaluation and approval, then dispatched daily to the fleet. Though the position was less prestigious than being an analyst—analysts assessed intelligence information and decided which commands had a need to know—Pollard didn't mind. Working as a watch stander gave him plenty of access to SCI information. In fact, after thinking it over, he decided that he just might like this job full time.

From June to October Pollard reported to Rich Sullivan, who thought Pollard was pretty savvy and solid—a "real sharp" analyst, a fellow who acted as if he'd been around the intelligence community most of his life. After Pollard had been a watch stander for four months, seven positions opened for regional analysts in the ATAC's threat analysis division. He promptly applied. Sullivan was on the review board, along with Bedway and Tom Filkins, a civilian employee of the NIS.

"My recollection is that I didn't want to hire Pollard, but I may in fact have voted for him. I can't be sure, but I'd like to think I said no," Sullivan told me.[7] Whichever way Sullivan voted, Pollard got the job. As a member of the board responsible for hiring him, Sullivan remains bothered to this day that he did not check the analyst's clearances. Apparently, employees nominated for duty in the ATAC were not vetted against NIS investigative or counterintelligence files; only their personnel records were reviewed.[8]

The NISC's civilian personnel office produced Pollard's official file, which contained nothing concerning his grievances, his fitness-for-duty evaluation, or his affiliation with TF 168 or NIS. There were no red-flag espionage indicators, only promotions, performance reports, his application for employment, and the personal qualifications statement he had completed to obtain his clearance. No one reviewing his official records noticed the inconsistencies in the dates of employment entered in his personal qualification statement and his personnel file.[9]

The records were quickly evaluated for signs of poor performance or anything that might stand out as a potential problem. According to his performance reviews, the candidate was highly intelligent and possessed an excellent analytical mind.

No one who had worked at NIS headquarters in 1980 still did in the fall of 1984. For one reason or another, all the managers and supervisors who might have provided more insight into Pollard had either left the organization or moved on to other assignments. Every person in the Code 22B division—the division that had handled the polygraph test Agent Addison administered to Pollard—was new, but that was immaterial. It wouldn't have occurred to the ATAC review board to check the files at this elite, highly secretive division. Furthermore, no one from Pollard's command had ever informed the navy special security officer of the analyst's work with TF 168. No one thought to check the files of TF 168 any more than they thought to check Code 22B files. It just wasn't common practice.

And so, on 14 October 1984, the NIS hired Pollard permanently as a desk analyst responsible for reviewing and interpreting classified information concerning potential terrorist activity in the Americas, which included the Caribbean and the continental United States.

Pollard was given a courier card, renewable annually, signifying that he had an SCI clearance, and his credentials were forwarded from the NIC to various government agencies, including the CIA, the DIA, and the NSA. The courier card allowed him unfettered access to all government libraries housing sensitive information. With it, Pollard could carry TS/SCI code-word material—provided it was properly wrapped—without fear of being searched.

In addition to free access to intelligence agencies, Pollard had access to data explaining sophisticated intelligence-gathering systems and to intelligence collected by those systems. ATAC personnel could use the repositories housing this information and retrieve sensitive data for specific reasons, but only if they had a need to know for a given job or project. They were basically operating on an honor code, meaning the government trusted them to limit their access on a need-to-know basis. Even though Pollard worked the Americas desk—one of his responsibilities was to cover domestic terrorism, another was to produce intelligence reports for deployed U.S. battle groups—he continued to access highly classified documents having to do with the Middle East. He violated the code with abandon.

Once again, Pollard had slipped through the cracks. The NISC had eliminated a headache, and now that headache fell once again on the NIS.

Chapter 6

THE ISRAELI CONNECTION

B etween 1981 and 1984, while Pollard was moving from one job to another, he was also disclosing, or attempting to disclose, classified information to people with no need to know. The way he went about it was clumsy, if not downright naive. Pollard pushed information on anyone who showed the least bit of interest—even on those with no interest at all. Did he do this in hopes of monetary reward, or simply to impress people with his knowledge and access? Probably both. He was mired in debt, and certainly, ever since childhood, his peers had ostracized him. Maybe Pollard was thinking he could help Israel and at the same time pick up some easy cash. No one would be hurt or the wiser.

In one of his earliest bumbling attempts, he approached an Australian officer who was working on a temporary basis in the NISC under a personnel-exchange liaison program run by the Royal Australian Navy (RAN) and the U.S. Navy. Pollard began disclosing highly classified information to the officer that was coded NOFORN, for no foreign dissemination. As time went on Pollard grew bolder, revealing more and more documents. The RAN officer—who had no need to know—became so distressed over this that he called his supervisor back in Australia. Allegedly, the Australians began to wonder if this might be some sort of CIA ruse. Perhaps Pollard was trying to get them to take the bait. Being close allies, the Australians could not imagine the Americans setting such a trap. Nevertheless, they decided to bring their naval officer back before things got out of hand.

Not until Pollard was apprehended years later did the Australians realize he was a spy. As soon as they heard about the arrest, they contacted U.S. government authorities to explain the RAN officer's encounter with him. Pollard subsequently admitted in an NIS debriefing report following his guilty plea that he had provided classified information to an officer of the Royal Australian Navy. But, he claimed, it was only a single secret message, a copy of the official U.S. position regarding disengagement from New Zealand, originated by the Department of Defense Joint Chiefs of Staff. [1] Later he would alter his story, saying that his supervisors ordered him to show the RAN officer classified information because the Australians were close allies. There are no known facts that suggest the Australian naval officer engaged in any improper or illegal activity. No further investigation was conducted, nor was Pollard charged with a violation in this case.

In another disturbing incident, Pollard disclosed classified information to nongovernment employees who had no need to know. In the introduction to the government's memorandum in aid of sentencing it states, in part,

> With respect to defendant's claim that he was motivated by altruism rather than greed, a number of articulable facts demonstrate that this claim is superficial rather than substantial. Initially, it must be recognized that defendant's espionage relationship with the Israelis is not the only instance where defendant has disclosed classified information in anticipation of financial gain. The government's investigation has revealed that defendant provided to certain of his social acquaintances U.S. classified documents which defendant obtained through U.S. Navy sources. The classified documents which defendant disclosed to two such acquaintances, both of whom are professional investment advisers, contained classified economic and political analyses which defendant believed would help his acquaintances render investment advice to their clients. Defendant also gave classified information to a third social acquaintance who defendant also knew would utilize it to further the acquaintance's career.
>
> Defendant has acknowledged that, although he was not paid for his unauthorized disclosures of classified information to the above-mentioned acquaintances, he hoped to be rewarded ultimately through business opportunities that these individuals

could arrange for defendant when he eventually left his position with the U.S. Navy. In fact, defendant was involved in an ongoing business venture with two of these acquaintances at the time he provided the classified information to them. . . .[2]

Pollard approached all sorts of people in his eager quest to impress others and share classified information, but he singled out one group for special consideration: the Israelis.

In tracing the history of his contacts with the Israelis it is difficult to sort fact from fiction. Some of the information we have comes from Pollard's own mouth, in the form of confessions made after his guilty plea. This was probably one of the few times he felt compelled to tell at least a good portion of the truth, for he wanted to get his wife's sentence reduced. But Pollard has changed his stories repeatedly, either consciously or because he is so tangled up in far-fetched tales that he himself can no longer distinguish between truth and fantasy.

Pollard, whose loyalty since his teens had been split between the United States and Israel—ethnic paranoia, he called it—toyed with the idea of immigrating to the Jewish homeland. But because his parents resisted, he decided to assist Israel in some other way.

In 1981 the Mossad's files showed that he had informally applied for a job with the

Israeli flag —ELECTRONIC MEDIA

American Israel Public Affairs Committee (AIPAC) in Washington, D.C. During his interview he told members of the committee "a very detailed story of AIPAC being watched by the Department of Justice, maintaining that its phones were bugged." Pollard was turned down for the job.[3] No one in the U.S. government will ever know for sure what Pollard told the AIPAC. There are no facts to show or suggest that AIPAC was involved in any way with Pollard. In fact, they wanted nothing to do with him.

The following year Pollard sat in on an exchange conference attended by the Israeli Defense Force and the U.S. military—or so he claimed in an NIS and FBI debriefing that took place in July 1986, following his guilty plea. According to navy officials, the idea that Pollard, a lowly analyst, ever attended a high-level official conference between Israel and the United States is ludicrous.[4] At any rate, Pollard insisted that he had been present, and furthermore, that he had been horrified by certain anti-Semitic remarks coming from the mouths of American analysts. In his mind, U.S. disclosure documents didn't reflect the tenor of the agreements for the exchange—in other words, the U.S. Navy was withholding information about terrorists that was vital to Israel's defense. At one point, he maintained, he heard an American exclaim, "Let 'em lose a couple of pilots and they'll figure it out!" The combination of anti-Semitic remarks and the U.S. Navy's refusal to share information was too much to bear. In his own words, Pollard "snapped." "I watched the threats to Israel's existence grow," he said, "and gradually came to the conclusion that I had to do something."[5]

At the same conference, Pollard approached the Israeli military attaché and, addressing him in Hebrew, pitched an offer to spy. The attaché made no overtures to take him up on his offer. Pollard saw the same man at another conference in October 1983, but the two never spoke. Frustrated, Pollard thought perhaps he should approach the military attaché at the Israeli embassy in Washington. That would require an intermediary, and he didn't have one. Once again Pollard entertained the idea of immigrating to Israel, but when he proposed this to Anne, she dug in her heels, adamant about not going. His next thought was to work in the United States for an Israeli defense company, but that didn't happen either. Then, he "considered quitting the intelligence community and going to work in the private sector, taking with him a stockpile of classified documents to pass to Israel, but he decided this was unprofessional."[6]

How could he provide secrets to the Israelis? Pollard was eager to forge ahead. He was an analyst with an almost photographic memory and a great fund of knowledge. He was a good liar and he had the gift of gab. He was an expert at manipulation. He had the access, he knew the security procedures. Most important of all, he had the courier card to transport TS/SCI anywhere in Washington, D.C., without being searched or questioned. His opportunity was just around the corner.

Dr. Morris Pollard was a good friend of Gustav Stern, a former owner of Hartz Mountain Food who had thrown parties to raise funds for Morris's research programs in microbiology at Notre Dame.[7] Gustav's son, Steven, a wealthy stockbroker in New York, was about the same age as Jonathan and had attended several of the parties. Pollard renewed his association with Stern sometime in 1983.

Late in that year, Steven called Jonathan from New York to discuss prospectuses on an Israeli military company and a Belgium mutual fund. The two also discussed the effect on the oil market of a possible Persian Gulf/Strait of Hormuz closure.[8] Through the spring of 1984 they stayed in touch, discussing business prospects and the plight of Israel. Steven was deeply impressed with Pollard's analytical abilities and his knowledge of world affairs.

At one point Steven attended a Zionist conference at L'Enfant Plaza in Washington, D.C., and the two arranged a brief social meeting. Anne went along.[9] Soon thereafter, around the time Pollard transferred to the ATAC, Steven called from New York to say that he had met an interesting colonel in the Israeli air force who had spoken at a lecture promoting bonds for his country. His name was Aviem Sella and he was pursuing a graduate degree in computer science at New York University. According to Steven, Colonel Sella was a bona fide Israeli war hero. Steven sought him out after the lecture and informed him of Pollard's passionate loyalty to Israel.

Steven asked if Pollard would like to meet the air force colonel. "Pollard recounted that he immediately said to himself, 'That's my opportunity to begin providing information to the Israelis.'"[10] A real war hero! The answer was yes, and they arranged for Steven to give the colonel Pollard's phone number.

When the Pollard case broke in November 1985, Steven E. Stern told FBI officials that he never thought Pollard intended to spy for Israel and that the introduction arranged between Sella and Pollard was strictly because of Pollard's love for Israel. The FBI follow-up investigation found no connection between Stern and Pollard's spying for Israel. The investigation of Stern was not pursued and no charges were brought against him, nor was he considered a conspirator or possible accomplice in the Pollard spying activities.

It was early June 1984, and Pollard had just started working as a watch stander in the ATAC. No more than a couple of days after Steven had broached the subject with him, Pollard got a call in his apartment. Aviem Sella was on the other end of the line. Pollard could hardly contain himself. The colonel came across as mild-mannered and articulate on the phone. Would Pollard like to have lunch? Sella would be flying into Washington anyway to attend a conference at the Hilton Hotel, just a few blocks from Pollard's apartment.

The answer was an enthusiastic yes.

Thinking it would be advantageous to have someone help him with the logistics of providing intelligence to Israel, Pollard decided to recruit a friend who had roomed with him for a semester at the Fletcher School. His plan was to present to Israeli intelligence a preexisting ring that could begin spy operations with minimal start-up time. His friend, a Jew sympathetic to Israel, worked at the Voice of America, was well traveled, and had access to highly placed individuals.

Although Pollard and Anne Henderson were not yet married, she was the girl of his dreams, and he shared everything with her. When he told her about his plan to pass secrets to Israel and to recruit the ex-roommate, they discussed the wisdom of the move. In Anne's *60 Minutes* interview with Mike Wallace on 1 March 1987, he asked if she and Pollard had discussed spying for Israel. Anne replied, "Oh yes, we did"; she further admitted she knew exactly what she was getting into.

After a lengthy discussion, they decided that Pollard should approach the fellow. That wasn't all. Though she would initially deny it later, Anne herself planned to participate in Pollard's spy ring and to join him in the recruitment attempt.

And so, one Saturday evening, Anne and Pollard showed up unexpectedly at his ex-roommate's doorstep. No sooner had the visitors set foot inside than they began berating him for his pedestrian lifestyle and hinting that he could "live better." Pollard told him there was money to be made if he would help him deliver certain classified documents. For whom? the friend inquired. "The brothers," Pollard answered, referring to the Israelis. He went on to say that Anne was going into business for herself, and he wanted to help her. When the friend asked how much money he would make, Pollard replied, "Oh, this would be roughly two to three thousand dollars." Apparently he meant monthly.[11] Then he repeated, "Anne needs assistance." Pollard explained that his friend would be responsible for delivering and disseminating documents.

Finally, Pollard cut to the chase. "Well, do you want to join us?" he said bluntly. Taken aback, the acquaintance gave a noncommittal answer.

As they were driving home, Anne turned to Pollard in distress. "This was a bad idea," she said. "I think you should just forget that you had this conversation."[12] He might have been an ardent Zionist, but the ex-roommate hadn't shown any enthusiasm for Pollard's idea, nor had he displayed any expression of sympathy.

The next day the friend called and met with Pollard and told him that he wanted nothing to do with this scheme, adding that if the analyst was serious about it he was going to the authorities. "I was just telling stories, if anyone ever asks," Pollard replied, as if nothing had happened.[13]

Anne initially denied any attempt to recruit Pollard's former roommate in a memorandum in aid of sentencing presented by her attorney on 26 February 1987. In it attorney James F. Hibey picks apart the government's accusations that Anne participated in a recruitment attempt. He argues it was just a conversation taken out of context by a friend who cannot be deemed reliable. The memorandum reads, in part,

> . . . in order to imply that Mrs. Pollard was involved in the planning stages of Mr. Pollard's scheme, the government describes in detail a visit by the Pollards to a friend's apartment.
> . . . The government alleges that, in the course of this visit, Mrs. Pollard and her husband jointly attempted to recruit the friend to participate in Mr. Pollard's activities, However, the government's account of this visit, based on the account of the "friend," is simply inaccurate and untrue. It represents the use of incredible information to make a serious allegation of criminal conduct without any safeguards of reliability. . . .
>
> The Pollards went to visit their friend on a Saturday evening in the spring of 1984, hoping to persuade him to go out to dinner with them. . . .
>
> It is true that Mr. Pollard attempted to solicit his friend's participation in whatever might come of Mr. Pollard's initiative to work for the Israeli government. . . . Mr. Pollard and his friend

discussed a proposal to aid the Israelis. . . . Mrs. Pollard did not participate in this discussion, although she had accompanied her husband to the friend's apartment and apparently overheard parts of it. . . .

Disjointed quotes about "Anne's going into business for herself" and Mr. Pollard's proposed plan being "for the Brothers" (meaning the Israelis) are strung together as if there were a relationship there. What that relationship could possibly be is a mystery that even the government does not attempt to explain. . . .

Furthermore, the friend's story is contradicted by the Pollards' account of the visit, and by their insistence, verified by separate polygraph examinations that Mrs. Pollard never attempted to "recruit" anyone. The friend has not submitted to a polygraph examination; he has not been cross-examined. The Court should discount the friend's version of events, as used by the government, as inherently untrustworthy and incredible.[14]

In order to end this matter once and for all, the government filed with the court a "government's reply memorandum in aid of sentencing" on 3 March 1987, just one day before her sentencing, stating, "Not only is her statement denying her activities in this regard patently false, but no such claim was ever certified by the government's polygraph examiner." The government decided to reveal her recollections of the reasons why Pollard thought he needed a backup to help him in his spying activities. The following excerpts are taken from the court record of the FBI polygraph examiner, Special Agent Barry Colvert:

Anne Henderson Pollard stated that the Washington friend had grown up in Detroit in a predominately black neighborhood and his "Jewishness" had been an impediment to him while growing up and in later life in seeking employment. . . . She described the Washington friend as being violently "anti-Arab" and espousing, at least in private, the same views with regard to the need for the security of the state of Israel as her husband Jonathan Jay Pollard.

Anne Henderson Pollard stated that during the spring of

Anne Pollard leaves U.S. District Court on 4 June 1986 after she pleads guilty to two charges brought against her by the government. —WASHINGTON TIMES

1984 a number of terrorist incidents had occurred throughout the world that were directed at Israeli citizens and American Jews. These escalating incidents greatly disturbed both Jonathan Jay Pollard and Anne Henderson Pollard. Jonathan Jay Pollard became upset with the fact that he was unable to provide any assistance to the state of Israel. . . .

Anne Henderson Pollard stated that Jonathan Jay Pollard had tried to assume the nature of this assistance and had anticipated that he might need a "backup" . . . and that in the event he was unable to make these trips he would need someone to go in his place. He felt that it was extremely important that this person be as committed to the state of Israel as he, Jonathan Jay Pollard, was. . . . Both Jonathan Jay Pollard and Anne Henderson Pollard considered the Washington friend to be reliable, intelligent, a "quick study," and felt that he was as completely "pro-Zionist" as they were. . . .

She stated that she had gone to the Washington friend's

Israeli Consulate on the corner of East 42nd Street and Yitzhak Rabin Way, New York City, NY—TODD CAMERON WESTPHAL

apartment with Jonathan Jay Pollard knowing in advance that he would at some time during the evening ask the Washington friend for his assistance. . . . When Jonathan Jay Pollard ultimately asked the Washington friend for his assistance, he was unable to provide any exact details as to the nature of this assistance, only that he would need his help. The Washington friend's response, according to Anne Henderson Pollard, was one in which he did not say "yes" [and] did not say "no." Anne Henderson Pollard stated that she felt very negative "vibes" about this conversation as the Washington friend did not show any enthusiasm for the idea presented by Jonathan Jay Pollard. She noted no expression of sympathy and felt immediately that Jonathan Jay Pollard should never have brought this subject up with the Washington friend.[15]

Pollard's disappointment did not last long. He was, after all, scheduled to meet Colonel Aviem Sella, a man who had flown combat missions during the Six-Day War, led the daring air raid on the Osirak nuclear reactor facility in Tuwaitha, Iraq, and masterminded an air assault in the 1982 war in Lebanon during which Israel shot down ninety Syrian MiGs. Before arriving in New York to pursue his degree, Sella had served three years as chief of Israeli air force operations.

Sella wanted to meet Pollard too. Quite aware that this was a delicate matter requiring discretion, he decided to contact Yosef "Yossi" Yagur at the Israeli consulate in New York City. Yagur reported to the scientific intelligence-gathering unit of the Israeli prime minister's office, the Lishka Lekisherey Mada (LAKAM). LAKAM gleaned its scientific and technical information from governments and corporations around the world, its operatives attending events such as trade shows and business meetings and combing through news articles and other public sources. Some information was also collected in clandestine operations.

Yagur was concerned about Sella meeting Pollard. After all, they didn't know anything about this American. Furthermore, Sella was a war hero, not a clandestine operative trained to run foreign agents in the field. But Sella was eager to meet with Pollard. Yagur, after getting permission from a higher-up, gave the air force pilot the go-ahead, with a warning to be careful. Sella's decision to meet Pollard would prove to be fatal. It eventually ruined his career, made him a fugitive from justice, and caused a serious riff between the United States and Israel.

Chapter 7

THE POINT OF NO RETURN

F ollowing his initial meeting with Colonel Sella, Pollard immediately set out to locate documents that would impress the
Israelis and convince them that he was serious. Sella returned to
New York and briefed Yagur about the meeting. Yagur in turn briefed
the man in charge of the operation, Rafael Eitan. Born in 1926, Eitan
had a long, colorful history. Reportedly he had fought in the Jewish
underground in the 1940s and in the war for Israel's independence
in 1948–49, during which he was severely wounded. Eitan had run secret
intelligence operations for Mossad
for twenty-five years, most notably the
operation that captured Nazi war criminal Adolph Eichmann in Buenos
Aires, Argentina, thus making Eitan an
Israeli national hero.

Though Eitan gave Sella permission
to proceed with the operation, he told
the colonel to be watchful and gauge
whether Pollard could really produce.
Within a week or so, as planned, Sella
called and gave Pollard the Hebrew   Rafael Eitan —DANIEL BAR-ON, BAUBAU PHOTOWIRE
letter for one of the phone booths close to his apartment. The analyst
ran all the way and picked up the phone, out of breath. They arranged
to meet again at the Hilton near Pollard's apartment.

This second meeting occurred on a Saturday in July 1984. Pollard drove
to the nearly deserted ATAC, gathered a briefcase stuffed with TS/SCI
material, returned home, then walked to the Hilton with the briefcase.

When he met Sella in the lobby the colonel said he wanted to go somewhere else to talk, and Pollard suggested Dumbarton Oaks.[1] Dumbarton Oaks is a famed research library with an adjoining public park situated on the crest of a wooded valley in Georgetown. In the hotel garage was Sella's rental car with New York plates. The two men went downstairs, got into the car, and set off. When they reached their destination, they parked the car and found an out-of-the-way picnic table near the back of the park where they could talk without being overheard.

Pollard opened his briefcase and pulled out a bulky three-volume series on Saudi Arabian ground forces and a ground logistics study classified TS. Scanning this material, Sella couldn't believe his eyes. "I've never seen anything like this before," he remarked to Pollard. The most sensitive documents Israel possessed on Saudi Arabia were Exxon maps.[2]

With the enthusiasm of a child, Pollard reached into the briefcase again. Watching Sella for his reaction, the analyst pulled out his prize: satellite photographs from the pilot's raid on the nuclear reactor facility in Tuwaitha, Iraq. Because the photographs still had satellite-positioning information in the margins, they were marked TS. Sella's mouth dropped open. This fellow really did have access.

Sella proceeded to specify what sort of technical and scientific information Israel needed. For example, "air defense information on other countries, such as cockpit layouts, uplink and downlink communication systems, radar and navigation beacons." He stressed, however, that Israel "did not need much terrorist information from the United States."[3] (This is something Pollard's handlers would tell him repeatedly in the future because he persistently turned a deaf ear and insisted on supplying such information.)

Presently Sella brought up the issue of money, but nothing was decided. The colonel gave all the documents back to Pollard with the exception of the satellite photographs, which he kept. Maybe these were souvenirs, or maybe he wanted to show Yagur an example of what Pollard could produce for Israel.

Pollard wasted no time preparing for his next meeting, gathering highly classified message traffic on anything he could get his hands on that the Israelis might want. If he couldn't copy it, he would write it out. Over the next two weeks he took numerous Middle East and North African summary (MENAS) traffic messages. He also accessed every national intelligence daily message from the NISC. He took an NSA study on Egyptian air defenses classified TS and screened every hard copy report from U.S. defense attaché offices in the Middle East. All this and more Pollard stockpiled near his desk with what appears, in retrospect, to have been reckless abandon. He would later explain that he was able to get away with this because stacks of TS/SCI material were lying all over the ATAC offices.[4] It was common practice to amass such material and no one thought twice about it.

Pollard was sweating bullets to impress the Israelis. This was no longer child's play. He had reached the point of no return.

About a week after their second meeting, Sella called Pollard again. This time, he told the analyst to bring his documents to the Holiday Inn in Chevy Chase, Maryland. On or around 21 July, Pollard duly met Sella in the garage there, parked his vehicle, and climbed into the same rental vehicle the colonel had driven before.[5] Carefully watching to make sure no one was trailing them, they headed to a house on Deborah Street in Potomac, Maryland. Sella told Pollard to remember the route so that in the future, he could drive there by himself.

Seasoned spies often use the "dry-cleaning" process to shake off possible pursuers. In dry cleaning, the spy employs both fixed-point surveillance, pulling over and parking, and mobile countersurveillance, taking a circuitous route before heading to a meeting site. It is doubtful the two neophytes practiced dry cleaning.

You would think, at the very least, that Pollard and his Israeli handler would have devised a more sophisticated system for passing secrets. During the Cold War, one of the tried-and-true methods was to deliver an envelope containing classified documents, or film taken of classified material, to a drop site, or dead drop, for later pickup by the handler. As for payment, the handler would leave money at either the dead drop, or some other designated location, with a marker—such as a small piece of tape on a mailbox, or a brand-name soda can at a specific location on the side of the road—indicating that it was ready to be picked up. This reduced the risk of exposure because the spy and the handler didn't meet each other.

Not so with Sella and Pollard. Incredibly, for their third meeting the analyst brought with him, not just a bulging briefcase, but two large suitcases stuffed full of highly classified national defense information, as if he had just arrived in town and was settling in for a long stay. This, despite the fact that he had attended several counterintelligence awareness briefings given by the NIS that alerted the audience to various methods spies used to deliver documents to their handlers. Subtlety was not Pollard's forte.

As they entered the residence, the analyst noticed that all the blinds and curtains had been drawn. A man came up to Pollard and greeted him without introducing himself. Not until later would Pollard learn that the man was Ilan Ravid, scientific consular at the Israeli embassy in Washington. Ravid and Sella began rummaging through the contents of the suitcases, astounded by the wealth of materials.

Soon a third, unknown person began shuttling documents to the second floor for copying. Pollard informed his handlers that they needed to return just the highly classified documents, those code-worded TS/SCI which he had to sign out from the intelligence agencies. He would return those documents and manuals the following Monday morning. The Israelis could keep the rest of the material, the message traffic, because he didn't have to sign for them. There would be no paper trail.

Pollard and Sella sat at the dining room table discussing Israel's current state of readiness—Sella gave him a lengthy briefing on this subject—and reviewing the documents. After each was reviewed, the unknown man took it upstairs for copying. Pollard noticed a large Hasselblad camera in his possession. At one point the man took color film out of the refrigerator before going back upstairs. He also photocopied Pollard's NIS analyst credentials and courier card.

Sella told Pollard that he would have to make a trip abroad to meet the man in control of the field operation, Rafael Eitan. "The old man," as Sella called him, would define more precisely Israel's collection priorities. Pollard was warned that at the meeting Eitan would also try to replace Sella with a new handler, Yosef Yagur. The colonel, who didn't want to be removed from the operation, asked Pollard to intervene and try to persuade the old man not to make the switch. Pollard agreed.

At the same meeting, Sella said, Eitan would determine the compensation Pollard was to receive. How much did Pollard need? The analyst jokingly told Sella two hundred thousand would be nice. That wasn't going to fly, Sella told him flatly. Ravid questioned Pollard about his current salary and instructed him to bring his government pay stub and Anne's, without her knowledge, to the next meeting. (At the time

Anne was working in the press room of the National Rifle Association producing brochures on firearms safety for hunters, among other duties.) They discussed a "salary" based on Pollard's income of thirty thousand without going into specifics.[6]

As they continued to sit at the dining table, Sella explained that a meeting in Paris was scheduled for November 1984. He instructed Pollard to make plane reservations for himself and Anne, to whom he had become engaged on the Fourth of July. Pollard should book a suite at the Paris Hilton Hotel. The Israelis would reimburse him. It was impressed upon Pollard that Anne must not know a thing about the operation, and he lied, assuring them she did not. As for how Pollard should explain his newfound wealth and the trip, Sella told him to tell Anne that a rich relative who owned a jewelry business was paying for the trip, and this was to be an engagement gift. The Israelis would get Anne a good-paying job with a Jewish firm when this was over, Sella promised.

Before the trip to Paris, Sella wanted Pollard to arrange a dinner meeting at the Four Ways restaurant near his apartment so that the colonel and his wife could meet Anne and better assess her. Sella would introduce himself as an old college chum and a potential business contact.

After all the copying was done, Pollard packed up his two suitcases and departed with Sella. Later, he would have to bring a whole stack of the same classified documents back to Ravid's house because the original film had been overexposed.

LAKAM was daring beyond belief—or simply incompetent. It was bad enough that they had an American spying against their close ally on that ally's home turf, but to bring him into an Israeli consular's residence with suitcases full of highly classified material was incomprehensible. Furthermore, the operational security was blatantly flawed, violating every clandestine contact procedure and other spy modus operandi. One can only conclude that the Israelis felt it was safe because the FBI didn't conduct surveillance of embassy personnel from allied countries. LAKAM must have believed that no one would ever suspect Israel of betraying its trust by spying against the United States of America in its own backyard. They were right.

Not long after the first meeting at Ilan Ravid's house, Pollard called Anne in Ohio, where she was attending a business meeting, to ask her if she could cut her trip short and return to Washington. He had set up a dinner meeting with Aviem Sella and his wife, and they wanted to meet her. Shortly afterward Anne caught a flight back to Washington. In addition to assessing Anne's devotion to Israel, Sella wanted their future contacts overseas to be relaxing. Anne should feel comfortable with Yehudit (Judy) when Pollard was in meetings.

Four Ways Restaurant, Washington, D.C. —NIS PHOTO

This was the first time Anne was to play her part, feigning ignorance of the operation. In fact, Pollard had already disclosed to his fiancée the plan to go to Paris and meet "the old man" in charge. On 28 July, the two couples met at the Four Ways restaurant, not far from Pollard's apartment.[7] The dinner was a success. As Pollard knew she would be, Anne was impressed with Sella and Yehudit, and, likewise, Sella approved of Anne. The colonel informed her that a business trip to Paris was being planned and she would be invited to accompany Pollard. Later, he cautioned Pollard again that Anne could not be told anything about the operation.

Sella and Pollard began making deliveries at Ravid's house every two weeks or so, and there was no attempt to be any more discreet than during the initial trip. Again, instead of a single briefcase, Pollard toted suitcases filled with highly classified documents. The deliveries included three separate, running intelligence summaries the Israelis wanted: the MENAS originated by the NSA, the Indian Ocean littoral summary, and the Mediterranean littoral summary, the latter two originated by the navy's Sixth Fleet ocean surveillance information facility in Rota, Spain. From the Sixth Fleet facility alone, Pollard took away thousands of highly classified messages—in fact, every message the facility generated, from the time the ATAC was placed on distribution in early August 1984 until his arrest in November 1985.[8]

Meanwhile, Pollard's financial troubles worsened. On 5 July 1984, while he was still on temporary duty at the ATAC and officially employed by the NISC, the Suitland, Maryland, branch of the Consolidated Civilian

Personnel office had received a letter of indebtedness regarding an employee named Jonathan Jay Pollard. The letter, from the Navy Federal Credit Union, specifically stated that "his payments for a personal loan and a line of credit loan were both three months in arrears." The navy personnel office forwarded the letter from the credit union to the NISC with a reminder that "the employee should be informed of the navy's policy concerning indebtedness and that failure to pay a just debt may result in adverse action."[9] Although the letter did not specify what, the rules allowed for disciplinary action and even removal of an SCI clearance. The NISC in turn requested that Pollard's command counsel him on this matter and forward the results to the personnel department at the Suitland branch.[10]

In theory, if not always in practice, the U.S. government does not allow people who cannot take care of their own finances access to its most sensitive information. The command later counseled Pollard, and he signed a memorandum to that effect. Under pressure to make good on his loans, on 30 July he paid the credit union $300 for the share check loan and $592.80 for the line of credit loan. Both payments were made in cash.[11] While Pollard was being transferred from the NISC to the ATAC, no one at the NISC provided copies of Pollard's letter of indebtedness to the navy special security officer or to anyone at the NIS.[12] Another red flag was ignored.

In November and December 1984 Pollard again missed his rent payments. While the apartment manager was preparing to file an eviction notice, Pollard made good on the payments. That winter, the NIS security officer asked Pollard to submit a new statement of personal history to initiate an updated special background investigation because his TS clearance had expired. He never complied with this request.[13]

Pollard returned home one night and found a tag hanging on his doorknob informing him that maintenance had been performed in his apartment. Furious that someone had gone into his apartment without his or Anne's knowledge, he immediately went to the manager with his complaint. Apparently, a maintenance man had fixed some windows. Pollard told the manager never to allow anyone in his apartment again without him being present because he had "some stuff in there." He worked for the government, he explained, and sometimes brought home classified material.[14] The manager had no legal responsibility to report Pollard's admission to having classified documents in his apartment. Once again, fate seemed to smile on the amateur spy: no call was ever made.

Chapter 8

A THIEF IN THE NIGHT

Ｗith his trip to Paris fast approaching, the ATAC analyst was elated. He would be meeting Israel's espionage master-mind, Rafael "Rafi" Eitan. After leaving Mossad at the behest of his good friend Ariel Sharon, Eitan had served as the head of LAKAM. He had also been the counterterrorism adviser to Prime Minister Yitzhak Shamir. Working for Eitan would be the thrill of a lifetime. Unbeknownst to Pollard, the legendary spymaster who had been responsible for capturing Eichmann would soon be making history again, and Pollard would play a role in it.

Still cautioning him not to let Anne know anything, Pollard's handlers also told him that he would have to wed her because Judaism did not condone common law marriage. So, in November 1984, the two lovers traveled to Paris with plans to buy an engagement ring. They checked into a suite at the Paris Hilton International that cost three hundred dollars a day. Little did Sella

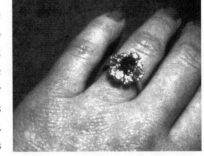

Sapphire and diamond ring worn by federal agent for evidence photo —NIS PHOTO

know that Pollard's fiancée was not only aware of the operation, but she had also given it her personal stamp of approval.

The day after Pollard and Anne arrived, the colonel phoned them at the Hilton. It was decided that Sella's wife would take Anne shopping while he and Pollard prepared for the meeting with Eitan.[1] The two men went over classified items Pollard was providing to the Israelis, reviewed background information on Syrian MiG pilots training in Russia, and discussed the effect on the balance of power in the Golan Heights if Syria were to deploy a certain type of missile.[2]

Afterwards they met the women for lunch at the hotel, then went to Mappin and Webb, a jewelry store on Place Vendome, to look at a ring Anne had seen earlier in the day. The ring, with a two-carat sapphire surrounded by two carats' worth of small diamonds, cost ten thousand dollars.[3] Anne had fallen in love with it, but Pollard said he couldn't afford it.

Luxuries were showered on the couple during their stay in Paris. The operation was anything but subtle. That evening the two couples went on a dinner cruise, and at one point a roving photographer, without asking permission, took pictures of them together. Furious because it would compromise the operation if the press got a picture of him and Pollard together, Sella ripped the camera out of the photographer's hands and seized the roll of film.[4] Instead of being inconspicuous, the novice spies were attracting still more attention to themselves.

The colonel was upset, and not just about the photographer. Apparently, Eitan wanted to assign someone else as Pollard's handler. For the second time, Sella asked Pollard to intervene. Would he talk with Eitan, try to convince him not to make this switch? Again, Pollard agreed.

Several days into the trip, while Anne went shopping again, Sella took Pollard to meet Eitan. The ride from the Paris Hilton took about thirty minutes and they ended up in a residential area with lots of apartment buildings. For some reason Pollard was under the impression that the apartment he and Sella visited belonged to an elderly German couple, but no doubt it was an Israeli safe house used to meet undercover operatives. Yosef Yagur, who had long wavy hair and dark, penetrating eyes, met them at the door and introduced himself, using only his first name. Pollard followed him into the living room and there he was, seated in a chair, the legendary spymaster. He was a short, chubby man, balding, with a pleasant smile and thick glasses that magnified his eyes.

Pollard crossed the room and held out his hand. "You're one of us," Eitan said, shaking it. He told Pollard that the material he was providing Israel was vital to its survival.[5]

After a small ceremony during which Pollard was sworn in as an Israeli citizen—there was no documentation to make it official—he was handed a detailed briefing paper on the forces arrayed against Israel in the Middle East. The document, in Hebrew and classified TS, appeared to Pollard to have come from an Israeli prime minister's briefing paper.

Eitan leaned forward in his chair with an intent look and began questioning his guest. Did the CIA have any dirt on Israeli cabinet members? Any psychological studies on them? Could Pollard identify any Israeli "rats" working in the country? Did he know anything about the Syrian order of battle? Pollard didn't answer these questions.

Their conversation consumed the entire morning. Following a catered lunch, Eitan discussed the "essential elements of information" that Israel wanted Pollard to obtain—documents, for example, pertaining to Soviet aircraft, air-to-air missiles, and surface-to-air missiles, and any chemical and biological weapons in Arab hands, including neutron bombs. One item the Israelis were keenly interested in was the so-called radio signal notations manual or RASIN manual. This was a roadmap to signal intelligence that described America's global listening profile, geographic slice by geographic slice. At the time, however, the Israelis didn't quite know what it was or where it came from. Pollard's handlers wanted the spy to locate and copy the most up-to-date edition. Pollard said he would try to find out what it was and who had originated it.[6]

Over the next few days several more meetings took place. Repeatedly, Pollard was told that he would be "taken care of" if apprehended by U.S. authorities. Eitan assured him that the U.S. response would be "contained," in other words, the United States would take no action because of the close relationship between the two countries. Pollard, Eitan reiterated, was "one of them."

The spymaster directed Pollard to provide passport photos of himself and Anne. They were Israeli citizens now, the spymaster said, and he wanted to make everything kosher.[7] The name on Pollard's passport would be Danny Cohen, after the famous spy Eli Cohen, who in the 1960s had gone undercover to Damascus and was later executed by the Syrians. Pollard was on cloud nine. Cohen—it was a name to be proud of, the name he would use after the operation when he moved to Israel.

The Israelis told Pollard that they were going to buy Anne her engagement ring. Sella had gone back inside the jewelry store and convinced the shop owner to reduce the price by three thousand dollars. Still, it was clearly expensive, and not yet purchased. They needed to make up a story so that no one would wonder how Pollard, on his salary, could afford the ring. Pollard came up with a subterfuge about an Uncle Joe Fisher, the black sheep of a family of diamond brokers in Europe. He dictated a fake letter from Uncle Joe to Anne, and Sella scribbled it down on Hilton letterhead stationery. In the letter Uncle Joe said he was sorry that he wouldn't be able to attend Pollard's wedding, and that he was sending the engagement ring as a gift to Anne. He ended the letter saying, "I hope that this 'surprise' will make up for my absence. Wear it in good health! Your Uncle, J. Fisher." Anne, the Israelis told Pollard, was to carry this letter with her at all times to prove who had given her the ring, in case she was asked. She would not actually receive it until after returning to the United States.[8]

During the meetings the Israelis also provided Pollard with basic training—just the bare bones. For example, if he was ever asked to take a government polygraph exam, he should resign his position first. Pollard didn't need to be told twice about that. The last thing he wanted was to endure another polygraph. He hadn't told the Israelis he had already taken two, neither of which turned out well.

Again he was assured that Israel would take care of him if he were ever caught. He could escape by way of the Israeli embassy in Washington, they said. But they never provided Pollard with a plan— not even the most basic countersurveillance techniques, none of the instructions he would need to get out of the United States in a hurry, no code words to use when calling his handler to implement an escape, no secondary contact numbers in the event he couldn't get in touch with his handler. Without realizing it, Pollard would be left out in the cold.

Eitan, like Sella before him, expressed little interest in the terrorist and counterterrorist information that Pollard had persisted in supplying to the Israelis. They already had sufficient information on that subject, they reiterated; Pollard shouldn't waste his time.

When the topic of Pollard's new handler came up, the American urged Eitan to reconsider and keep Sella on. He was comfortable with Sella, Pollard argued. But Eitan was adamant that he be cut out. He told Pollard that the colonel had some important matters to tend to at his airbase and that he had to be "isolated" from the operation. End of discussion. Pollard had been led to believe that his new handler lived in Israel, but he now found out that Yagur was in fact the scientific attaché to the Israeli consulate in New York City. In the future, when they had meetings in Washington, Yagur would be arriving from the

Big Apple, not Israel. Eitan wanted the two men to continue having operational meetings in Europe, but Pollard disagreed, saying the navy special security officer might get suspicious about all his trips overseas.

To reimburse him for this first trip to Paris, the Israelis gave him approximately ten thousand in cash. Eitan also established Pollard's "salary": fifteen hundred a month, a figure based on his navy pay.[9] The figure was woefully below what Pollard had hoped for, but the Israelis didn't want him to have too much unexplained cash. They knew the FBI looked at unexplained or sudden affluence as an indicator of espionage. Despite their concern, they did not provide Pollard with any training on how to conceal his extra earnings.

After leaving Eitan with an itinerary, Pollard and his fiancée departed Paris and traveled around Europe for three weeks, staying at luxury inns. Their hotel charges alone exceeded four thousand dollars, and the restaurant bills, as they ate their way through France, Italy, Austria, and Germany at four-star establishments, were equally high. With all the fine dining and little exercise, Pollard started to put on weight. His belly now protruded over his belt, his cheeks were chubby. He was sporting a mustache and his hairline had receded, which made him look older and more mature.

Back in the States, Pollard and Anne played fast and loose with their extra cash, blowing it mostly on food, drink, and drugs. They were living the good life now. Neither seemed to realize the gravity of the step they had each taken or the consequences should they be discovered. Instead of lying low, Jonathan and his fiancée were virtually advertising their crimes to the world.

As for Sella, he was none too pleased about being replaced as Pollard's handler. In the coming months he would maintain frequent contact with the spy in America's capital, but only socially. Neither could have predicted that the colonel who had launched Pollard's clandestine career would eventually play a key role in its termination.

Once the three-week European vacation ended, Pollard returned to spying. During one of his next deliveries to the Israeli diplomat's residence in Potomac, he was given the ring purchased for Anne in Paris, along with the letter from "Uncle Joe" to carry with her at all times.

The DIA was one of the facilities hardest hit by Pollard, his "gold mine."[10] He spent a lot of time in its central library, which stored all Defense Attaché Office messages and other intelligence reports, including military intelligence from the Middle East and around the world. Pollard combed this repository and took whatever he wanted, meaning everything he could carry out at any one time.

The normal procedure for analysts who wanted specific classified documents from the DIA library was to fill out a certified request form and send it to the library, which would arrange to have the documents ready for pickup. But Pollard wasn't interested in just a few specific documents. In his search for as much information as possible, he skipped the request forms and hunted for documents himself. He would stroll into the library, scan the computer system for defense attaché officers' reports from Baghdad, Damascus, Riyadh, Cairo, Algiers, and Pakistan, pull up the reports on the computer, copy them, and put them in his briefcase with no audit trail. Unlike intelligence information reports, TS and SCI documents were available only in hard copy, and Pollard had to sign them out. For these, he would complete a check-out form and drop it off at the desk before exiting the building. No one ever verified what he had in his briefcase. Because of his courier card he was never challenged. If it was too late to return to his office, he would store the material at his apartment.[11]

Another of Pollard's methods was to retrieve messages from the Special Intelligence Communications (SPINTCOM) center in the basement of NIS headquarters. He would order material from his computer terminal upstairs in the ATAC. Once the center obtained the material, they would call and tell him it was ready for pickup. As at the DIA library, he had to sign for TS and SCI material. After doing so, he would return to his office and place the material in a drawer until he had enough to transfer into a sturdy briefcase that could hold at least four to six reams of paper.

Sometimes, in a single day, Pollard would make two or three trips to his car, a 1980 Ford Mustang with a fold-down backseat that gave him access from inside the vehicle to the trunk, where he kept a suitcase. On occasion he drove over to Sam's Car Wash in Suitland, right outside the back gate of the NISC (from which he also removed information). While the vehicle went through the wash cycle, he transferred material from his briefcase into the suitcases in the trunk. On other occasions Pollard would find a secluded park in Maryland and transfer the documents into his suitcases. If he were taking material from the SCI libraries at the DIA, he would park in a secluded area on Bolling Air Force Base to transfer it.

In his quest for highly classified information, Pollard was an expert at deceit and manipulation. Early in the operation when the Israelis wanted to get their hands on intelligence about the joint Egyptian-Argentine Condor missile, he called an acquaintance at his former place of employment, the NISC, who steered him toward a DIA analyst who happened to have information on the subject. After contacting this person by phone, Pollard visited him at DIA headquarters.

As a cover story, Pollard told the DIA analyst that the NIS was working on a technology-transfer case involving an Egyptian missile engineer who was approaching U.S. companies on the West Coast looking for information. Without questioning Pollard or verifying his comments, the DIA expert provided him with a complete, highly classified folder on the Condor and even showed him where to find the copy machine. Pollard would later claim that the Israelis had been aware merely that Egypt was attempting to build a medium-range ballistic missile. They wanted him to fill in the gaps.[12]

Wednesday, 23 January 1985, would be one of Pollard's last drops at Ilan Ravid's residence in Potomac, but he didn't know that yet. Still feeling elated from his trip to Paris two months earlier, he wanted to make a big impression. Following his previous drop-off at the house, he had continued to collect highly classified information for almost two weeks and had stored it in the ATAC. He was supposed to make the delivery on 21 January, but that evening he and Anne, along with some friends, attended an inaugural ball for President Ronald Reagan at the Shoreham Hotel.

At about 6:00 PM on Tuesday, 22 January, Pollard drove back to his office, knowing everyone had left for the day except two ATAC watch standers. His office was located on the second floor of the NIC-1 building, which also housed NIS headquarters. The security setup and layout in the SCI facility were flawed, allowing Pollard easy access. The area was supposed to be highly secured, but classified material did not have to be locked up. Sometimes it would accumulate several feet high and be left for the night, stacked on the floor or under analysts' desks. The two watch standers stood duty on the far side of the ATAC, answering phones and gathering intelligence reports from classified computers. Pollard's cubicle was located at the other end of the center. There were two doors into the ATAC, one near the watch standers, another at the far end through which Pollard could enter. His cubicle was no more than twenty feet from this door, separated from it by a small office and adjoining space, and the watch standers wouldn't be able to see him enter and exit because their view was obstructed by cubicle partitions.

Pollard was determined to remove every document he had stacked up in his work area during the previous two weeks. He segregated the messages from TS/SCI publications, which had to be signed out and returned. Carrying either his briefcase or a box stuffed to the gills, Pollard hauled the material down the corridor to the elevator and rode it to the first floor, then walked past the security guard and out to his car parked near the entrance to the building. Once in a while he would go and strike up a conversation with the watch standers, in case they were growing curious.

The security guard at the front desk did present a slight problem. The courier card authorized Pollard to remove classified material without a search, but to get back into the building after each trip to his car he had to ring a doorbell, it being after hours. The guard would have to get up, leave his small office, and open the door. To alleviate the problem, after a couple of trips Pollard informed the guard he was moving material from NIC-1 to NIC-2—the building next door—for a project he was working on. Pollard was lucky. The security guard didn't want to keep getting up to open the door, so he put a block down between the frame and the door to prop it open.

Pollard made some fifteen to twenty trips to his car, filling five suitcases to the brim. It took him nearly five hours to complete the task. Just before 11:00 PM, he finished and went home.[13] The security guard never made an entry into the logbook about Pollard's unusual actions that night, nor did he notify his relief. Security was lax, procedures were ignored; no one had the common sense to harbor suspicion.

On 23 January Pollard made his drop-off at Ravid's house. Ravid, Yagur, and a third person whom Pollard had never met were there. The

Israelis had already had a taste of what their operative could produce in volume; this time, the spy had outdone himself. Two suitcases contained TS- and SCI-coded publications that Pollard had to return on Monday morning, and right away the Israelis attacked those, pulling out the documents and running upstairs to copy them. The other three suitcases held highly classified messages that didn't have to be returned. At this meeting his handlers provided the analyst with two black leather briefcases in which to carry additional documents.

Van Ness Apartments, Washington, D.C. —SHANNON OLIVE

Up to this point the Israelis had felt fairly secure using Ravid's residence, but the material being passed was so voluminous and highly classified that they decided it would be prudent to choose a new temporary drop-off location. Irit Erb, who worked as a secretary at the Israeli embassy, had a place in the Van Ness Apartments at 2939 Van Ness Street N.W., not far from the embassy. Her apartment was quickly outfitted with a high-speed Xerox machine, and Yagur instructed Pollard to drop material off there in the future. After being furnished with keys to Erb's garage and apartment, in the event she wasn't home, Pollard began drop-offs every other Friday evening, unless there was a publication or a message he felt the Israelis needed ASAP.[14]

During his next encounter with Yagur, Pollard was introduced to an Israeli agent referred to as Uzi. Eitan had decided Uzi would soon be taking Yagur's place as Pollard's handler. The analyst never learned Uzi's real name. They needed a meeting place other than Erb's apartment, Yagur and Uzi said. The embassy had asked an American-Israeli lawyer who lived in Israel to purchase an apartment for embassy business. One was purchased in the Van Ness complex for $82,500.[15]

This new apartment was equipped with several sophisticated high-speed copying machines, and Erb began photocopying material there during weekends. Pollard would typically deliver the classified documents to Erb's apartment on a Friday evening. Erb would copy or have copied the documents for which Pollard was accountable, in order that he could retrieve them, usually on Sunday, for return to their classified repositories the following Monday. Materials such as messages or cables which Pollard was not accountable for were left with Erb.[16] On the last Sunday of every month, Yagur would fly or drive from New York and meet with Pollard at the newly purchased apartment to give him his monthly salary of $1,500 and to issue new instructions.

It was at one of these meetings that Pollard complained about his compensation. The work he was doing for Israel was dangerous, he argued, and the quality of the information he provided was better than anything Israel had ever seen through intelligence exchanges with the United States. He wanted more money. Unbeknownst to Pollard, the Israelis had already decided to raise his salary but they hadn't told him. How much? Yagur wanted to know. "Up it by a thousand," Pollard replied.[17] Yagur passed the request on to Eitan and it was approved. Now Pollard would start receiving $2,500 a month.

During this same meeting, the issue of the radio signal notations (RASIN) manual resurfaced. The only thing Pollard had been able to find out was that the manual dealt with extremely sensitive signal intelligence. Later, at a meeting in February 1985, Yagur showed him a copy of the first chapter of the manual. After looking it over, the analyst realized it was an NSA document. According to Pollard, Yagur told him that using this first chapter the Israelis had been able to access the uplink of the Soviet Military Assistance Group in Damascus, and that they "needed the whole manual to see if it was economically and technically feasible to decrypt the uplink signals."[18]

How did the Israelis get their hands on the first chapter of the RASIN manual? This question, and the fact that the Israelis were asking for documents by exact title, sometimes even by identification number, later led U.S. investigators to suspect that there had been someone else besides Pollard passing information to Israel. The news media would dub this mystery figure Mr. X, but his existence has never been proven. Still, the hypothesis raises interesting questions that persist to this day.

Chapter 9

THE FALL GUY

I n 1983 Kurt Lohbeck was working as a congressional staffer, rubbing elbows with high-ranking politicians and young people who had taken jobs in Washington on the coattails of the new president, Ronald Reagan. It was a heady time in the nation's capital, but Lohbeck was bored. One day he met a young woman who was well versed in the Afghanistan conflict. At that time Lohbeck knew precious little about the landlocked Muslim nation that the Soviets had invaded in 1980. She told him that since the Soviet invasion, American news coverage of the war consisted of a total of fifteen minutes. It was astounding, she said, that the invasion of a neighbor by a country the size of the Soviet Union wasn't getting more news coverage. Lohbeck, once a journalist who had freelanced for local television and radio stations in Texas and New Mexico, was stunned himself. After doing some research and discovering that no one wanted to cover the story because it was too dangerous, he raised some money to go to Afghanistan and make a documentary about the conflict. Before he knew it, he was in Pakistan meeting with top government officials and members of the Afghan resistance.[1]

One of the mujahideen (Islamic guerrilla commanders), Abdul Haq, believed that Afghanistan could some day prevail, forcing the Soviet invaders out. Over the years Lohbeck and Haq formed a lasting bond of trust. Because of the doors Haq opened for him, Lohbeck was allowed to interact with the mujahideen during every phase of the war and to shoot inside video footage. His was the first real coverage of the war from the point of view of the resistance. CBS, impressed by his footage and incredible stories, hired him on as their "man in Afghanistan."

Lohbeck eventually spent years in Afghanistan with the resistance fighters, returning to the United States for about three weeks a year.

Embassy of the Islamic Republic of Pakistan, Washington, D.C. —ELECTRONIC MEDIA

During one of those visits, in January 1985, he attended a party at a friend's house in Washington. The friend happened to be a close friend of Newt Gingrich, then-Speaker of the House of Representatives. At the party a person Lohbeck had never seen in his life walked up to him and said, "Oh, I'm glad you're safe. We've been following you and we've been worried about your safety." The guy was with a short, attractive redhead. Confused, Lohbeck asked who he was, and the fellow introduced himself by whipping out a picture with a caption that read, "Jonathan Jay Pollard employed as an analyst with the Naval Investigative Service." Pollard introduced the woman as Anne Henderson, his fiancée.

Why would any intelligence agency be interested in his activities in Afghanistan? Lohbeck wanted to know. After all, he was reporting everything to CBS, telling the world everything that was happening. This wasn't a secretive operation.

"We've been following you," Pollard repeated. "We can't talk here, there are too many people, but we have to get together."

They made arrangements to meet for dinner the following night at a German restaurant in the vicinity of New York Avenue. When Lohbeck arrived, Anne and Pollard were already waiting at a table for him. Out of the blue, the analyst pulled out a stack of classified situation intelligence reports, primarily CIA reports on Afghanistan. Lohbeck, along with some other journalists, was already getting such reports every Monday morning in Afghanistan, most of which were classified. The difference was that the situation reports offered by Pollard identified source and place of origin. To protect sources, such information is almost never revealed, particularly not in sensitive documents.

Lohbeck read over the reports, telling Pollard this was interesting stuff but adding: "A lot of it is bullshit. I know for a fact during that time period the Soviets weren't doing this in that part of the country, it was in another part of Afghanistan." Other information in the reports seemed credible. After dinner they parted ways, agreeing to get together again.

No sooner had he returned to his apartment than Lohbeck called Sam Roberts, then foreign editor of CBS News in New York, and told him about Pollard showing him classified information on Afghanistan. What should he do? "Come up to New York and talk it over," Roberts replied. [2]

During their meeting Roberts was quite stern. He told Lohbeck that because of his unique situation in Afghanistan, "everybody will try to co-opt you intelligence-wise." [3] Frequently, reporters knew more about what went on than the intelligence agencies. Roberts guessed that Pollard was an intelligence operative trying to recruit Lohbeck into passing information to him about Afghanistan. Lohbeck agreed. Roberts said, in so many words, that if the reporter wanted to stay on with CBS News he could not allow himself to be co-opted. Roberts kept insisting that Lohbeck couldn't let Pollard think he was going to become an intelligence agent, because he was not, he was a reporter. The lecture sank in. Lohbeck understood him loud and clear.

Throughout 1985 Lohbeck's visits to the States became more frequent. Every time he returned, he met the analyst for lunch or dinner several times. Pollard continued showing him classified documents, mostly coded secret but with some TS information. The intelligence dealt primarily with Soviet troop movements and plans for Afghanistan and Pakistan. One day over lunch, Lohbeck recalled, Pollard brought in a particularly memorable item. About an inch thick with a cover, photos, and drawings, it was a Soviet document, translated into English, that dealt with military plans for Pakistan once the invaders had solidified their control over Afghanistan. Pollard studied Lohbeck as he read it over. Then out of nowhere the analyst said, "Do you think you could sell this to Pakistan?"

"Jay," Lohbeck replied firmly, "my relationship with the Pakistanis is that they give *me* information, I don't give them information. I have a fairly good relationship with the Pakistani intelligence service. This relationship is the reason I can get in and out of Pakistan and Afghanistan. They're not going to pay me for anything."

On another occasion, at a coffee shop near Pollard's apartment, the analyst brought along a publication dealing with U.S. communications ability, classified TS. Lohbeck sat drinking coffee and skimming through it. Then he handed it right back and said, "Jay, I don't want to walk out of this coffee shop with this in my hand."

Pollard responded, "Well, we could sell it to somebody."

"Not *we!*" Lohbeck shot back. "I don't want anything to do with this." The reporter said that he informed CBS about Pollard trying to sell this publication, but nothing was ever said about it again.

On one occasion Pollard took Lohbeck to a location he believed was NIS headquarters. The analyst pulled into the parking lot and told him to come along. Inside the building Pollard flashed his identification. Lohbeck waited in the lobby while Pollard got on the elevator. When he returned about fifteen minutes later they got back into his car. The analyst reached into his overcoat, pulled out a stack of classified documents, and said, "Look at this, it's some good stuff." Pollard starting laughing at how easy it was to sneak the material past the lax security at NIS headquarters.

Lohbeck took the material home to peruse it and gave it back to Pollard the next day. "Jay's only comment was to say I was missing an opportunity to make a lot of money," Lohbeck told me.[4] He didn't know what Pollard ended up doing with the material.

Pollard also proposed a scheme to Lohbeck to sell foreign arms to Afghanistan via Saudi Arabia, which apparently appealed to the reporter because that way he could help the resistance fighters as well as make some money on the side. They would both get a commission. But Lohbeck steadfastly refused to sell the maps and other bits of classified information Pollard put into his hands.

Despite Lohbeck's refusals the two became fast friends, no doubt in part because the analyst was interested in Afghanistan, Lohbeck's passion. Pollard wanted him to be the best man at his wedding. At one point the reporter was getting ready to go back to Afghanistan when Pollard called him from Paris to say that he was getting married there. Lohbeck suggested that since he was flying to London the next morning en route to Afghanistan, he could take a short detour to Paris for the wedding.

When Lohbeck arrived in London, he called Pollard's room at the Paris Hilton. A man answered the phone and Lohbeck asked if Pollard was there. "Who's this?" the voice came back.

"This is Kurt Lohbeck."

"What do you want?" the man demanded.

Lohbeck said, "I want to talk to Jay. I'm supposed to meet him tomorrow."

The man on the other end of the line said, "Oh, he left." Lohbeck finally got around to asking who the man was and he responded, "Uh, this is his uncle, but Jay has left." Lohbeck often wondered who that man was on the other end of the phone. He is now convinced it was Rafael Eitan.

Lohbeck skipped the jaunt to Paris, and as it turned out, Pollard did not get married there. The next time Lohbeck saw Pollard and Anne in the States, she was sporting a huge blue sapphire surrounded by diamonds, and they still weren't married.

"How the hell did you buy that?" the reporter asked.

"My uncle paid for it," Pollard replied.

Pollard continued his attempts to make contacts with other countries. One time Lohbeck went with him to see Argentina's defense attaché on Connecticut Avenue. Pollard appeared to be good friends with the guy; they greeted each other by first name. Pollard asked the attaché whether the Argentines would sell their Cobra antitank weapon to the Afghans if he found someone to pay for it. The answer was yes.

Pollard then took Lohbeck to the South African military attaché's office near 19th and M streets. He and the attaché appeared to know each other well. The South African suggested a scheme by which they could make the weapons sale to Afghanistan happen. The Argentines would sell the weapon to the South Africans, who would pay for it and then sell it to the Afghan fighters. Lohbeck and Pollard would get the commission. Anne, at Pollard's request, had obtained Bureau of Alcohol, Tobacco, and Firearms forms so that they could register as international arms brokers. When Lohbeck found out about the forms he became upset, fearing that a background check would be initiated.[5] But no price was ever set, the deal didn't happen, and as far as Lohbeck knew, the Cobra antitank system never surfaced in Afghanistan.

The only other country Pollard talked to Lohbeck about was Taiwan, which he said had antitank weapon systems that might be equal to or better than the Argentines' Cobra.

Later, after his arrest, Pollard revealed to investigators other contacts he had made in hopes of gaining commercial contracts. He claimed to have met with a South African diplomat at a hotel off Dupont Circle to discuss the sale of night-vision scopes for the mujahideen. Supposedly, the sales would take place through a trade organization called NIMROD International. Within days the South African diplomat contacted Pollard with a price breakdown, which he later showed Lohbeck. According to Pollard, Anne attended both of those meetings. The arrangement was for the analyst, through Henderson, to receive a percentage of the sale as a commission if a contract was executed.[6] Again, no deal went through.

Pollard later told investigators that in addition to the Argentines and South Africans, he had contacted people from the embassies in Washington of these countries:

- Taiwan's. He approached the Office of Special Liaison to discuss obtaining the Bumblebee wire-guided missile.
- Brazil's. He and Anne went to this embassy and spoke with a woman about obtaining the Cobra missile.
- France's. Here he made inquiries about purchasing the short-range Mistral air defense infrared missile for the mujahideen.
- Sri Lanka's. He approached this embassy regarding ultralight aircraft but never followed up.
- Kenya's. He inquired about ultralight aircraft but never followed up.[7]

While all this wheeling and dealing (or rather, would-be wheeling and dealing) was going on—Pollard had a lot more success passing classified information to the Israelis than turning himself into a big-shot arms trafficker—Pollard continued to do drugs. Lohbeck witnessed several instances of cocaine use. Pollard carried around a one-gram vial of the stuff, and he and Anne would snort it through a rolled-up dollar bill, not only in front of Lohbeck, who didn't participate, but also sometimes openly in restaurants.[8]

The analyst was living recklessly, and it should have served as a warning to Lohbeck, but it didn't. During the period of their friendship, he had no idea that Pollard would eventually attempt to make him the fall guy for the crimes that Pollard himself was committing.[9]

Chapter 10

THE TEN-YEAR PLAN

■■

I n the summer of 1985, Yagur informed Pollard that he and his fiancée should prepare for another trip abroad, this time to Israel. Again he pressured Pollard to marry Anne. The Israelis offered to pick up the entire cost of the trip to Israel as well as the honeymoon. Pollard was thrilled. He hadn't been to Israel since attending the Weizmann Institute in 1971. Anne would finally get a chance to see the country where, he hoped, they would spend the rest of their lives and maybe have children. Getting married in Israel would be a dream come true.

When Yagur found out about Pollard's plan, he nixed that idea. When two people get married in the Jewish religion, a rabbinical investigation is conducted to prove, among other things, their Jewish heritage. Pollard couldn't get married in Israel because doing so would require such an investigation, and Yagur and Eitan were afraid it would draw attention to the couple. That was fine with Anne, who wanted the wedding to take place in Venice. The couple planned to take several weeks off, traveling first to Israel, then to Europe for the wedding and honeymoon. It would be an expensive trip, but they didn't have to worry about it taking a toll on their finances. They made arrangements through Cal Simmons Travel Agency in Georgetown, planning to stay in nothing but first-class hotels.

That wasn't going to work while they were in Israel, however. Pollard would have an operational contact meeting in Tel Aviv. For fear of attracting too much attention, Yagur told him not to ask for a suite at the Tel Aviv Hilton. Instead, Pollard should pose as a tourist of modest means and stay in a regular guest room.

In late July Pollard and Anne flew directly from New York to Tel Aviv on El Al Airlines because security was better on an Israeli carrier—at least for someone spying for Israel. Nevertheless, as Pollard recalled, "El Al security in New York almost did not let Anne on the flight because she did not look Jewish."[1] Pollard did not elaborate on this statement. Perhaps because of her Irish family name and her red hair, the Israelis believed Anne was not Jewish.

Upon their arrival in Tel Aviv, Pollard and Anne checked into the Hilton. Yagur called and made arrangements to meet them that evening.

Pollard and Anne attended a dinner held in their honor at Uzi's residence; Yagur and Sella and their wives were also there.[2] During this dinner and subsequent meetings with Eitan, the analyst was encouraged to double his espionage efforts. He learned that Uzi, being groomed to take over as his handler, was an international arms dealer who sold weapons to Iran. Pollard's antennae shot right up. Still harboring the pipe dream of selling arms to Afghanistan, the analyst talked to Uzi about a contact he had with the South Africans. It was incredibly careless of him to broach this subject. No handler wants an agent doing international arms deals on the side that might attract attention and compromise his effectiveness as a spy. The only element of discretion Pollard can be said to have observed was in not telling Uzi that this situation had once gotten him in trouble on an NIS polygraph exam.

The next morning Anne went shopping and sightseeing with Yagur's wife while he and Pollard visited Eitan, who was in the ophthalmic ward at Beilinson Hospital for eye surgery because of an injury he had received earlier that summer. Security for this undertaking was extremely tight. The Israelis had to "clean" the entire floor, that is, remove anyone who might question Pollard's presence and make sure no Americans were in the area.[3] As he and Yagur were about to enter Eitan's room, a guard in civilian clothes started to search the analyst, but stopped when Yagur gave the order.

Eitan's room was cramped and sparsely furnished, just a bed and no chairs. When Pollard and Yagur walked into the room, a nurse was cleaning out Eitan's eye. After the nurse departed, Eitan and Yagur went over a computer-generated list of the material the analyst had passed them so far. The publications were meticulously sorted by title and serial number, the messages by date-time groups, the intelligence information reports by originating defense attaché office and number. It was a lengthy list, to say the least, and Pollard didn't know why they were reviewing it with him.

When Eitan produced photographs from the NPIC, Pollard noticed that the photo of the bomb damage inflicted on the nuclear facility in Iraq he had given to Aviem Sella was missing. Sella must have kept it for himself after the meeting at Dumbarton Oaks, Pollard thought. The analyst didn't mention it to Eitan.

Eitan praised Pollard for the excellent job he was doing, which far exceeded expectations. The spymaster, who had once been under the impression that the U.S. security system was as good as Israel's, could hardly believe his good fortune. Since their last meeting, Pollard had provided the missing chapters of the precious RASIN manual. The manual, which according to Eitan had already been put into partial operational use, had helped "break out" the specific signals the Israelis were interested in without a big waste of time and money. They were working on exploiting the satellite uplink signals at the Soviet Military Assistance Group headquarters in Damascus. Eventually, they would be able to read the signals, Eitan added, and "then the fun would begin."[4]

The spymaster described the information the Israelis hoped to glean from the uplink as an "indications and warnings" asset, which in the event of hostilities would be crucial. Because they had the RASIN manual, the Israelis would be forewarned on exactly what the Syrians and Russians might be planning. Israel believed the Soviets would be completely integrated into the Syrian military command.

Pollard had also provided the Israelis with a DIA study that detailed an invasion scenario in which Syria attacked Israel at a point along the Golan Heights. Eitan told Pollard the Israeli planners were upset about this document because it didn't fall in line with their own scenario.

Later that afternoon Pollard revisited the question of what would happen if he and Anne were caught. Eitan told him not to worry, that "no drastic action would be taken against [you]—it hasn't happened in the past. We haven't taken action on the U.S. collecting here." If something did go wrong, the Israelis would take care of him. When Pollard asked for specifics, Eitan dismissed the topic.[5]

Raising his voice, the analyst pointed out that he was taking great risks. He was worried about his safety. He was providing Israel with a wealth of information. He wanted assurances, and he deserved a raise. The argument became so heated that the guard outside the door looked in to make sure everything was all right. Eitan refused to increase the analyst's salary because of the risk that he would be discovered with unexplained income; it was much too dangerous. Rather than offering Pollard more, the spymaster fueled his anger by pushing him to "redouble" his espionage efforts.

As the argument continued, however, Eitan did offer a carrot. Instead of giving their informant a pay raise in cash every month, the Israelis would establish a Swiss bank account in the name of Danny Cohen. This would be part of a ten-year plan. Pollard would continue his services to Israel, and in return, every year for the next ten years, they would deposit thirty thousand dollars into the Cohen account. Pollard wouldn't have access to this money until the operation was over, at which point he would be given the signature cards that allowed him access to the accumulated funds. Eitan assured Pollard that thirty thousand a year was what he would make if he were living and working in Israel. They were taking a long-range view of this operation. After ten years Pollard could bow out and relocate to Israel. Yagur hung his head when Eitan made these remarks.[6]

It happens in the career of every spy: The initial excitement and intrigue wear off and disillusionment begins to set in. Pollard was emotionally devastated by Rafi Eitan's revelation that the operation would continue for ten more years, and he was unable to respond. Though he appreciated the offer, he was still upset. Ten more years of this was more than he had ever bargained for.

On the ride back to the hotel Yagur said to Pollard, "You're obviously not ready for this." No, he wasn't. Yagur counseled him to put this behind him for the time being and enjoy the rest of his visit in Israel.[7] Should any U.S. personnel in Tel Aviv recognize him, the

Israeli cautioned, he should say he was there for a trade conference or for his honeymoon. The next day Pollard and Anne moved into the King David Hotel in Jerusalem and were provided with a tour guide who spoke perfect English, as well as the use of a car for three days, all expenses paid. They visited the Golan Heights, Massada, Jericho, and a Palestinian refugee camp. At one point during the tour, the driver commented that they must be VIPs because it was unusual for the prime minister's office to call and arrange for Israel's best tour guide for three days—all expenses prepaid.[8]

Yagur's advice about enjoying himself had fallen on deaf ears. Pollard was having a difficult time concentrating on the tour. He was worried, really worried. Newspapers around the world were plastered with headlines about spies being arrested. Several spies operating in the Department of the Navy had been arrested in recent years, not to mention others uncovered in the NSA, the CIA, and the FBI. At the time the most infamous case in the navy was the Johnny Walker spy ring. Walker, who had recruited his son Michael, his brother Arthur, and his friend Jerry Whitworth, had been arrested on 19 May 1985. Pollard could hardly sleep at night.

Two days into the tour, distracted and anxious, he called Yagur at home and demanded to see the old man again. In addition to assurances that the Israelis would provide him with safe asylum if he were detected, Pollard wanted to rehash the subject of money. Yagur promised he would arrange another meeting. The analyst should go to the Tel Aviv Hilton and Yagur would pick him up there. While Pollard and Anne were on the road from Jerusalem to Tel Aviv, a car pulled up behind them and the driver began honking. By chance—or perhaps because of surveillance—it was Yagur. The tour car stopped and Pollard switched cars while his fiancée stayed behind.

Yagur drove him straight to the hospital. This time, instead of going to Eitan's room, Pollard was directed to the security office. Eitan stormed into the room, holding one hand over his bad eye, agitated by Pollard's demand to see him again. The whole operation "stunk," Pollard complained, and demanded to know how it was decided the operation would last ten more years. He had to have more money. Eitan repeated that he could not give him more money. The Swiss bank account would be set up, and if something did happen they would take care of Anne. In the midst of Pollard's continued badgering, Eitan abruptly ended the conversation. "Okay, look," he said shortly, "take two thousand more and have a good time in Europe. End of discussion. I've had it! *I'm* running this operation," and he stormed out.[9] The meeting lasted no more than fifteen minutes.

There was nothing more Pollard could do or say. Yagur drove him to the Hilton, where he caught a cab back to Jerusalem. That night, while Pollard and Anne were having dinner with Yagur and his wife, Pollard was handed an envelope containing twelve thousand dollars, two thousand more than he was initially going to get for his travels.[10]

Pollard departed Israel with no concrete reassurance that the Israelis would, in fact, rescue him should he be caught. There was still no escape plan, no emergency phone number, no safe house in which to hide until arrangements could be made to sneak him and Anne out of the United States.

From Israel the couple traveled to Venice, where they were married on the ninth of August. After the wedding their itinerary took them to Vienna, Zurich, Paris, and London, a trip so exhilarating that Pollard put all concern about his safety behind him. They enjoyed luxury accommodations in every city and even in between, spending one night on the Orient Express in a cabin that cost seven hundred dollars.

After they returned home, the biweekly deliveries resumed. At a meeting with Yagur, Pollard was shown the Israeli passport bearing his picture and the name Danny Cohen. The document was a demonstration of gratitude for his services. Pollard was pleased, doubly so when Yagur told him that right after leaving Israel he had flown to Switzerland and made a deposit of thirty thousand dollars.[11] Yagur would hold on to the passport and the bank signature cards for the time being, until Pollard emigrated to Israel.

The Israelis had lured Pollard, and now they had him hooked. The ten-year plan was a means of stringing him along and maximizing the volume of intelligence he gave them. Why should they enrich him all at once? That would only invite detection (because sudden wealth would serve as a red flag) or outright defection. His payment—$2,500 in cash every month and $30,000 every year for ten years accumulating in a Swiss bank account—was paltry considering the grave risk he was taking, and the Israelis knew it. For the incredible volume and quality of intelligence Pollard was feeding them, the money he received amounted to nothing more than thirty pieces of silver.

Chapter 11

TALL TALES

■■■■■

D
espite Pollard's worries about getting caught, he continued
to spread stories abroad that were a bizarre mix of fact and
fiction. It is not clear what his motives were. In some cases he
seemed to be trying to impress people, in other cases, trying to deceive
them. And then there were stories so fantastic that they appeared
merely to reflect the workings of a delusional mind. Whatever his
motives, one thing was certain: Pollard was raising eyebrows.

One evening, around the time the analyst returned from his
honeymoon, the NIS's assistant director for counterintelligence, Lanny
McCullah, was working in his corner office on the second floor of the
NIC-1 building, some forty feet from the ATAC spaces. It was about
five o'clock. Exhausted after a twelve-hour day, he was still doing
paperwork when Pollard suddenly popped into his office. The analyst
asked whether McCullah knew anyone who could help him. When
McCullah asked what was wrong, Pollard told him that his fiancée
had been kidnapped from a gun show and was being held hostage in a
motel nearby. He said he had reported the license plate number to the
FBI, but they weren't doing anything. McCullah, too preoccupied to
pay him much heed, glanced up, told Pollard to follow-up with the FBI
because he wasn't going to get involved with them, then turned back to
his work. Pollard thanked him and left. McCullah told me years later
that he wished he had paid more attention to Pollard's comments. They
would have signaled his instability.[1]

On another occasion Rear Admiral Cathal "Irish" Flynn, director
of the NIS at the time, was in the ATAC making small talk with the
analyst when suddenly Pollard told him that he had once been arrested
in Damascus and thrown into jail, where he was tortured. He didn't

say for what. Israeli hero Eli Cohen was tortured by the Syrians and hanged for treason. Perhaps Pollard was fantasizing that he himself was Cohen. The name, after all, appeared on his fake passport. Or perhaps he was delusional. Whatever the case, Flynn was taken aback. Pollard seemed quite serious. Babbling on, the analyst claimed that he knew people in the Israeli security service and that the Israelis bugged hotel rooms.

Then, Pollard jumped to an entirely different subject: the NIS's vulnerability assessments of port security. The assessments were nothing but a big joke, he told the admiral brazenly. This erratic conversation happened in the course of ten short minutes. Pollard, Admiral Flynn concluded, was disgruntled. In fact, he seemed to hate the NIS.

Not long afterwards, over dinner at a navy function, Flynn expressed his concerns to Jerry Agee, the ATAC commander. Agee shrugged it off, commenting, "That's just Pollard."[2]

According to Richard Sullivan, a supervisor in the ATAC at the time, Pollard told him that he had earned an advanced degree in mathematics, and that his father, Morris, had been the CIA station chief in Prague, Czechoslovakia, during the spring of 1960.

While Pollard continued to tell tall tales, his work, once highly praised by supervisors, began to go downhill. Though he worked the Americas desk, he was still obsessed with the Middle East. When he began neglecting his intelligence reports, Sullivan and two other analysts in the division, Ron Brunson and Robert Bouchard, repeatedly had to massage them in order to get intelligence out to the fleet.[3] Pollard was also missing deadlines for status reports and product reviews, and it was discovered that he was several months late in filling out a security update form. His supervisor, Tom Filkins, taking heat from Commander Agee, gave Pollard a verbal warning regarding his performance and said that if it didn't improve, he would receive a written warning. To Pollard, however, warnings were like water off a duck's back.

I didn't know Jonathan Pollard in the summer of 1984 when I was transferred into a job with special operations at NIS headquarters.

I had been assigned as a desk officer at Code 22B responsible for counterespionage operations against nations that were either Communist or hostile to the United States. I was never sure why I'd been transferred into special operations—probably because of my involvement in a string of successful operations as a counterintelligence squad leader in Naples, Italy. Personally, another field office would have been my choice, but I made the best of the transfer and quickly adapted to the headquarters way of doing business.

One project I became involved with—way out of my purview—was to make a Navy Department presentation on reporting suspicious activity. The old counterintelligence awareness briefings, called collector's briefings, that presented the methods Communist and hostile countries used to try and recruit U.S. sailors and Marines were sorely outdated. I wrote a proposal for a short training film on counterintelligence awareness and submitted it. To my surprise, it was approved. The film featured a sailor who was tricked into committing espionage after falling in love with a "swallow" (spy lingo for a female agent who seduces people for intelligence purposes) KGB agent and explained how the trap worked. Ten months later the film was set to go into production.

In June 1985 I lived in Virginia and commuted to the office with Frank Bloomingberg, head of the NIS's polygraph program, and Victor Palmucci, the NIS's executive assistant director. The promotion board was to meet that day and Palmucci was a senior player on the board. Up for a promotion, I kept my thoughts to myself during the drive in.

I had been late getting up that morning, and in my haste I grabbed my shoes from the closet, shoved them on, and hurried out the door into the predawn darkness. It was Bloomingberg's turn to drive that morning; Palmucci was sitting in the passenger's seat, and I was alone in the back. When we had almost reached headquarters, the sun started to rise and I happened to glance down at my shoes. There, staring back up at me, was a black shoe on my left foot and a dark maroon shoe on my right. Both were the exact same style. You've got to be kidding me! I thought, my heart sinking. If there were any chance of my getting a promotion, it would be over when Palmucci saw this. I could just hear him saying, "You want to be promoted to a supervisory position and you can't even match your shoes—forget about it!"

When we arrived at the office, we climbed out of the car and I let my fellow car-poolers walk about twenty feet in front of me, then hurried into my office and removed my shoes. It was seven o'clock, and the closest shoe store wouldn't open until nine. For two hours I padded around the office in my socks, worried that my boss, Special Agent Phil Comes, would see me and spread the story of my stupidity all over headquarters.

Lucky for me, that didn't happen. I ended the day on the promotion list, which was disseminated to all NIS offices and headquarters' divisions, and a few weeks later was offered a job as assistant special agent in charge of counterintelligence at the NIS's Washington Navy Yard field office. This was a prestigious position that carried with it major responsibilities. I was elated.

At the time, Pollard was working in the ATAC. We still hadn't formally met, though I recall passing him in the hallway because the ATAC was located just down the corridor from the Code 22B offices. This was about three or four weeks before my August transfer to the field office. One day, out of the blue, Pollard showed up in the Code 22B spaces, introduced himself, and congratulated me on my pending promotion. No sooner had I thanked him than he launched into a story about—what else?—a good friend of his who was the naval attaché at the South African embassy in Washington. It was a drawn-out account of how this attaché might be able to get me information on arms sales to the mujahideen in Afghanistan.

The first thing that popped into my mind was, Is this guy a nut? But the more I listened, the more he sounded like someone who knew what he was talking about.

Pollard was still chattering away when I interrupted him to say that I didn't think there would be a navy connection. Instead of information on arms sales to the mujahideen, would this attaché friend of his be able to give me anything on planned terrorist attacks against navy personnel and installations in the United States and around the world? That was the type of information I could use. (This reminded me of one of our missions in Naples. We were to collect information on terrorist threats against the Department of the Navy. The Italian police allowed Special Agent Joe Riccio and me to interview a member of the *Brigate Rosso*

[Red Brigade] and a member of the *Prima Linea* [Front Line]—terrorist organizations at that time. The two members were under arrest and cooperating with the police. They gave us intelligence on their plan to ambush and kidnap or kill Admiral William J. Crowe Jr., commander in chief of Allied Forces, Southern Europe. It was a big coup for the Naples office and for us.)

Yes, Pollard said, the attaché could provide well-placed intelligence about planned terrorist attacks. Listening to him, I started imagining what a big impression I would make at the field office if I were to get my hands on some good intelligence. Of course, before using this attaché as a source of information, I would have to get permission from headquarters and the Department of Defense. In the meantime, I asked myself, what harm would it do just to talk to the guy? Pollard said he would approach his friend and arrange a meeting.

The story seemed too good to be true. After all, I didn't know Pollard, and why would he want to help me? But hope overrode my natural inclination to be suspicious.

A week passed. By now we were on a first-name basis. Every time I ran into him in the hallway I would say, "Hey, how are you doing, Jay? Did you talk to your contact yet?" Every time his answer was no, and he had a different excuse.

One day he told me he was going to set up a meeting in a small movie theater somewhere in downtown Washington. Well, the only small movie theaters I had heard about in D.C. were devoted to porn. I told Jay that wouldn't work because it would be too dark in a theater, we couldn't have a proper conversation. I preferred a restaurant. He agreed and said he would let me know the details. The last time our paths crossed before my transfer to the field office, he said he would continue trying to set up the meeting, but it never materialized.

After my transfer in August I didn't hear from Pollard again, nor did I try to call him for an update. He was nothing but a storyteller who liked to impress people with his supposed contacts, I concluded, and didn't give the matter another thought. Besides, I had my hands full with my new job. Without knowing it, I adopted the same distorted thinking as everyone else who encountered Jonathan Jay Pollard. I wrote him off as harmless.

As assistant special agent in charge of counterintelligence, I had my work cut out for me. The educational film I had written on counterintelligence awareness, "The Waiting Man," was now in production, and the director had me playing myself. My agents and others at headquarters appeared in portions of the film, while local professional actors played the main characters. Everyone did a great job of acting—everyone, that is, but me. Take the worst spaghetti Western you ever saw, then take the worst actor in it, and his acting would be Oscar caliber compared to mine. The film was later shown to U.S. Navy sailors and Marines around the world, and it took the better part of a year to live down my performance.

One other item on my agenda, besides supervising upwards of eighty counterintelligence investigations, was to conduct protective service details for foreign defense officials. This fell under "extra duties" at the field office. And it just so happened that in November the minister of defense for Israel, Yitzhak Rabin, was coming to town to conduct fundraisers for Israeli bonds.

To coordinate the detail, some of my agents and I met with the chief security officer at the Israeli embassy. The officer, whose name escapes me, was extremely difficult to work with. He kept demanding changes to our protocol, and he wanted to dictate where Israeli agents would be placed while Rabin was in motorcades and walking around. He seemed to forget that he was in our country, not his. I didn't agree to most of his demands. After all, if something went haywire, it would be my reputation on the line. Furthermore, although there was a threat against Rabin's life in the Middle East, there wasn't the slightest hint of a threat against him in the United States. For that reason, I told the security officer, we could put only a third of our agents on the protective detail. The security officer said this was unacceptable.

Back at the office one of my agents, Rich Cloonan, told me to stand by. He said every time Israeli security was planning for the arrival of their minister of defense, it played out the same way. The NIS would try to reduce the detail owing to a lack of threat and, lo and behold, within forty-eight hours the ATAC would receive a phone call from the State Department indicating that an unidentified individual had made a threat. Sure enough, the threat came in no more than twenty-four hours later. Whether it was real, perceived, or contrived made no difference.

I had to initiate a full detail with more than thirty agents, reducing our resources at the field office to a skeleton crew.

So far, I was doing well in my new job. It was much bigger than I had anticipated, but I liked challenges, and a challenge is exactly what was in store for me. Though there was no way I could have known it at the time, the Jonathan Jay Pollard case was about to blow wide open, right in the middle of my watch.

Chapter 12

A SECRET TIP

━━━

I t was just a matter of time before the analyst was discovered. Even spies who are trained in their craft and possess the utmost discretion run the risk of arrest. Pollard had neither training nor discretion.

The man who can be credited as the first both to notice Pollard's suspicious activity and to take it seriously enough to follow through by reporting it was a coworker of the analyst's who did not want his name revealed. To this day, few know his identity. During an interview I had with him, I didn't ask why he wanted to retain his anonymity. It was none of my business, and besides, I understood that without a guarantee of anonymity, much suspicious activity in the intelligence community would never be reported. At any rate, he is a true hero, the only person I know of in the whole sordid saga of Jonathan Jay Pollard who had the courage and patriotism to come forward and report that something "was out of the ordinary and just didn't seem right." This chapter is his story, and the story of the dedicated supervisor to whom he reported.[1]

On Friday, 8 November 1985, shortly before 5:00 PM, Pollard's ATAC coworker wasn't feeling well. He decided to go home a few minutes early. Just before leaving the office, he spotted Pollard holding up a list of document titles attached to the front of an envelope. The envelope contained TS/SCI message traffic he had just retrieved from the SPINTCOM center in the basement. The messages, as always, were double wrapped and sealed with brown masking tape. Pollard was telling some other analysts how stupid he was for requesting all the wrong documents from the center downstairs. He was upset; now he had to go back downstairs to the computer room and destroy the documents.

An ATAC analyst could order TS and SCI material from a special computer with links to all intelligence agency networks, military or civilian. Once the requested documents had been gathered, a SPINTCOM employee would call the analyst to say they were ready for pickup. The analyst would then go downstairs to the computer room, show his or her credentials and courier card, sign for the messages, and pick them up. An analyst who was finished with a TS/SCI document had to sign it back in. Most of the time returned material was destroyed under the two-person rule; that is, the person who ordered the material would have someone witness it being shredded, then sign a notice verifying that it had been destroyed.

Naval Investigative Service (NIS) Headquarters, Suitland, Maryland. —NIS/FBI AERIAL PHOTO

The coworker wasn't paying much attention to Pollard. He left the ATAC, got into his car, which was parked directly across from NIS headquarters, and waited for his wife, who happened to work in an office nearby.

While waiting, he observed Pollard's wife drive into the half-circle parking lot and pull up directly in front of the entrance to NIS headquarters and the NIC-1 building. She got out of the car and set off toward the building when, suddenly, Pollard emerged from the lobby and came down the steps to meet her. In his hand was an envelope sealed with brown masking tape, just like the one he had been complaining about a few minutes before.

The coworker thought to himself that Pollard could never have gone down to the computer center in the basement and destroyed the material so fast. This must be the same package. Where was he taking it? Thinking the analyst was probably going to drop it off at another intelligence agency, the coworker was about to blow it off. Then Pollard got into the car with his wife and headed away from the NISC. Maybe he's going to the DIA, the colleague thought. But Pollard's car turned in the opposite direction.

On the drive home with his wife, who also had a security clearance, the coworker told her what he had witnessed and voiced his suspicion. All kinds of crazy ideas were running through his head. Why had Pollard's wife picked him up? Would he show the material to her, or worse, to a foreign country? Should he report what he had seen? And if so, to whom? If he told someone, his name might be brought up during an investigation. What if he was wrong and falsely accusing Pollard of something he hadn't done? What if the word spread throughout headquarters and he was labeled a snitch? His colleagues would no longer trust him. He would be shunned, and risked losing his job.

Then he began to rationalize his coworker's actions, coming up with excuses. What if Pollard had been authorized by his supervisor to take the classified material somewhere? Pollard would never commit a security violation. Stop overreacting, he told himself.

While he agonized over the matter, his wife listened. Finally, she told him that if he felt so strongly there was something wrong, he needed to report it. Although still fearful that his suspicion might be unfounded or not believed, he decided to call his supervisor, Commander Agee, when he got home.

Before being promoted to commander of the ATAC, Jerry Agee had been assigned to the Sixth Fleet in the Mediterranean. In 1983 he was off the coast of Lebanon analyzing the terrorist intelligence reports that streamed in from across the region. He had also recruited military personnel from Communist countries for collection operations.

The coworker made up his mind not to tell Agee exactly who it was he had seen. This would prevent a lot of embarrassment if he were wrong. All he would say was that he had seen someone take something out of the building, it was late in the afternoon, and the person did not head in the direction of one of the intelligence agencies. No big deal.

Back at home, he phoned Commander Agee, hoping he was still at work. When Agee answered the phone, the coworker cautiously told him the story of what he had seen. Agee asked him who the person was, and when he didn't respond, the commander said jokingly, "Was it Ron Brunson?" referring to a hardworking analyst in the ATAC who also happened to be a prankster. The coworker didn't think it was funny. Suddenly it dawned on him that by withholding the name he might force Agee to start a witch-hunt that would eventually blow up in his face. He had no choice. It was Jonathan Pollard, he admitted, then pleaded with Agee to conceal his identity. He was anguishing over this, he said, afraid he might be accusing Pollard of something he hadn't done. Agee told him not to worry.

In an attempt to get this resolved quickly, the coworker suggested, Agee might want to check Pollard's office to see if there was a torn manila envelope in his wastebasket, on his desk, or somewhere else in his cubicle. That would indicate that Pollard had removed the material in the package and left it in his office rather than removing it from the building. If not, Agee might want to go downstairs to the Special Intelligence Communications center and see whether or not Pollard had returned the materials and had them destroyed. There was no getting around the fact

Jerry Agee. —RON OLIVE

that the coworker had seen Pollard take a package out of the building taped the way TS/SCI documents were always taped. He knew Pollard had classified information; he just didn't know where he had taken it.

Commander Agee thanked him and told him again not to worry; he would keep this to himself. While there might be a reasonable explanation for Pollard's behavior, Agee had no doubt that the coworker had accurately reported what he had seen. He was not one to overreact in any situation.

As soon as he hung up, Agee took the elevator down to the communications center to see whether Pollard had picked up or returned some SCI documents that day. The logbook showed that the analyst had indeed picked up SCI message traffic at about 4:00 PM, but there was no indication that the documents had been returned or destroyed. He had signed out numerous lengthy messages, and their subject matter, interestingly, did not lie within his area of responsibility. The documents dealt with intelligence in the Mediterranean and the Soviet Union.

Commander Agee hurried back up to Pollard's cubicle and began poking around, first checking his wastebasket for an empty manila envelope. Nothing. Nor was there a torn envelope on top of Pollard's desk. He did notice some papers on the Middle East but didn't think much about them. Next he checked the "burn bag," used for disposal of classified information. When full, a burn bag is sealed and taken to a secure location awaiting transportation to the Pentagon. Once at the Pentagon it is deposited in an incinerator for destruction. There was no empty manila envelope in the burn bag. Then Agee glanced under the desk. Highly classified documents and message traffic were arranged in two-foot high stacks, but again, no envelope.

Back at his desk, Agee sat down and began to work through what he knew. Late in the day Pollard had definitely signed for highly classified materials whose subject lay outside his purview. They had not been returned and could not be found in or around Pollard's desk. His immediate conclusion was that the ATAC employee's report of events was probably true. Pollard had the security documents with him. Then the question was, why had he left with those materials, where were they, and why would he commit such an egregious security violation?

It was about eight o'clock on Friday night. Tired, Agee realized that he could have missed the materials during his quick search, or that Pollard could have locked them up in his safe. Should he simply call Pollard and ask him where the materials in question were? No, he quickly decided. First, Pollard was a notorious fabricator and unlikely to tell the truth, and second, it would give him the opportunity to return the materials quietly and claim they had never left the ATAC. Agee decided to wait until Tuesday (Monday would be Veterans Day) to approach Pollard, without telling him the source of the information. It was late. Tomorrow was Saturday and the commander was looking forward to a restful weekend.

On his way home to Annapolis, however, he couldn't stop mulling over the problem of Pollard. The analyst's behavior had been remarkably eccentric over the past year, and in spite of that he had been assigned to work the terrorism problem on the Americas desk at the ATAC. Although Pollard had requested an assignment to the Middle East desk, he was refused because he lacked the experience. Besides, another analyst already held that job. Was Pollard unhappy? He had been missing deadlines for reports, and his supervisor, Tom Filkins, had given him the verbal warning regarding his performance. Agee himself was upset with Pollard for being months behind in producing a paper on the Caribbean. Yet the analyst was obviously working diligently, out of the office a lot collecting materials and meeting with analysts at various intelligence organizations. On the other hand, if Pollard was going to such lengths to collect information, why would he delay writing up the Caribbean report?

When Agee finally made it home, his wife, Karen—also a naval intelligence analyst—asked why he had been delayed. He explained that he had a problem with one of his employees. A serious security violation might have occurred. She asked what "serious" meant.

Over a late-night dinner Agee laid out his concerns, and Karen's "comments laid bare the issue he faced." She was blunt about the need to pursue this further. Agee knew she was right, but the question still facing him was how.

Commander Agee couldn't sleep that night. It was three o'clock in the morning and a gut feeling told him he needed to go back to work. So much for his restful three-day weekend. By five he was in his car and by six he was back in the ATAC. He asked the watch standers if they had seen the kind of manila envelope that held TS/SCI material discarded in the trash or lying around. No, they answered. And so Agee began a cubicle-by-cubicle search of the ATAC, looking in every trash can and burn bag, on top of and underneath every desk. He searched Pollard's cubicle again. No envelope.

While in Pollard's space Agee decided to check out the stack of highly classified documents, books, and message traffic he had noticed the night before. He started sifting through the material. To his shock, which swiftly turned to aggravation, he noticed little under Pollard's desk that dealt with his area of responsibility. In fact, the material dealt almost exclusively with the Soviets, their missile systems, and the Middle East. It came from various intelligence agencies, but mostly from the DIA. In all, Pollard had thousands of pages of highly classified information. *What is he doing?* Agee thought angrily. The more he saw, the more questions he had.

Pollard was a strange bird. He said crazy things. He was missing deadlines and delaying production in the ATAC. Agee had caught him in lies. The analyst had been given a form to update his SCI clearance that was due in August. It was now November, and the form still hadn't been turned in. What if Pollard had been removing messages? What if—no. Agee stopped in the middle of the thought. He feared something was wrong but couldn't bring himself to admit it. Just like his employee had done the night before, Agee was rationalizing away his suspicions.

Returning to the communications center to determine just how much classified information Pollard had been signing for and what type of information it was, he confronted the staff member at the window. "I can't tell you why I'm asking and you can't say anything to anyone," Agee told the sailor. He wanted a computer printout of the titles of everything Pollard had requested during the previous six months.

When Agee saw it, he almost did a double take. The list was incredibly long. Every week for six months the wayward analyst had been picking up message traffic packages, almost all coded TS or SCI, and almost all dealing with the Middle East and the Soviet Union. Just as significant, most of the packages were picked up on Fridays.

The ATAC commander's stomach turned. Clearly, Pollard's action of the previous Friday was not a random event but part of a deliberate pattern of behavior. Each Friday evening he probably took the classified material out of the facility. *He has to be giving this stuff to somebody,* Agee thought.

Kurt Lohbeck? About six months earlier Pollard had told Agee about the freelance reporter who was slipping over the mountains from Pakistan into Afghanistan, reporting on the Afghan insurgency against the Soviets. Pollard wanted permission to task Lohbeck with getting information about arms sales to the Afghans, but the ATAC commander said no and told him to discontinue his contact.

By now, Agee was convinced the Pollard affair was no simple security violation. It was much more serious than that—possibly even espionage.

As he gathered more data, Agee tried to piece together the evidence in a rational manner. The volume and nature of the materials Pollard had accumulated indicated more than a passing interest in the terrorist threat in the Middle East. In fact, the materials had to do with U.S. military operations in the Mediterranean and the latest Soviet weapon systems. In Agee's analysis, although the Soviets were probably keen to know more about U.S. military activities in the Mediterranean, they wouldn't be acquiring technical material on their very own systems. Moreover, many countries in the eastern Mediterranean possessed those same Soviet-produced systems. There was only one country that would have an interest in all the materials Pollard had in his possession, Agee thought. Yet that would be difficult, if not impossible, to prove.

The implications of an allegation would reach far beyond the U.S. Navy and its intelligence organizations. The manner in which the NIS handled this explosive situation was critical, Agee realized. He went back up to his office and, knowing he couldn't keep this to himself until

Tuesday, thought of calling Lanny McCullah, NIS's assistant director for counterintelligence. At first he hesitated. After all, Agee was a commander in the navy. If he were wrong, his career could be over. For that matter, if he were right it could be over. Either way, he had to do something, and right away.

McCullah was an outstanding assistant director with broad experience in the intelligence community. He had worked for the Menlo Park, California, Police Department in the early sixties, and later as a special agent with the

Lanny McCullah in memoriam.
—PROVIDED BY DARLENE MCCULLAH

Office of Naval Intelligence. In his position with the NIS, he had sat on numerous intelligence committees and had testified before the House and Senate intelligence committees on policy recommendations and navy spy cases.

So, on a sunny Saturday morning in early November, Agee called to say he needed to discuss something with him that couldn't wait. McCullah told Agee to drop by his house. Agee hurried over to McCullah's suburban home, pondering how to break the news to him. Shortly after he arrived, they shared a beer on the back porch while Agee briefed him.

The two doubted that Pollard was actually engaged in espionage. What country could be so foolish as to recruit someone like Pollard, of all people?[2] McCullah told Agee that on Tuesday morning he would brief Admiral Cathal Flynn, director of the NIS.

That weekend, neither Agee nor Pollard's anonymous coworker could have realized the incredible events that were about to unfold. Had it not been for these two conscientious men, U.S. national security would have suffered an even more severe blow, and Jonathan Jay Pollard might have escaped to Israel without ever having to pay the price.

Chapter 13

THE WHEEL BEGINS TO TURN

On Tuesday morning, 12 November, Assistant Director McCullah arrived early to work so he could get his foot in Director Flynn's office before anyone else. Flynn was a colorful figure who had attended schools in Ireland, France, and Spain before graduating from Trinity College, Dublin, in 1959. After spending thirty years with the navy SEALs, he was promoted to rear admiral and took over as head of the NIS.

After briefing Admiral Flynn on what had taken place since Friday, McCullah said he didn't know whether a foreign government was involved, but something was definitely wrong—so wrong that Flynn would probably have to tell the Chief of Naval Operations, Admiral James D. Watkins, and Secretary of the Navy John Lehman. Following his talk with Flynn, McCullah arranged a meeting with the FBI for late Tuesday morning.

NIS headquarters called that morning and summoned me to an urgent meeting. Because of the Rabin detail and other pressing commitments, I asked if someone else could attend in my place. In that case, I was told, I should send one of my best agents.

Special Agent Lisa Redman —RON OLIVE

Special Agent Elizabeth "Lisa" Redman, not on the Rabin detail, was without doubt one of my best agents. I had once wondered what made a quiet, seemingly timid woman like her become a federal agent in the first place. Then something happened she didn't like—an investigation gone awry—and it was as if a fire had been lit under her. Without yelling, she made her point of view known. Agent

Redman was extremely competent and thorough in everything she did, which was why, years later, she became the assistant inspector general for investigations with the Department of Homeland Security.

I told her about the meeting at headquarters in Suitland and asked her to attend in my place. She was to brief me upon her return. Others at the meeting that Tuesday morning were Agent McCullah and his deputy, Agent Lance Arnold; Commander Agee; Lieutenant Commander Thomas Connelly, an NIS attorney; and several FBI agents.[1]

After Commander Agee briefed everyone on the events that had unfolded since Friday evening, Agent McCullah told the FBI he wanted them to open an investigation on Pollard. Their response was lukewarm. They had other cases in the works, they said, and couldn't spare the manpower. What they didn't mention was that these included two major spy cases that were about to break wide open.

McCullah was adamant. The NIS was dealing with a serious security violation at the least—espionage, at the worst. He wanted the FBI to open an investigation and surveil Pollard, using helicopters or fixed-wing aircraft in the air and its Special Surveillance Group on the ground. The FBI agents insisted they couldn't spare the time.

According to McCullah, one supervisor from FBI headquarters asked if Pollard was at work. When informed that he was, the agent said, "Let's just pull him in here and talk to him about it. I'm sure he'll have a reasonable explanation."

McCullah, whose underlings affectionately called him the Prince of Darkness, prided himself on never chewing out anyone who didn't deserve it. His management style was like Wyatt Earp's. He held people to the highest professional standards but never asked anybody to do anything he wouldn't do himself. When he heard the FBI agent suggest that they have a casual chat with a man suspected of possible espionage, his fist came slamming down on the table. "Damn it," he exclaimed, "if you don't want to conduct this in a professional manner, then we'll handle it ourselves without you!"[2]

Taken aback, the FBI agents agreed to open a preliminary investigation; the meeting was adjourned.

In a preliminary investigation, the FBI's procedure was to gather background information on the individual in question through the National

Crime Information Center (NCIC). Not until FBI headquarters authorized a full-field investigation could the Washington field office obtain a search warrant or order wiretaps, which it did through the Foreign Intelligence Surveillance Court. The problem was, it could take months for FBI headquarters to authorize a full-field investigation.

Later in the day McCullah asked Commander Connelly about the legality of putting a surveillance camera in Pollard's work space. Would that intrude on his right to privacy? Connelly answered that there was no "expectation to privacy," that Admiral Flynn could issue a command-authorized search based on probable cause. The equivalent of a federal search warrant from a magistrate judge, this would allow for a video camera, but no sound.

Unfortunately, Admiral Flynn had already left town on other business. Connelly would have to go up the chain of command.

The first thing out of Redman's mouth when she came back to brief me was, "They think Jonathan Pollard might be a spy."

"Gee-sus krist, you gotta be kidding me," I said.

Having worked at NIS headquarters, I knew the people there had a tendency to make mountains out of molehills. Why would this be any different? But that didn't matter. Mountain or molehill, once the investigation opened, my squad would be handling the case. NIS headquarters had oversight and made policy; investigations were usually left up to the field offices.

Personally, I never had a problem with the Prince of Darkness. If someone was right or presented facts that made sense, McCullah would usually listen and back down. Nonetheless, I didn't want to find myself being chewed out on his red carpet, and to avoid that I vowed to continue at full speed with the investigation.

I told Agent Redman to open an initial action lead sheet, that is, a short report describing why Pollard was being investigated. Of course, being suspected of and committing a crime were two different things. The action lead sheet indicated that an inquiry was being initiated to prove or disprove the allegation. We didn't have to wait for a green light from NIS headquarters to proceed; unlike the FBI, we could move forward with a full investigation.

To keep things quiet, I decided to classify the action lead sheet as a secret/no-foreign-dissemination document, and to provide it to headquarters through a back channel.

Redman informed me the FBI was opening a preliminary investigation. Since the FBI had jurisdiction over civilian cases like this, we usually had to follow their lead. With the FBI involved, this case could go on for months or years without closure or arrest. In normal espionage cases, evidence was gathered slowly, piece by piece, secret search warrant by secret search warrant, until a solid case could be made. I was somewhat relieved not to have to deal with it all. What I didn't know was that NIS headquarters, Lanny McCullah to be exact, had a different idea of how this case was going to be conducted, an approach that would cause me many sleepless nights and repeated bouts of heartburn. Alka-Seltzer became my best friend.

On 13 November Agent Redman visited the FBI's Washington field office at Buzzard's Point, in a run-down neighborhood on the banks of the Anacostia River, to discuss the case. She also checked Pollard's personnel records but found nothing of significance.

The command-authorized search was issued, allowing the NIS to place two pinhole video cameras in Pollard's cubicle in the ATAC. The cameras were to be installed in the drop-ceiling panels. The first would give an overhead view of the entire cubicle: Pollard's L-shaped desk, his desk drawers, and his safe. When Pollard worked at his computer, positioned at the inner corner of the L, the camera would show a left-side view of him. It would be placed in such a way as to catch him storing documents and other material. The second camera would give a view of a small passageway leading to Pollard's cubicle. In this area, some ten feet from his cubicle, was a wooden mailbox with slots where ATAC members picked up message traffic and administrative materials. The camera's eye allowed a side view of the mailbox.

The trick now was to find a way to install the cameras without causing suspicion in the ATAC. Being an SCI facility, it was manned around the clock with no fewer than two people in the spaces at any time. The ATAC never shut down. To get the cameras into place the NIS technical services branch, Code 26, was called into action. The agents in Code 26 were experts at covert surveillance. They devised a plan in which Commander Agee would inform ATAC employees that, owing to an increase in the electrical load from more and more personnel and computers, the power would be shut down and the ATAC rewired.

The bugging itself would actually be completed at night, when only two watch standers were on duty. This would minimize suspicion and prevent a total disruption of ATAC activity. And so, for about two hours on Wednesday, the ATAC shifted to another location, its staff limiting their work to answering phone calls. Later, the technicians ran wiring through the drop ceiling and rigged up the closed-circuit television cameras with a view of Pollard's cubicle and the small passageway leading to it.

The camera monitor was set up in the office of Special Agent Jack Tuckish, assigned to photography and tech services. His office was almost directly across the hall from the ATAC and his doors were always locked. Both cameras operated around the clock, taping every minute, and the monitor was always on, its black and white split screen giving simultaneous views of Pollard's cubicle and the small passageway. Because most of the field office was still on the protective service detail for Israeli Defense Minister Rabin, NIS headquarters took the job of rotating its agents to watch the monitor. Agent Redman set up the schedule.

NIS headquarters also wanted outside surveillance on Pollard. McCullah initiated this with headquarters personnel and told me about it as an afterthought. Special Agents Robert Cathcart and Pam Connelly were tasked to watch Pollard's car in the parking lot and follow him in the event he went anywhere during his lunch hour.[3] I was none too happy about the use of headquarters personnel for this task because it meant that headquarters would make some decisions outside of the field office. To compound the situation, my special agent in charge, John D'Avanzo, was still on vacation. Without him, I thought I wouldn't have much influence with headquarters should a major decision have to be made.

At the surveillance monitor in Tuckish's office, the agents watched black and white images of Pollard at work, putting papers in his desk and in envelopes and packages, but they couldn't read any of the documents because of the poor resolution. This was 1985—the image was comparable to that produced by a camera recording a bank holdup.

On Thursday, 14 November, the analyst ordered a large batch of classified documents from the SPINTCOM center. Commander Agee arranged to withhold these from Pollard to see how he would react. In fact, I believe Agee stored the documents in his safe. He told someone at the center to make up an excuse as to why the documents were delayed—and to make it sound good. When Pollard called down to the communications center asking for the documents, he was told that because of a computer glitch his package wasn't ready. He could pick it up on Monday. Reportedly, Pollard was furious.

Friday, the fifteenth, the camera monitor caught something significant.

It started at 10:51:00 in the morning, according to the monitor's time clock. Pollard stepped into the passageway outside his office, glanced into the cubicle across from the mailbox, then walked out of sight of the hallway camera. Twenty-four seconds later he returned to his desk with a briefcase, which he placed upright on the floor, half under his desk. The briefcase was a standard size, some five inches deep. It had two roller combination locks on top, one on each side of the handle. Pollard left his cubicle and returned six and a half minutes later.

Then the following sequence of events occurred:

10:57:48   Pollard shoved the briefcase under his desk, out of sight of the person in the cubicle next to his, sat down, and appeared to open the briefcase.

10:58:36   He opened the lower left-hand drawer of his desk, removed some papers, reached in again, pulled out a batch of documents about two inches thick (approximately five hundred sheets), then reached under his desk and placed the documents in the briefcase.

10:58:58   He was removing a three- to four-inch stack of documents from the same drawer when suddenly, seeing something out of the corner of his eye, he stopped and started to close it. The analyst in the opposite cubicle entered the passageway and moved out of sight. Pollard went back to what he was doing, using both hands to pull a large bundle from the drawer, then bending over and reaching under his desk again. The coworker came back down the passageway and turned into her cubicle. Pollard, busy cramming documents into his briefcase, didn't seem to notice her.

10:59:11   He began shuffling papers in the drawer, then pulled out another stack and, with some difficulty, for now the briefcase was getting full, shoved it in. After much squirming and shifting about in his chair, he finally closed and locked the briefcase. Finally, he sat up, looked back in the drawer, which was still a little over half full, and quickly thumbed through the remaining pages.

11:00:29   He closed the drawer and removed a folded piece of paper from his shirt pocket. (The NIS later inferred that this was a "shopping list" of documents the Israelis had requested.) After looking over the paper, he opened the drawer again, dropped the paper in, and closed it.

11:00:56   Getting up from his desk, he tucked his shirt in and put on his sport coat. Finally, he slid the briefcase from under the desk and, bringing it along, briskly walked down the passageway and out of sight of the camera.[4]

Based on the standard of five hundred sheets in one ream of copying paper, it was estimated that in the short space of about three minutes, Pollard had removed up to three thousand pages of highly classified information.

Murphy's Law states that anything that can go wrong will go wrong. The person assigned to the monitor for that period, whoever it was, happened not to be watching during this three-minute episode, and it wasn't discovered until months later. I found out about it when everyone else did, during a viewing held for the assistant U.S. attorney's office to determine if the film contained any evidence useful for a possible trial. "Gee-sus, tell me this isn't so!" I exclaimed when I realized the oversight. I was just as shocked and angered as my colleagues.

To make matters worse, the surveillance agents outside had failed to pick up Pollard leaving the parking lot. As it turned out, the analyst departed early without permission from his supervisor and didn't return to work that day.

The Israelis must have had a busy time copying material at the Van Ness apartment over the weekend. At least they got an earlier start on that particular Friday.

When Pollard failed to return to work on Friday afternoon, Lanny McCullah was fit to be tied. It didn't help that the FBI hadn't moved forward an inch on Pollard. While they were dragging their feet, he might have had a spy sitting right down the hall from his office. I received a call from Lance Arnold, McCullah's deputy assistant director, informing me they wanted surveillance on Pollard after work on Monday. Arnold also called the FBI field office and FBI headquarters to inform them of the plan.

Throughout the weekend the hidden cameras were monitored, but Pollard didn't return to the ATAC. That was fine with me. I had a chance to rest up, which proved to be a good thing. That weekend would be the last time I'd be getting any R&R for quite some time to come.

Chapter 14

THE BEGINNING OF THE END

O n Monday morning, 18 November, I called the FBI's Washington field office and laid out the last-minute plans for the surveillance. Having missed the meeting on the previous Tuesday, I was under the impression that, at a minimum, the FBI would have their fixed-wing small aircraft in the air, their Special Surveillance Group on Pollard, and at least a dozen agents assisting. Not so, I was told. They could spare only two agents and they would be lucky to dig up a single vehicle. "What the hell are you talking about?" I said. This was crazy. The FBI field office numbered about seven hundred agents, a little less than the NIS's entire worldwide organization. Surely they had resources to spare.

Apparently, every agent in the FBI office was out on other investigations, everyone, that is, except Special Agents Lydia Jechorek and Kenneth Farmer, who were made available for the Pollard case. On our end, only Elizabeth Redman and I could tend to Pollard because my other agents were winding down the protection service detail on Defense Minister Rabin.

I wondered how we would conduct a moving surveillance from Suitland, Maryland, to Dupont Circle in Washington, D.C., at the five o'clock rush hour, with less than a handful of agents. Commander Agee was going to have the communications center release to Pollard the documents he had ordered the week before. It didn't take me long to nix the operation. If our suspect disappeared in the hectic commuter traffic, which was highly probable, we stood to lose even more SCI material. In addition, McCullah would come down on me hard. I told my FBI colleagues that it wouldn't work, pointing out that if Pollard went into an apartment complex other than his own with the material and came out empty-handed, we would lose the classified material.

But McCullah had insisted that we get to the bottom of this right then. That being the case, our only option was to wait until Pollard walked out of headquarters with the package that afternoon and then approach him when he started climbing into his car. We would have no reason to arrest him at that point. Though we knew the coworker had seen Pollard leave with classified documents on Friday, 8 November, he could say he dropped them off with an analyst at another agency, picked them up Tuesday morning, and brought them back. All we could do was ask him to speak with us voluntarily to clear up some questions. If he were innocent, Pollard would have no reason not to feel comfortable talking to us.

I discussed this option with NIS headquarters and they agreed the surveillance was too risky. We would take our chances with the interview. I was surprised that McCullah, who had been so dead set against an interview just one week before, agreed to this plan.

That Monday, Special Agent Bob Cathcart and Deputy Assistant Director for Counterintelligence Lance Arnold were monitoring the cameras surveilling Pollard. He spent the entire workday at the ATAC, reading his message traffic, thumbing through documents, and stuffing various papers in the same drawer from which he had taken papers the Friday before. At one point Arnold observed Pollard pull a note from the bottom left-hand drawer of his desk, check it, then begin rifling through files. He peered at the note a second time, then a third, then returned it to the drawer.[1] In the afternoon the cameras caught the following sequence of events:

15:24:00   The monitor showed a note taped to the front of Pollard's chair, informing him his package was ready to be picked up from the communications center. Pollard had already seen the note and was retrieving the documents.

15:25:34   He arrived back at his cubicle with the package, removed the note from the chair, pulled a folded piece of letter-sized paper from his pocket and read it intently, tore it in half, then put it in the burn bag under his desk.

16:39:57   He entered the cubicle with large envelopes. After removing two small stacks of classified information, earlier retrieved from the communications center, from his bottom left-hand drawer, he placed them in an envelope. After borrowing Scotch tape from a nearby cubicle, he taped the envelope shut and inserted it into another, larger envelope, approximately thirteen by fifteen inches, secured it with masking tape, and placed the large envelope in a basket on his desk.

17:02:41   Pollard stopped at his mailbox and began to read message traffic. Commander Agee came up and stood next to Pollard, likewise reading his message traffic. Neither man looked at the other or spoke.

17:06:58   Back at his desk, Pollard finished a cup of coffee, rubbed his forehead, and sat for a minute in deep concentration. He then stood up, opened his left-hand desk drawer, and turned the small combination lock on the top edge of the drawer. He retrieved a tissue and appeared to be wiping the lock off as if he spilled something on it, then closed the drawer again. He tucked the back of his shirt in—he wasn't wearing a sport coat that day—and after retrieving the envelope with the documents inside, turned off the light. In the aisle outside his cubicle he checked his mailbox one more time before disappearing from sight. The time on the monitor read 17:08:36.[2]

While this was happening, Redman and I climbed into separate vehicles in the parking lot. At about 4:30 PM, FBI agents Farmer and Jechorek arrived in a banged-up van that looked as if it might have been seized at the first Woodstock music festival; all it lacked was graffiti. I gave them an extra radio so Redman and I could communicate with them. Inside NIS headquarters, everyone involved had radios too, including McCullah.

By now, several people had gathered around Cathcart and Arnold to follow Pollard's moves on the surveillance cameras. I was the only one stationed outside who could recognize Pollard. McCullah tried to reach me on the radio to say that the suspect was on his way out of the building, but Murphy's Law took hold again and his radio didn't work. While McCullah cursed his bad luck and told Agent Connelly to contact me immediately, Pollard exited headquarters. I saw him come down the front steps and head toward the large parking lot across the street.

Unbeknownst to me as I sat there watching, Pollard was playing a high-stakes game with the Israelis. He had good reason to be concerned. Between January and October 1985, ten spies had been arrested for espionage—navy spy Johnny Walker, his son Michael, his brother Arthur, and friend Jerry Whitworth; an air force enlisted man by the name of Edward Buchanan; CIA spy Sharon Scranage; navy spies Bruce and Michael Tobias; Stephen Hawkins*, an enlisted navy man; and Francis Pizzo, a civilian working for the Navy Department—and more arrests were imminent.

Had it not been for his arrogance and greed, maybe Pollard would have listened to the instinct that told him his behavior was turning more reckless by the day. But he didn't. He missed his chance to cut the Israelis off. Little did he know that over the course of the next few minutes, the fears he had expressed to Rafael Eitan would be realized, and the cushy life he and Anne had built for themselves would come tumbling down.

Clutching his taped-up package, Pollard closed the distance between himself and his car. I radioed Redman and Jechorek and described Pollard. We pulled out of our parking spots and from our separate locations zeroed in on the suspect, driving slowly so as not to alert him. It was critical that he not be given the opportunity to start his car and pull off before we stopped him. Upon reaching his vehicle, Pollard opened the front door. As he slid into the driver's seat, Redman walked up and, flashing her badge and credentials, identified herself as an NIS agent. Then the FBI agents converged on Pollard.

---

* Stephen Hawkins admitted that he had taken secret messages and confessed to the idea of selling them to a hostile intelligence service (espionage). He was charged with wrongful removal of classified material and wrongful destruction of a top secret message.

At first he looked confused. When I joined the group and caught Pollard's eye, neither of us acknowledged the other. Redman and the FBI agents said they wanted to talk with the analyst about some issues that needed straightening out and asked him politely if he would mind returning with them to NIS headquarters. Without hesitation, Pollard agreed. We escorted him to a space on the first floor of the building that had been set up for an interview. It was in the NIC-1 area (NIS headquarters was housed on the second and third floors). Once inside, I informed Pollard this wouldn't take long; we just needed to talk to him about a couple of matters.

I had decided not to join the interview, which left three people to conduct it. This was still too many in principle, but I wanted to make sure my agent was present. Redman, Jechorek, and Farmer began the session at approximately 5:30 PM. Since Pollard was not under arrest or accused of anything and had voluntarily agreed to the interview, he was not advised of his rights. At any time he was free to go. All he had to do was say, "I've had enough, I'm going home." The interviewers asked him what was inside the envelope he was carrying. He responded by giving them general titles. The agents decided not to open the package because Pollard had not yet been accused of a crime. Instead, they began posing questions about his job and the ATAC.

In the meantime, I went upstairs to see how the search was going. On my way I informed Arnold of what was going on on the first floor. The area around Pollard's workstation had been cordoned off with crime scene tape. Cathcart and another agent, Al Sipe, who was working the Walker family spy case with the FBI and had been pulled off to assist with the search, got to work. Cathcart was the first to look over the material on top of Pollard's desk, which included a lot about Soviet weapons capabilities. Though tempted to look in Pollard's desk, he decided to wait until the command-authorized search from the navy came through.

At about six o'clock I hurried down the hall past the office of Director Flynn, who was out of town on business. Flynn's executive assistant, Special Agent David L. Brant, appeared in the hallway and asked what was going on. "Right now I don't have time to talk," I said as I shot by him. Looking back, that was probably a mistake because Brant was on the fast track at the NIS and would eventually become civilian director of its successor, the Naval Criminal Investigative Service (NCIS).

Back downstairs I waited around outside the interview room. Agent Redman came out and informed me that Pollard said he had intended to drop off his package at the NISC to be analyzed by a friend with whom he used to work. According to her, Pollard said he did this all the time, giving information to analysts in other commands to compare their conclusions about the contents to his own. Pollard had given Redman the name of the individual, and she gave it to me. It was a plausible story, I thought, but it seemed late in the evening to be dropping off highly classified material. Regardless, it had to be checked out, not later, but right then.

I phoned Gerry Nance, the assistant special agent in charge of general crimes at the NIS's Washington field office, who had been put on standby in case we needed him. Nance was a mild-mannered agent who knew his job well. Explaining the situation, I asked him to come over to NIS headquarters. He radioed Jeff Jenkins, a hardworking young agent who at the time was conducting a search of an officer's residence, and told him to drop everything and head over to headquarters. As soon as they arrived, I sent them over to the NISC to check out Pollard's story. About twenty minutes later they called to tell me that the individual whom Pollard had named had left the building hours ago.

"Contact the duty officer in charge," I told Nance. "Get his home phone number and address, and go over there and interview him."

About an hour later, Agent Nance contacted me and said the person had not seen Pollard in more than six months, had had no dealings with him on any analytical issues during that time, and was not expecting him to drop off a package at his desk that evening. According to this individual, Pollard knew he always left work at four in the afternoon. Not good. I passed this information on to Redman, and she confronted Pollard with it. He explained that when this person was not available to analyze material, he would deliver it to another analyst, someone at the DIA, and he gave Redman that individual's name. This version of his story would also prove to be false.

Pollard admitted to nothing. While he was explaining away every question the agents asked him, ready with an excuse for all his actions, authorization for a search had arrived from the navy. I dashed back upstairs to find Cathcart and Sipe, now joined by Arnold, in the analyst's cubicle packaging evidence. They seized what seemed to me to be everything Pollard had on, in, and around his desk and safe. I told Arnold and Commander Agee what was happening downstairs. McCullah was nowhere to be seen, but I didn't think much of it at the time.

Downstairs again, I ran into Jechorek and Farmer taking a break from the interview. I took them aside and told them that we desperately needed authorization from Pollard for a permissive search of his apartment. A permissive search is one voluntarily agreed to, conducted without a warrant and with the suspect present. The FBI agents were highly skeptical. They didn't know how much longer they could hold Pollard. They were now about two and a half hours into the interview and he continued to deny any wrongdoing. As I watched them go back into the interview room, my hope began to fade.

During the next break Redman stayed in the room with Pollard. The FBI agents told me that just as they had feared, the analyst declined to give them a permissive search. Without probable cause that a crime had been committed, it would be tough to get a federal search warrant for Pollard's apartment. Without any evidence of a crime, they went on, they were probably going to have to terminate the interview.

"You can't do that!" I said. "We have to keep talking to him because he has these documents for a reason—he was taking them somewhere, and his explanation doesn't check out." Furthermore, I pointed out, Pollard hadn't told his supervisor or anyone else he was leaving to drop the documents off. Of course, he was free to go at any time, but we needed to stall him for as long as possible.

"We'll have to ask our supervisor," Farmer said.

The answer was what I'd feared: They couldn't hold Pollard too much longer if he didn't admit to something.

Redman emerged from the interview room and said that Pollard, who was late for a dinner engagement with his wife and someone else, had asked to call her. Redman allowed him to make the call but remained by his side. Pollard phoned Anne and informed her that he was tied up at work. Redman heard him say, "Why don't you go to dinner without me? . . . Go ahead and take Chris the *cactus*, you know, the *cactus* we bought for her birthday?" Anne said something on the other end to which Pollard responded with a curt yes before hanging up.

A few minutes later, he asked if he could call his wife back because he had forgotten to tell her something. Again, he was told it was all right. This time Pollard told Anne not to forget the *wedding album* because the neighbors hadn't seen their wedding pictures.

All of this struck Redman as odd. Men weren't in the habit of reminding their wives to show off wedding photos—if anything, it would be the wife reminding her husband—and as for the cactus, Redman thought it sounded like a code word.

"You might be right," I said. "Make sure you take notes on exactly what happened."

Redman's hunch was correct. As we would later find out, on the very eve before the interview, Pollard, who seemed to have had a premonition that he was on the verge of arrest, had spoken with Anne about what to do in case he was ever in trouble. He came up with the code word *cactus*, the name of a new weapon system that had recently been popping up in classified message traffic. If he ever uttered this word in any context, it meant that he was in trouble, that she was to clear the classified documents out of the apartment, and then contact Avi Sella or Yosef Yagur. *Wedding album* was another code, to remind Anne that their wedding album contained classified documents pertaining to China. At the time, Anne was still looking for a job with the Maryland-based public relations firm CommCore, which hoped to get a contract with the Chinese embassy in Washington. Pollard had taken these documents to help her with a proposal she was going to make to the company and the People's Republic of China's embassy.[3]

It was now three or four hours into the interview and Pollard was still denying that he had done anything wrong. According to Redman, he was rambling on about his life and his job. At approximately nine that night, the FBI agents emerged from the interview room and said they couldn't hold Pollard any longer. When I asked if they'd had any more luck securing a permissive search, they told me Pollard wouldn't give one. His reason was that his wife sometimes smoked marijuana to ease the severe pain caused by a stomach disorder, and there might still be some marijuana in the apartment.

"We have to keep talking to him," I insisted. "We need that permissive search. If we don't get it, the case could fall apart."

They trudged back into the interview room and I set about trying to get a search warrant based on Pollard's spontaneous comment regarding the marijuana, asking Nance if he or one of his agents on the drug squad could get in touch with the D.C. police narcotics division. Was there a magistrate in D.C. who would give us a search warrant based on Pollard's slip?

Later Nance got back to me and said he'd contacted the D.C. narcotics detectives. The good news was they could probably find a magistrate to issue a warrant. The bad news was that it probably wouldn't hold up in court. Suddenly I was faced with the old "fruit of the poison tree" dilemma. If we found classified documents based on a bad warrant for drugs, the evidence would be inadmissible in court.

"Great," I said with a hefty dose of sarcasm. There was no way I was going to take that chance.

By now it was around ten at night. One more time Jechorek and Farmer emerged from the interview. "This is it, we *have* to let him go."

I urged them to hold out just a bit longer, telling them this was the last chance we might ever have to snag someone who might have committed serious crimes against the United States. While they called their supervisor again, I went back upstairs and told Arnold and Nance that the FBI was about to pull out and go home. I couldn't stall them much longer. Commander Agee, who overheard the conversation, said he needed to get Pollard's badges and have him sign a waiver that his clearances would be suspended until further notice and he was not to come back into the building until this was straightened out. He couldn't leave until this was done.

"Why don't I talk with Pollard while we take care of all this administrative stuff?" he said.

Our options were running out, and nobody was getting anywhere, so I reluctantly agreed to let him talk with Pollard. Agee was the officer in charge of the ATAC, not a federal agent, and to my knowledge he wasn't trained in conducting interviews, but I decided to break the rules and let him do it. This was a huge investigative blunder on my part that could have backfired in everyone's face. I didn't realize how much Agee hated Pollard.

"Go on downstairs," I said. "Tell Agent Redman I said it's okay for you to take care of this administrative business."

All the agents left the interview room. Agee had Pollard sign the forms and he took his access badges and courier card. It didn't take long for the ATAC commander to start accusing Pollard of spying. Before I got back downstairs, Agee had lost his temper and was screaming at him. Agent Jechorek, hearing the commotion, had to bust into the room and physically escort Agee out of the room, leading him by the arm. Another break was announced and Pollard went to the rest room on the first floor.

I was crushed, thinking I had blown it. Up to this point Pollard seemed to be enjoying the attention he was getting. He kept rambling on and on, but at least he was talking, buying us time and increasing the chance that he would let slip some vital piece of information. Now, however, there was the danger that Agee had upset him and that Pollard would clam up. Nobody accused of being a spy, given what had happened, would continue to cooperate. To make matters worse, Farmer and Jechorek told me their boss had ordered them to terminate the interview in no more than thirty minutes. Thirty minutes, period!

When Nance found out the FBI was leaving in thirty minutes, either he or Arnold called McCullah. According to Nance, McCullah began yelling and threatening to handcuff Pollard to his chair until morning. It was probably just hyperbole, but knowing McCullah, I couldn't be positive. One thing I was sure of: If Pollard were let go, the assistant director would be furious.

The three interviewers were waiting for Pollard to return from the rest room when I saw him coming around the corner. I was directly in his path, and our eyes met. Deciding I had nothing to lose, I reached out and stopped him. He had tried to befriend me once with his story about the South African attaché, and although we hadn't talked since I'd left for the Washington field office, it was time to use that slight connection to try and turn the tables on him. Our conversation went something like this.

"What's going on, Jay?"

"I don't know," Pollard replied. "Everyone's asking me what I was doing with those documents. I keep telling them but they won't believe me. Then Jerry Agee comes in and starts yelling at me, accusing me of being a spy."

I ignored that comment. "Look, Jay, you know and I know this is all bullshit, so why are you doing this? Why don't you just give us a permissive search? Nobody's going to find anything. We can get this thing straightened out and call it a day." I was pulling stuff out of the air, talking as fast as I could to see what, if anything, he would respond to. He didn't say anything; he just listened.

"If it's about the marijuana, forget it!" I went on. "Just between you and me, I don't give a damn about marijuana in your house. I'm not going to nail you on some measly marijuana charge, Jay. We just need to search your place to see if there are any documents there, and if we don't do the search, your life and my life will be miserable. You know we won't find any, so what's the big deal? Don't do this to yourself. Go back in there and give them permission to search your apartment. I'm tired and you're tired. Let's just get this over with and we can both go home."

Pollard stood there, poker-faced and dead silent. A few seconds ticked by, then he turned on his heels and walked back into the interview room. I lost him, I told myself. I blew it and it's over.

A short while later, sometime before eleven, Redman emerged from the interview room with a gleam in her eyes. "Pollard gave us permission to search his apartment," she announced.

I couldn't believe my ears. It was as if a huge burden had been lifted off my shoulders. Not until later did it occur to me that Pollard, rather than being persuaded by my argument, must have figured that after all his rambling talk, he'd given Anne plenty of time to get rid of the classified information. Apparently, he felt it was safe to go home.

Thank God, we've overcome the first major hurdle, I thought. We hurried out into the parking lot and headed to our cars, not wasting any time. Not, that is, until the FBI agents started up their battered hippie van. The headlights wouldn't come on. So, Farmer jumped into Redman's government vehicle and Jechorek climbed into my car and we set off, following Pollard home.

In the meantime Anne, frightened out of her wits, had been scrambling around the apartment trying to follow her husband's vague command. *Cactus, wedding album. . . .* She wasn't practiced in the art of disposing of classified documents, certainly not the reams and reams of documents that Pollard had amassed. And what happened while her husband was being interviewed for nearly six long hours at the NIS was a twist of fate so uncanny that even the most experienced counterintelligence agents in the business were astounded when they heard the story.

Chapter 15

A TWIST OF FATE

W hen she hung up the phone, Anne's head was spinning. Cactus? Wedding album? She and Jay had only just worked out the code words. Was there something her husband knew that he hadn't told her? Was the FBI onto them? Whatever the answer, Jay was in trouble. Anne had been getting ready to go out for dinner. Aviem Sella, Pollard's original Israeli handler, and his wife happened to be in Washington, and they were supposed to meet the Pollards for dinner.[1] Chucking those plans, she hauled the nylon-cloth suitcase out of storage, one of several Jay used to make deliveries to the Israelis, and frantically began stuffing it with

classified documents. There were so many! She had to make sure she got every single page. She couldn't forget the classified documents on China she had been working on.

Working against the clock, not knowing how much time she had left, she clapped the suitcase shut and dragged it to the front door of their apartment. Her plan, devised without the luxury of forethought, was to throw

Small nylon suitcase containing classified documents —NIS EVIDENCE PHOTO

the suitcase in a dumpster located in the alley behind their apartment building. That was easier said than done. The suitcase weighed about seventy pounds, and Anne, in addition to being petite, was out of shape, her girth having spread from their month after month of fine dining.

With much huffing and puffing, and now feeling sick to her stomach, she dragged the suitcase down three flights and out the rear entrance of

Alley behind the Pollards' apartment —RON OLIVE

the apartment building. The dumpster was on the other side of the alley. Glancing to her right and left before crossing over, she spotted a car at the end of the passageway. Her heart almost stopped beating. It had black-wall tires and two antennas on the trunk, the engine was running, and she could hear the dry, scratchy sounds of radio static. Two men sat in the front seat. The scene matched everything Jay had told her about government agents and their unmarked cars. They had to be FBI. She and Jay were under surveillance!

The evidence in the suitcase had to be destroyed, but how? Certainly she couldn't take it back up to her apartment. For all she knew, the FBI would come knocking on her door at any time. Besides, the suitcase was too cumbersome to drag back up the stairs. No, it would have to be moved elsewhere. At her wit's end, Anne decided that the only course of action was to approach the neighbors. Surely her need for help could be explained in a manner that would not arouse their suspicion. And so she lugged the suitcase back into the building and across the floor, placing it under the first-floor stairwell.

She then hurried upstairs and knocked on her neighbors' door. Christine Esfandiari—the woman with whom Pollard had told his interviewers at the NIS he and Anne would be dining that evening—poked her head out and beheld a very distraught-looking woman. Ms.

Esfandiari asked Anne to come in but she refused, launching into a frantic, breathless explanation of how her husband was in big trouble and she needed help removing a heavy suitcase from the building. When Ms. Esfandiari questioned her about the suitcase, Anne said that she had asked Jay to help her out with some information on the Chinese embassy and that the suitcase contained classified documents.[2] They were going to burn them but never got around to it, she added. Please, could Christine help her?

By now the husband, Babak Esfandiari, an Iranian studying in the United States, had come to the door. Eventually, he agreed to help out. Anne asked him to retrieve the suitcase from under the first-floor stairwell and transport it to the Four Seasons Hotel in Georgetown. She would meet him there in the lobby, take the suitcase, and somehow destroy the documents.[3]

Four Seasons Hotel —RON OLIVE

After slipping Babak ten dollars for the taxi ride, Anne left and walked around the neighborhood for a short while to see if anyone was following her. Thinking the coast was clear, she hailed a cab, but just to be on the safe side, she made the driver take a circuitous route to the hotel. She had him drop her off a block away from the Four Seasons, and then walked in circles in case she was being trailed. In the meantime, Mr. Esfandiari retrieved the suitcase, caught a cab, and went directly to the hotel. He looked for Anne in the lobby, then the bar, thinking she might be having a drink. After waiting for what seemed like a long time, he went outside and took a cab back home, bringing the suitcase with him. Shortly thereafter, Anne arrived and began looking for Babak.

Seeing no sign of him, she started to panic and called the Esfandiari residence to find out if Babak had left his apartment yet. Yes, Christine replied, he should be at the hotel. Frightened, Anne finally called Aviem Sella at the Holiday Inn in Bethesda, Maryland.

O'Donnell's Seafood restaurant located half a block from the Holiday Inn in Bethesda, Maryland —RON OLIVE

It was around ten o'clock. Sella answered the phone. He was worried, he told Anne, because she and Pollard hadn't shown up for dinner. Anne said she had to meet right away, alone—it was urgent. They arranged to meet at O'Donnell's, a restaurant about half a block from the Holiday Inn. There they sat in a private booth and Anne spilled the whole story.

"Are you sure he's in trouble?" Sella asked.

"Yes! You have to help me."

Sella seemed unresponsive, so Anne began raising her voice. Presently, Sella told her to wait where she was, he had to make a phone call.[4]

No doubt Sella's impassivity was a facade hiding panic inside. The Israelis supposedly believed Anne knew nothing of her husband's spy activities, but certainly they weren't that naive. After getting up from the table, Sella made a beeline for the nearest pay phone and put in a call to Yosef Yagur.

When he returned, Sella informed Anne that he couldn't stay. He asked her if she wanted to leave with him. No, she replied, Jay needed her. Sella gave her Yagur's phone number and told her to have Pollard call his handler later if he got the chance. Anne was not to worry; everything would be all right. His parting comment was, "You don't know me; you've never met me; you've never heard my name."[5] Though confused, Anne nodded in agreement. Sella said he would call her later at the apartment to see if everything was okay, then hastily departed.

Sella had no diplomatic immunity in the United States. If caught, he would go to an American jail. He had to flee the country. Because of the late hour, however, National Airport had no outgoing flights and the rental car agencies were closed. Not wasting time, he contacted the Israeli embassy, and someone there procured him a car. After one more call to Anne, he decided, he and his wife would hightail it to New York and jump on a plane back to Israel.

It was close to midnight. A thousand thoughts raced through Anne's head. Where, oh where, was Jay? Was he all right? Was he in jail? She was afraid to head back to the apartment but had nowhere else to go. Maybe Jay would be there when she returned. She hoped so, because there was no one else who could help her. In her entire life, Anne Pollard had never felt so alone.

If Anne had known the identity of the person those FBI men in the alleyway behind her apartment building were really looking for, she might have done something different with the bulging suitcase. She might have simply called a cab herself, climbed in with the suitcase, and made off somewhere with the evidence. But that is not what happened. What happened was an extraordinary coincidence, one that would prove to be the linchpin in bringing Jonathan Jay Pollard to justice.

On 1 August 1985, Don Kidwell was the counterintelligence officer in the CIA's Rome station. While he was reading a debriefing report about a high-ranking KGB officer who was missing the tips on two of his fingers, Kidwell received a phone call from the marine security office.[6] Someone wanted to see him. He headed downstairs to a waiting room on the first floor. Right away Kidwell noticed that the tips of his visitor's two middle fingers were missing. The man introduced himself as Colonel Vitaly Yurchenko, the number-two KGB officer in charge of Soviet spy operations in North America. He wanted to defect.

During Yurchenko's debriefings, he told intelligence agents about three American spies he knew of who were currently operating for the Soviets. One was Edward Lee Howard, a CIA employee. When this news filtered down to the FBI they immediately put surveillance on Howard at his residence outside of Santa Fe, New Mexico, but it was too late. Howard managed to elude FBI surveillance and flee to Moscow before an arrest.

Another spy—or so Yurchenko thought—was a sailor who went by the name of Thomas E. Hayden, stationed in Naples, Italy. What the KGB defector did not know was that Master Chief Hayden was a double agent whom I had vetted, recruited, and trained with the help of Special Agents Joe Riccio and Brent Barrett in a counterespionage operation dubbed Sackett Land. Hayden's mission, launched in 1983, was to portray himself as a traitor willing to sell out his country for money. He had been feeding his Soviet handlers a string of classified information the navy had approved for the operation, and they took the bait.

Operation Sackett Land ended in August 1985 after Yurchenko flew in from Moscow to meet Hayden. Yurchenko drilled the sailor, asking him if he knew any NIS agents who gave briefings on the base. Hayden stood fast in denial, frightened that his cover had been blown. The next day Yurchenko defected. The NIS believed he had been looking for the name of an NIS agent to facilitate his defection. For his service to his country, Hayden would later receive the U.S. Navy Legion of Merit medal.

The third spy Yurchenko named, Ronald Pelton, had been operating within the NSA. Like Pollard, Pelton was an intelligence analyst with a brilliant mind and a photographic memory. He had been passing TS/SCI information to the Soviets, and Yurchenko was his initial contact in Washington, D.C. One of the most damaging pieces of information Pelton disclosed dealt with a sensitive navy operation to gather intelligence on Soviet communications. He would later be convicted and sentenced to three concurrent life sentences.

When Anne went to the alley on the night of Monday, 18 November, to dispose of the suitcase, she saw what she thought were FBI agents on surveillance. She was right about that, but they weren't watching Anne or her husband. The agents didn't know the Pollards from Adam and Eve. In fact, they were on the outer perimeter working with other agents who were surveilling the residence of Ronald Pelton's girlfriend, where the Soviet operative often stayed, which just happened to be in very close proximity to the Pollards' apartment.

Who would ever have imagined that the fate of the man who would prove to be one of the most notorious spies in the annals of American history would be sealed because the FBI, on a given night, happened to be surveilling another spy? The actions Anne took that night, mistakenly

Aerial view of Pollard (A) and Pelton (B) apartments —NIS/FBI AERIAL PHOTO

thinking she was being watched, set off a chain of events that enabled the NIS and the FBI to gather evidence against her and her husband that resulted in their expeditious arrest and subsequent prosecution. It was an incredible twist of fate.

When we arrived at the Pollards' apartment, it was close to midnight, and Anne was not yet home. The small apartment had a kitchen to the left of the hallway, a combined living room and dining area, and another short hallway that led to the bedroom, an unkempt space with dirty clothes piled several feet high in the closet.

While Farmer, Jechorek, and Redman searched the back bedroom, I stayed in the living room/dining area with Pollard, who wasn't talking much. He looked bedraggled and was too nervous to sit down. It was late and Anne wasn't home from dinner yet, which seemed strange. I made a joke about how long she'd been at dinner. "She should be home soon," he said curtly, without cracking a smile.

Sure enough, some twenty minutes later Anne returned. As far as I knew she was just coming home after dinner with the neighbors. Still, she looked pale and nervous, and I could tell something was wrong because of the way she shuffled over to the couch and sat down with her arms crossed over her stomach, as if in pain. Pollard asked her if she was all right and she said yes.

"We won't be long," I assured her. "We're searching the house and we'll be done as quickly as possible." She didn't say a word to me or her husband, and she studiously avoided my eyes.

While the search was in progress, Pollard's phone rang and Anne got up and answered it. It was late, and Washington wasn't the safest city; I figured the neighbors were calling to see if she had made it home safely.

"I can't talk, Uncle Joe," she said. "I've got unexpected guests. Yes. No, it isn't." Then she hung up.[7]

Pollard didn't ask who it was and Anne didn't say a word to him, which struck me as odd. Later, I would find out that Uncle Joe was Aviem Sella.

It took about forty-five minutes for the agents to complete their search. They emerged from the bedroom with approximately thirteen TS/SCI documents and fifty-plus documents classified secret, almost all which had been stashed in a box under the pile of dirty clothes in the closet. Some were found under the bed.[8] Most had old dates but were classified nevertheless. The FBI agents asked Pollard why he had all these documents in his house.

"Look, I'm an analyst and I have a lot of work that I can't always finish at the office," Pollard said, or words to that effect. "Sometimes I bring my work home with me. I just forgot about these."

As I scanned through the documents, either Farmer or Jechorek must have called their supervisor, because when I looked back up, they informed me that the FBI was backing out of this case and turning it back over to the NIS. I couldn't believe my ears.

"What?!" I said.

They went on to say this was obviously an administrative issue and they were letting us handle it, implying that Pollard posed no more of a threat to the United States than an absentminded professor.

I was so mad I couldn't see straight, but I kept my cool. "Okay, if you say so." To this day, I have no recollection of how the FBI agents got back to their office. Perhaps Agent Redman drove them. They certainly didn't catch a ride with me.

Pollard had been scheduled to take an NIS polygraph the next day, Tuesday, regardless of how it turned out with his interview. Before Redman and I departed, I informed him that he had to come into the field office the next morning to take the exam. He gave me a funny look and said okay.

"Be there at ten thirty," I said, and we left with the documents.

We now had both secret and TS/SCI classified documents from Pollard's apartment, which at a minimum was enough to get him fired by the navy for mishandling classified information, illegal possession of classified national defense information, improperly safeguarding SCI material, and several other charges. Now that the FBI had backed out, however, there was no chance the U.S. attorney's office would even think about prosecuting Pollard for illegal possession of national defense information. Their hands were full of "real" cases dealing with polished spies, not amateurs. They were gearing up for Pelton's arrest and were also poised to apprehend Larry Wu Tai Chin, a CIA analyst who had been spying for the Chinese in excess of thirty years and was later convicted on three counts of espionage. Prior to his sentencing date he hung himself in his jail cell.

After returning to the office to secure the classified documents, I drove home in the wee hours to get some desperately needed shut-eye. On the way there I mulled over the events of the past few hours. Assistant Director McCullah was going to hit the roof when he found out what had happened. I winced at the thought of telling him about the documents we'd found at Jay Pollard's residence, not to mention the FBI's decision to drop out of the case. In retrospect, McCullah should have been the least of my worries. If I'd known then about the incredible whirlwind of events that was about to whip up, I might have just stayed home.

No sooner had they been left alone than Anne filled Pollard in on what had happened to her. In the mistaken belief that they were still under surveillance, if not by the FBI then at least by the NIS, the couple went to an all-night coffee shop and looked around to make sure no one was watching them. Then, using a pay phone, Jay dialed the number Sella had given Anne. Yagur answered. Was Pollard all right? he wanted to know. Had Israel's involvement been mentioned or come up in the interview?

No, he wasn't all right, Pollard replied, and no, Israel had not been mentioned. Yagur told Pollard to stall for at least seventy-two hours, at which point he would get back to him. Then he hung up. Pollard was convinced that a mission was gearing up at that very moment to rescue him and his wife. He couldn't have been more wrong.

Chapter 16

POLLARD BALKS

S uddenly I found myself driving back to work, wondering where the few hours of sleep had gone. Tuesday, 19 November—it was going to be a bad day. I could feel it. Agent Redman was already in the office when I arrived, along with a cluster of agents who had been on Defense Minister Rabin's detail.

I went to the safe and retrieved the documents we had seized the night before. Lanny McCullah would be calling, and I wanted to confirm my earlier count of how many TS/SCI and secret-coded documents we had unearthed at the suspect's apartment. As predicted, McCullah called me from headquarters and wanted to know "what the hell" was going on. My account only stoked his fire. "How many agents do you have on this?" he demanded. "What's your next move? Where is Pollard now? Where are the documents?"

I informed him that the Rabin detail had ended, that now that I had my agents back, everyone was going to be working this case. We knew what needed to be done, and I was on top of it. I didn't feel on top of it, but that wasn't something I needed to tell Wyatt Earp.

Had the FBI stayed in the game I would have had to follow their lead, but they hadn't, and now the onus was on me. Only eight o'clock and already I was tense. "I'm going to put together a surveillance and investigative plan," I assured McCullah, sounding more confident than I felt. "But I'll need some time."

It bothered me that McCullah was taking his frustration out on me, but I understood how he felt. The Pollard matter was proving to be one giant mess. I would have been a lot more upset had I known the reason McCullah hadn't been at NIS headquarters when we brought Pollard in for the interview. Lance Arnold told me several months later that the assistant director had had tickets to the Redskins football game! Nothing was going to interfere with Monday night football live.

When he found out Pollard was coming in later to take a polygraph, McCullah calmed down. I told him I had to go, not to worry, we would keep him informed.

"Make sure you do," he said before releasing me. "I want to be updated on everything!"

With all the other pressure on me, I didn't need headquarters breathing down my neck, but I had no choice in the matter. Before hunkering down with the surveillance plan, I went into Gerry Nance's office to vent. He was still the acting special agent in charge.

"Gerry," I announced in a calm voice, "I have to ask you for a big favor. I want you to call headquarters." I paused, then yelled, "And tell them to quit calling me, to let me do my job, and to stay off my ass while I sort this out!" Of course, I didn't expect Nance to make the call, but I sure felt better letting off steam. It wasn't until years later that Nance told me he did in fact pass the message on to McCullah. I laughed. Maybe that's why no one called me from headquarters for the rest of that day.

Around ten thirty that morning, Redman came into my office to tell me there was a problem with Pollard. I sighed. "What's wrong with him now?"

"I've got him on hold. He says he isn't feeling well and doesn't want to come in for the polygraph."

"I can't believe it!" I said, hitting the desk with the palm of my hand. "Transfer the call to my office, will you?"

How was I going to handle the analyst this time? It was absolutely critical that Pollard not worm his way out of the polygraph. I had no idea he had already taken two such tests, one with the CIA and one with the NIS. Nor did I know of the hatred he harbored for the NIS as a result.

Pollard came on the line and I said hello and asked him what was going on. He answered that he hadn't gotten much sleep the night before and his stomach was upset. He didn't think he could make it in for the polygraph.

Still trying to make light of the investigation without being threatening, I informed him that none of us had slept well the night before either.
"It's in your best interest to take this stupid polygraph test, Jay. Let's get
this over with once and for all," I said, adding that once he had passed
the test he could go back to work with a clean slate. That was a white lie.
On account of the documents we'd found in his residence, he would never
go back to work in the ATAC—or anywhere else in the government. For
all intents and purposes, his work as an analyst was over.

Then Pollard made a comment that set off alarm bells in my head.
"Ron, I don't mind taking a polygraph if they only ask me about the
Soviet Union or the Soviet bloc countries."

If they *only* ask him about the Soviet Union or the Soviet bloc
countries? For the first time I had a gut feeling that something was
wrong—very wrong. My mind spun. Why would he make such a
statement to me on the phone? What did it signify?

Up to this point, no one was close to believing Pollard was an
outright spy, not Agent Redman, not myself, and certainly not the FBI.
Commander Agee and Assistant Director McCullah suspected him,
though of what they couldn't be sure. It was imperative that we look
at the case with open minds. Yes, Pollard could be fired for having
classified documents in his possession, but making a criminal case
out of it would take hard evidence, not subjective reasoning or panic-
based conclusions.

What if this really *was* a worst-case scenario? We couldn't let Pollard
off the hook. This might be our last chance to get him on the box. If we
couldn't convince him to come in and take the test and he was spying
for another country, he would flee the United States. There was almost
nothing we could do to prevent it.

Gathering my thoughts, I said in a lighthearted voice, "Jay, you're
absolutely right. There's no way you can't pass this polygraph when
they ask you about the Soviets and the bloc countries." I was shooting
from the hip again. What the analyst didn't realize—or what he'd
forgotten—was that the counterintelligence polygraph didn't ask about
specific countries, it was very general. The question was, Have you ever
committed espionage or sabotage against the United States? "Yeah,
you'll pass it," I went on. "I know that and you know that. That's why

you need to come in here and get this thing over with." I reiterated that it wouldn't take long and then he could move on with his life.

"I'm really too tired to drive in," Pollard said, digging in his heels.

It was time to get firm with him or lose him forever. "Look, Jay, if you're so tired, I don't want you driving down here anyway. Stay right where you are. I'll have agents from the office pick you up and drive you back home." Then I raised my voice. "This mess can't be put off any longer. We both have better things to do. So just wait there for my agents and don't leave."

At last, he agreed to come in and take the polygraph.

After hanging up the phone, I raced back to the office area where my agents were waiting. "Get to Pollard's apartment *right now*, with a red light and siren if you have to, and bring him over here for a polygraph test." They catapulted out of their seats and took off without further explanation. I wish I could remember their names today, but things were happening way too fast.

Thus we passed the second major hurdle with Pollard. Only later would I find out that he was stalling for time because his handler had instructed him to do so. Yagur's order had clouded his judgment. If Pollard wanted to save his skin, he should have fled the country for Israel the night before, after we'd left his apartment. The analyst was an exceptionally bright man, but it was none too wise to call me late in the morning and say he was too tired to take a polygraph. By now he could have been driving up the East Coast for a flight out of New York, or making his way to Canada. It was foolish, also, to believe that Sella or Yagur would bail him out—but then, just about every action Pollard had taken during his career as a spy had been foolish.

Possessed of a king-size ego and lacking all common sense, much less knowledge of the workings of foreign counterintelligence, he was his own worst enemy. The Israelis hadn't given him any security training. He'd been handing thousands of classified documents over to them every month, and they had done nothing to bring him under control. He had no escape plan. After all this neglect did he really believe, having gotten an order from his handler to stall for seventy-two hours, that someone from Israel would swoop down out of the sky and save him?

Gerry Nance came in shortly after my phone call with Pollard and, seeing how tense I was, asked if I wanted to join him for a quick bite at the officers club, within walking distance of our building. It would take the polygraph operators three or more hours to complete Pollard's initial test, so I had the time. About forty-five minutes later Nance and I took the elevator down and were on our way out when my two agents came through the door with Pollard.

The analyst stopped in his tracks. "Ron," he said in an urgent voice, "I need to talk to you before I take this polygraph."

"Sure, Jay," I said, taken aback. I looked at Nance and told him to go ahead without me, thanked the agents for picking up Pollard, then escorted him into the office spaces at the far end of the hallway that had been set aside for polygraph testing. I had no clue what the wayward analyst wanted to talk to me about. What I was about to find out would wake up the FBI and put everyone at NIS headquarters into a tailspin.

Chapter 17

THE CONFESSION

Entering the testing area, I ran into Ben Johnson, supervisor of the polygraph program at the Washington field office, and informed him that Pollard wanted to talk with me before taking the exam. Johnson's expression soured. Not only had he been waiting for the analyst for better than two hours, but he also had interviews of his own to conduct, part of a delicately balanced psychological lead-up to the polygraph test itself. I was about to foul this up. But I had seniority over Johnson, and in any event, my hands were tied. Pollard still hadn't been charged with any crime, and because he was here voluntarily, I had to do everything in my power to keep him cooperating with us. I expected my interview to be a short one. I had no idea that it would turn into a full-blown interrogation.

"Is there an interview room I can use?" I said to Johnson. Disgruntled, he pointed to a space off the hallway.

As Pollard and I made our way there, we passed the testing room, its door open and a polygraph instrument sitting on the desk waiting for its next victim. Those were the days before digital technology. The machine was an intimidating metal box the size of a briefcase. Inside were numerous knobs and five or six long, ink-filled mechanical arms that recorded the subject's reactions to questions on scrolling paper. Two pneumographs, accordion-like rubber tubes filled with air, would be connected to the interviewee's chest and upper abdomen to measure respiratory rate. A cuff around the arm measured blood pressure and heart rate, while two tiny cuffs attached to the fingers—and sometimes a metal plate under the fingers—would gauge the amount of sweat. Electric cords connected all these gauges to the polygraph instrument, which was plugged into the wall. By the time polygraph operators had a subject hooked up, he or she already felt guilty about something. It was enough to make the Pope feel intimidated, and not surprisingly, out of the corner of my eye I caught Pollard staring at it uneasily.

We walked into a small, musty office equipped with nothing but three chairs and a World War II–vintage green metal desk, probably made in some federal prison. The space had no windows, just a single fluorescent tube overhead.

It is Department of Defense policy that when someone takes a polygraph test, he or she must be reminded of his or her Miranda rights warning against self-incrimination, and although I would not be the one to administer the test, it occurred to me that it would be a good idea to read Pollard his rights then rather than later. That would protect us both. I thought of going back to Johnson to get a copy of the NIS's civilian waiver of rights form, but not wanting to leave Pollard alone, I looked in the desk drawer first. The metal screeched open and there, on top of a stack of papers, was the waiver form already filled out, with Brian Cropper and Ben Johnson listed as the agents who were going to advise Pollard of his rights.

Taking my pen, I scratched out their printed names and inserted mine above. On the line identifying what Pollard was suspected of, someone had written the following: "I am suspected of the unlawful solicitation, acquisition, and possession of classified U.S government defense information and/or the unlawful disclosure of U.S. government defense information." I read Pollard all of his rights, one by one.

1. I have the right to remain silent and make no statement at all.
2. Any statement I do make can be used against me in a court of law or other judicial proceeding or administrative hearing.
3. I have the right to consult with a lawyer prior to any questioning. This lawyer may be a civilian lawyer retained by me at no cost to the United States, or, if I cannot afford a lawyer, one will be appointed to represent me at no cost to me.
4. I have the right to have my retained or appointed lawyer present during this interview.
5. I may terminate this interview at any time, for any reason.

I asked Pollard if he understood what I had read. He indicated yes.

Then I gave him the form to read and asked him to initial each advisement.

Next there was a paragraph that read: "I understand my rights as related to me and as set forth above. With that understanding, I have decided that I do not desire to remain silent, consult with a retained or appointed lawyer, or have a lawyer present at this time. I make this decision freely and voluntarily. No threats or promises have been made to me."[1] Pollard verbally waived all his rights and said he didn't have a problem talking with me.

It was already 1:34 PM when Pollard signed the overall advisement waiver. The day was growing short. At last we began to talk. In retrospect, I suspect that Pollard wanted to speak with me because he was following Yagur's order to stall, but at the time I knew nothing about that and had to wonder what he thought a pre-interview interview would accomplish.

I asked him where he had intended to take the documents the night before. Circling the question, the analyst launched into a drawn-out story about his favorite subject, arms sales to South Africa and through South Africa to Afghanistan. This was déjà vu, but I was willing to see where he was going with it. It dawned on me that our supposed chat was turning into an interview, and putting aside my reservations about Ben Johnson sitting in his office waiting for me to finish, I groped around in the desk drawer, came up with a pad of legal paper, and began scrawling as fast as my fingers would go. Pollard went on and on, spilling individuals' names I couldn't pronounce, much less spell. I was having trouble keeping up with him and had to interrupt several times so that he would repeat what he had just said. This went on for about half an hour.

With almost two decades of law enforcement experience under my belt, I enjoyed conducting interviews—that's what I called them, not interrogations, which sometimes carried negative connotations of verbal and physical abuse—and through repeated practice I had built up a good reputation for garnering confessions from suspects and gleaning information from witnesses. In Pollard, however, I had more than met my match.

Suddenly, in the midst of his grandiose story about international weapons sales, it hit me right between the eyes. What in the Sam *Hell* are you doing, Olive? I said to myself (a phrase my late mother, a dear, deeply religious woman, used to utter both in jest and in earnest, except that she changed the *e* in Hell to an *i*). Pollard was the type of person who, when asked a question about anything, could make the answer last as long as the hours in a day. With just minimum knowledge of any subject, he could relate his views seamlessly, making things up as he went along and eventually convincing you that what he said was solid fact.

In my enthusiasm and desire to get information, any information, I had let my subject gain control of the interview. Rather than answering my question, he was just wasting my time and everyone else's.

As Pollard rambled on, his confidence rising, I slammed my hand down on the old metal desk, which startled him. "Wait a minute," I said abruptly, looking him straight in the eye. "This story has nothing to do with those documents. I don't give a damn about South Africa and their arms shipments to Afghanistan. I want to know where you were taking those documents, and I want to know *now*."

One of the interview techniques I'd learned over the years was that when you raised your voice, you should do so only briefly, to shock the suspect and get his attention. If you kept on yelling, you risked losing his respect. I paused, letting my words sink in, while Pollard just stared at me.

Apparently, he realized he had to deliver some grain of truth to string me along, for now he changed course, veering into a story about how two and a half years earlier he had been introduced at a party to a person by the name of Kurt Lohbeck. Lohbeck was a freelance photographer and reporter covering the war in Afghanistan and, Pollard claimed, he was under the control of a Pakistani defense attaché in Washington. According to the analyst, Lohbeck had asked him for sensitive information about Soviet forces in Afghanistan and Pollard agreed to his request. He said Lohbeck became his friend, and that he would drop a few pieces of classified material off to him once every week or two. "I wasn't paid for the material," Pollard emphasized. When I asked him how the documents were classified, he told me they were coded confidential and secret.

"Are you sure you didn't get paid?" I asked.

"Yes, I'm sure," he replied.

He continued in this vein for another minute or so, at which point I stopped him and in a sincere tone, appealing to his apparent need for recognition, told him he was one of the most intelligent people I had ever met in my life. I praised him for his intellectual resilience and analytical brilliance. However, I continued, there was one thing he might not know as much about as I did, and that was counterintelligence, criminal investigations, security violations, and espionage.

"I've been in this business a long time, Jay," I said, "and I know you're lying when you say you haven't gotten paid for classified material. You walked out the door last night with TS/SCI documents in your hand and you're telling me you had the intention of giving them to this Lohbeck guy for nothin'?"

Pollard just gave me another blank look. I kept pressing him, and eventually he did admit to having passed top secret material to Lohbeck about once a month and receiving a small amount of money.

"How much?"

"About a hundred dollars."

"That's bullshit, Jay! You don't get a measly hundred dollars for giving someone top secret information."

Briefly, the image of Ben Johnson impatiently waiting outside flitted through my mind, but I couldn't break off the interview just then. It would be an egregious violation of standard procedure to interrupt a suspect who had started to confess—to leave the room and give him time to think. And so I kept firing questions at him, calmly, persistently, challenging every answer that sounded like a lie. Every time I confronted him, the number of classified documents he claimed to have sold multiplied tenfold, as did the amount of money he had received.

I kept the pressure up, determined not to stop until I was reasonably certain he was telling me most of the truth. Well into the interview, about three hours later, Pollard claimed to have received $2,500 a month in exchange for passing thousands of secrets to Lohbeck, and said his contact had paid him a total of about $30,000 for expenses and travel. He named a few of the documents by exact title and provided detailed information from them, and he told me where he had obtained them, from collections that included the intelligence libraries of the NSA, the DIA, the CIA, the FBI, the NISC, and the ATAC.

Supposedly, he dropped the documents off at Lohbeck's girlfriend's house biweekly and later picked them up and returned them to their respective libraries. The most recent payment from Lohbeck, he maintained, had been received on 26 October 1985—left on his girlfriend's coffee table—and the last time Pollard had dropped off a batch of information was Friday, 15 November. The thousands of pages of classified message traffic Pollard didn't have to sign for, he said, Lohbeck kept.

What Pollard had told me so far, if we proved it, could land him and Lohbeck in prison with life sentences. The analyst had confessed to espionage, and I had to inform NIS headquarters what was going on. It was then around four thirty and people would start leaving work soon. This information couldn't wait any longer. I had no choice but to interrupt the interview and leave the room.

Telling Pollard I had to make a call and would be right back, I left and hurried into Johnson's office. He was sitting behind his desk, looking steamed. I couldn't blame him. Agent Johnson was extremely capable. He could have conducted an interview with Jonathan Pollard and come away with similar or better results, and yet here I was, three hours after telling him I was just going to have a short talk with the suspect, emerging from the interview room with a ream of notes. It didn't help matters that I stayed in Johnson's office only long enough to bark out an order.

"Call upstairs and get Lisa Redman and Gerry Nance—I need them down here, now!" Then I vanished back into the interview room.

Within a minute, Agent Redman appeared. I told her to sit with Jay for a couple of minutes, that he had just confessed to providing top secret information and getting paid about $30,000 for it. Redman's face turned slightly red. She performed every aspect of her job with the utmost discretion, but I could see by her expression that she shared my thoughts about Pollard.

I closed the door behind me and gave Agent Nance, who was waiting right outside, a brief account. "Gerry, I want you to drive over to Suitland headquarters as fast as you can and inform McCullah of the situation," I said.

There was no way I was going to personally tell the assistant director for counterintelligence what had occurred. My excuse, certainly a valid one, was that I couldn't leave Pollard because I had to get a statement from him down on paper. But I knew, too, that Lanny McCullah's blood was going to boil, and I didn't want to be in his crosshairs. Later Nance described McCullah's reaction to me. Apparently, cursing to high heaven, the assistant director hurled his inbox off his desk and kicked it across the room, sending it crashing against the wall. I probably would have done the same thing if I'd been in his shoes. After all, he'd had a spy operating right under his nose.

I poked my head into the interview room and asked Redman to wait while I called my FBI counterpart Nick Walsh. This was not over yet. Not by a long shot.

I confess to having harbored, at the time, a somewhat cynical view of the FBI. It was notorious among most federal, state, and local police departments for gathering criminal and counterintelligence information from other agencies, taking over cases, and after a conviction, taking every bit of credit for the investigation, arrest, and final outcome. Ironically, now, when I most needed the agency, it had backed out on me. Nonetheless, I had a good working relationship with the FBI in general, and I had had the pleasure of working with some of its most outstanding managers and street agents, people willing to collaborate for a common cause. Numbered among them were two assistant special agents in charge of counterintelligence at the FBI's Washington field office, Nick Walsh and Joe Johnson.

FBI agent Lydia Jechorek —RON OLIVE

Walsh was a kind, soft-spoken supervisor without an attitude. When I informed him that Pollard had just confessed to espionage, he wanted to know the country involved. The information might be going to Pakistan, South Africa, Afghanistan, maybe other countries, I couldn't be sure. Walsh said he would send an agent over right away. Expecting a small squad, I was dumbfounded when, about half an hour later, I found myself face to face with Agent Lydia Jechorek. After what had happened the night before my trust in her and her supervisor had dipped, but I was willing to give them the benefit of the doubt.

As the case came together over the days and months that followed, Lydia Jechorek proved to be a top-notch FBI agent. Except for a two-year stint in the FBI's Chicago office, she had been in the Washington field office working foreign counterintelligence and espionage investigations, and would eventually pass up many opportunities to fill supervisory positions at FBI headquarters so as to continue working on the street.[2]

After I had filled her in, we proceeded with the formal statement of confession from Pollard. This was critical, because Jechorek gave me no assurances that the FBI would place Pollard under arrest any time soon. We didn't need to get everything—that would take days—just the essential elements of the crime, the information that would prove and convict him of espionage: knowingly passing national defense information to a foreign government or an agent of that government; understanding that the information, based on its classification level, would do harm to the national security of the United States or work to the advantage of a foreign nation; and recognizing that passing national defense information to a foreign government or agent of that government was against the law. We also needed a brief description of what Pollard had passed, where it had come from, and how much compensation he had received in return.

We had Pollard move to another room where we had a computer. I told him I could type out his statement as he relayed it, but the analyst preferred to record it himself in longhand. I agreed, and as Pollard scribbled away, Jechorek and I asked questions to ensure that he included the essential facts.

In addition to identifying most of the libraries and archives from which he had taken classified information, Pollard recorded the classification levels and titles of various materials, explained how he was able to obtain them, and included his cover stories. Below is a summary of the collections and materials he mentioned.

- From the navy's SPINTCOM center he had taken all Mediterranean littoral operations intelligence summaries, all TS/NOFORN (top secret/no foreign dissemination) documents, and various WNINTEL (warning notice: intelligence sources and methods involved).
- From the NISC's sensitive-intelligence libraries and all departments within the NISC he had removed documents of every classification level from secret to TS/SCI. These were primarily lines-of-communication studies on the Middle East and intelligence-data-input studies dealing with Soviet equipment that might appear in South Asia.
- From the National Security Agency he had taken the TS/SCI-classified RASIN manual with updates and the

NIS unclassified civilian suspects acknowledgement and waiver of rights form signed by Jonathan Pollard —NIS

Non-Morse Operator's Handbook, allegedly to help the Pakistanis break Soviet communications in Afghanistan. For this heist he simply contacted an unwitting woman at the central document disbursement office who provided either originals or copies. Pollard passed his clearances, showed his courier card, signed for the documents, and walked out the front door. Two or three of the manuals he checked out were never returned. He claimed to have lost them.

- From the CIA he had taken documents dealing with Pakistani and Iraqi nuclear developments, their classifications ranging from secret to TS/SCI.
- From the DIA's Genser Library he had removed an Iraqi ground forces intelligence study, and from the DIA's Special Intelligence Library, intelligence summaries classified TS, NOFORN, WNINTEL, and ORCON (originator controlled).
- From the FBI he had taken quarterly counterintelligence summaries classified secret and NOFORN periodical reviews copied from classified summaries distributed by the FBI to intelligence agencies around Washington. He received these not from a library but from individual authors. He would contact an author and have him mail the materials directly to his office at the ATAC.
- From the ATAC he had taken intelligence summaries classified secret and TS/SCI.[3]

While he was writing all this out, Pollard rattled on about Lohbeck and his adventures in Afghanistan, and the drop-offs and pickups he had made at Lohbeck's girlfriend's apartment. The analyst actually appeared to pride himself on his crimes, and to relish the act of recording them.

When he finished the statement, eleven pages long, I had him swear that its contents were true. After signing it, he agreed to come back the next day and embellish what he had written about his methods of contacting Lohbeck.

Perhaps Pollard thought he was ahead of the game. He had avoided the dreaded polygraph machine and produced a confession that was a big red herring. No doubt he believed that before the next day arrived—before his promised return to the NIS interview room—he would be winging his way to Israel.

It was now about ten in the evening. Before leaving, Jechorek called her office to inform Nick Walsh that we needed a full surveillance on Pollard. That was a huge relief to me. Then the three of us climbed into my car and I drove Pollard home. Although we had a confession of espionage, we still needed solid proof. Furthermore, we needed to know what foreign country or countries were involved before an arrest could be made.

When we reached our destination, FBI agents were already in place surveilling Pollard's residence. This struck me as odd. I had never seen the FBI respond so fast to a surveillance request, and certainly not at such a late hour. At the time, I had no idea that they were also watching Ronald Pelton down the street.

Heading home that night, I mulled over the lengthy interview with Pollard and the confession he had made. Though convinced that for the most part the analyst was telling the truth, part of his story bothered me, and that was the involvement of Kurt Lohbeck. Why would a freelance photographer and news reporter become embroiled in a major espionage case? In all my years of experience in law enforcement, I'd never heard of a journalist taking reams of TS/SCI material and paying huge sums for it. It didn't make sense. There had to be a crucial part to the story Pollard had intentionally left out.

We had a confession, but we couldn't get a conviction on a confession alone. What we needed was hard evidence proving the act of espionage. Arriving home bleary-eyed, I dragged myself inside and fell into bed, thankful for an end to the day, however belated.

Meanwhile, unbeknownst to me, Pollard had managed to elude FBI surveillance and get himself to a pay phone. Earlier that day, before my agents picked him up for the polygraph, he had had Anne walk around their neighborhood in the hopes that someone would bump into her and slip her an escape plan. That hadn't happened, and now, concerned about not being contacted by the Israelis—what was taking them so long?—he put in a call to Yagur. The phone rang and rang and rang, but no one answered. Perplexed, Pollard contacted the Israeli embassy. As soon as he got through to someone, he identified himself and began explaining his situation. He needed help, now. But the Israeli on the other end of the line, who didn't have a solid command of English, told him to call back the next day.

Growing alarmed, Pollard returned to the apartment. The next day, a Wednesday, he sent Anne out one more time to walk around the neighborhood. Surely someone from the Israeli embassy would pass her a note with the instructions that would save them.

11-18-85
16:40:00

A FATAL BLUNDER

O n Wednesday morning, 20 November, Special Agent Lance Arnold phoned to give me some interesting news. He had received a call from a naval officer in Norfolk, Virginia, whose daughter had contacted him from Washington, D.C., about an urgent matter. Apparently, on Monday night her next-door neighbor had dropped off a suitcase full of classified documents and asked her to hold on to them. The daughter, who hadn't opened the suitcase, was worried and wanted advice from her father. Arnold told the officer he would have the NIS's Washington field office check into the matter. Not long afterwards, Special Agent Rich Cloonan received a call there. It was Pollard's next-door neighbor, Christine Esfandiari.

Esfandiari recounted how Anne had arrived at her doorstep on Monday night with a breathless story about her husband being in trouble and a suitcase stuffed with classified information they hadn't had a chance to burn. Esfandiari knew Pollard worked with classified information for the navy, and this concerned her. She related how her husband, Babak, had taken the suitcase to the Four Seasons Hotel but hadn't found Anne. Where was the suitcase now? Cloonan wanted to know. In her apartment, she replied. Cloonan told her to make sure the suitcase stayed there, and to have Babak meet him in forty-five minutes at the corner of Connecticut Avenue and 20th Street, near where they lived.

"I'll be by the flower stand," the agent said. "I'll be wearing a tan raincoat, carrying a *Time* magazine, and my name will be Edward Thomas. Have Babak greet me using his first name."

A few minutes later Cloonan and another one of my agents, Joseph Grahek, left the navy yard and proceeded to the designated meeting site. Before parking, they did a security check of the area, dry-cleaning it to ensure that nothing looked suspicious and that the Pollards wouldn't catch Babak talking to Cloonan. The agents scoped out the apartment building—they didn't notice any FBI cars in the neighborhood at the time—and found they had a good line of sight down the alleyway behind it.

A few blocks from the rendezvous, Grahek parked in front of a drugstore and Cloonan set off to meet Babak. As Mr. Esfandiari expanded on his wife's account of what had happened the night before, lo and behold, Anne appeared on the other side of the street, heading toward their apartment building. Esfandiari grew agitated. Anne might spot them and create a scene. Cloonan calmed him down, and she passed by without noticing them.

"Where's the suitcase?" the agent asked

"In the bathtub in my apartment," Esfandiari replied.

Cloonan told him to bring it to the back door of the apartment building, the door opening onto the alley. While Esfandiari went to fetch the suitcase, Cloonan cautiously worked his way to the rear of the building.

Soon thereafter, Esfandiari met Cloonan with the suitcase. The two men walked up the alleyway and out of sight, where they met Grahek with the vehicle and climbed in. After Esfandiari initialed an evidence custody document, the agents, resisting the temptation to open the suitcase—that couldn't be done until a search warrant arrived from the assistant U.S. attorney—sealed it shut with NIS evidence tape to preserve the chain of custody and to protect the evidence from unnecessary contamination.

Before leaving, Cloonan took a written statement from Esfandiari about what had happened, and Esfandiari "affirmed"—being a Muslim, he couldn't swear—that the information was correct to the best of his knowledge.

This was all unfolding while I was still conducting my initial interview of Pollard, before the FBI had been contacted about his confession. Cloonan knew the FBI had backed out of the case late on Monday night; thus, it came as a surprise to him when, a short time later, an FBI field office agent arrived on the scene and demanded that the suitcase be turned over to him. Apparently, the FBI had rejoined the investigation, if not yet officially. That was awfully fast work. Someone from the NIS field office must have contacted the bureau as soon as Cloonan left his office for the rendezvous, or shortly thereafter. The bureau agent had no evidence document with him to maintain a chain of custody, so Cloonan had him sign the NIS form showing the suitcase was being turned over to the FBI.

When Cloonan finished telling me this story, I was amazed.[1] Serendipitously, the very evidence that we needed had surfaced, and before my initial interview with Pollard had even been completed. Who would have believed that Christine Esfandiari's father would be an officer in the navy? Leaving the evidence with a neighbor was a fatal and unpredictable blunder on Anne's part, and it would prove to be a crucial piece of evidence in the indictment and conviction, not just of Jonathan Pollard, but also of Anne herself. A search warrant was later obtained for the suitcase and its contents, which happened to include five classified FBI reports on the People's Republic of China. The FBI laboratory discovered forty separate fingerprints of Anne's on the documents.

Documents found in suitcase that Anne attempted to dispose of —NIS UNCLASSIFIED EVIDENCE PHOTO

Documents from suitcase — NIS UNCLASSIFIED EVIDENCE PHOTO

After talking with Cloonan, I called my boss, Special Agent in Charge John D'Avanzo, who was still on vacation, and informed him of the whirlwind sweeping through the NIS. Could he cut his vacation short? We might need a special agent in charge to give us firepower in any negotiations with the FBI. D'Avanzo said he would be in right away.

At about 12:30 PM on 20 November, Pollard arrived at the NIS field office. After advising him of his rights one more time—again, he waived them—FBI Agent Jechorek and I resumed our interview. Trying to figure out just who Kurt Lohbeck was, we began by asking Pollard to expand on how he had delivered packages to the reporter. He described his modus operandi in detail, saying that usually every other Friday he would leave NIS headquarters and drive directly to Lohbeck's girlfriend's apartment to drop off classified information. If Lohbeck wasn't there he would leave the material on the coffee table. Lohbeck kept the message traffic, but the documents Pollard had signed for would be retrieved at the apartment the following Sunday and returned to their respective libraries and archives on Monday.

Pollard talked about three restaurants that Lohbeck supposedly patronized in the Adams Morgan district: Café Lautrec, the Red Sea, and Massawa, all located on 18th Street NW. Occasionally, Pollard went on, he would call Lohbeck twenty or thirty minutes after a meeting at the apartment and invite him out for a drink at one of these establishments. Lohbeck paid him in person the last Saturday of every month, an amount supposedly determined by somebody else, who deemed it sufficient to keep Pollard satisfied while not being so much as to arouse suspicion. When he raised a complaint with Lohbeck about getting only $1,500 a month, the reporter replied that he would check with his contacts to get approval for a raise.[2]

During the interview, Pollard signed a written consent for a permissive search of the large manila envelope he had been carrying the night of Monday, 18 November, when he was stopped in the NIS headquarters parking lot. The envelope contained twenty top secret messages, thirty-four secret messages, and six confidential messages. Because they weren't publications, he didn't have to return them to their libraries.

When asked if he had ever taken any documents, published or unpublished, out of the country, he said no. Nor had he ever met Lohbeck

Documents and messages found in the large manila envelope in Pollard's possession— opened on 20 November 1985 —NIS UNCLASSIFIED EVIDENCE PHOTO

abroad, although one time, he said, the reporter had requested that Pollard meet him in London or Paris. I asked Pollard to draw a floor plan of the inside of Lohbeck's apartment, which I attached to his statement.

I was just about to address my doubts about Lohbeck being involved in espionage when Pollard informed us that Anne wasn't feeling well, that she had a stomach disorder and was scheduled for an outpatient procedure the following morning, Thursday. He needed to get home. Before he left, we had him write out and sign a sworn statement, but because of the circumstances, it was only four pages long. Instead of drilling him on Lohbeck then, I decided to wait until the next day, when we would have plenty of time to pin him down. Pollard said he would come back following Anne's procedure, insisting he had additional revelations about specific classified documents Lohbeck had asked him to secure.

Off the record, he mentioned that Lohbeck had a "thing" for Anne and was in the habit of dropping by their apartment. Pollard feared that if Lohbeck found out he had ratted on him, the reporter might visit them again and his life and Anne's would be in danger. Could they be moved to a hotel? We considered his request but made no promises. With the FBI now back in the investigation, its agents were now surveilling him around the clock, and we didn't have to worry about Pollard slipping out of the country. At least, we thought we didn't.

Agent Jechorek's squad supervisor showed up at my office, a tiny room with only enough space for a four-drawer safe, a desk, and two small chairs for visitors. I waved him into a seat and mentioned the suitcase that had been seized the day before, what a twist of fate it was that Esfandiari's father was a naval officer.

"That's what I came over here to talk to you about," the supervisor said, looking upset. Suddenly, he launched into a lecture, telling me the NIS had had no right or authority to seize the suitcase from Pollard's neighbor. The FBI had jurisdiction in this case and was the only agency that could seize the evidence involved. He didn't want this to happen again!

Who in the hell did this guy think he was? Perhaps my unassuming office reinforced whatever impression he had that he could lord it over me. I suspected he was the same supervisor who, two days earlier, during our preliminary interview with Pollard, had told Agents Jechorek and

Farmer that we had to let the analyst go. I also suspected he was the person who had given them the order to back out of the investigation, leaving me standing in Pollard's apartment with dozens of secret and TS/SCI messages.

Biting my tongue, I proceeded to tell him in no uncertain terms that number one, the FBI had backed out of the case, and number two, it had been urgent that we act quickly. There had been no time to sit around making phone calls deciding who should or should not pick up a suitcase. My agents had done a professional job and acted quickly to gather and protect what could turn out to be vital evidence in an espionage case. Moreover, the NIS had an 1811 designation, which meant that we were a civilian federal law enforcement agency. As such, just like the FBI, we could seize evidence and serve and execute federal search warrants.

The supervisor backed down, and from that point on the two of us got along just fine.

Cutting his vacation short, John D'Avanzo made a beeline for the FBI's Washington field office. There he spoke with Nick Walsh and Joe Johnson, assistant special agent in charge of counterintelligence field support, who told him that the Department of Justice wanted the NIS out of the investigation. The FBI would take over from there. D'Avanzo was determined not to let that happen. We later found out through Assistant U.S. Attorney Charles Leeper, who would lead the prosecution of Pollard, that the Department of Justice did not want NIS agents, only FBI agents, testifying when the case went to trial.[3] Eventually, NIS worked this out with the FBI and the Justice Department. We would be a player in the investigation after all, an equal player, or so we thought.

Late on Wednesday evening I was still at my office when D'Avanzo called and asked if I could come over to the FBI field office for a strategy session. I drove over and met with D'Avanzo, Walsh, and Johnson. Both bureau agents had low-key, unexcitable demeanors. They asked if I thought Pollard was telling the truth about Lohbeck. I said I wasn't convinced that the journalist was Pollard's contact. Moreover, I had grave doubts about the destination of the classified material. There had to be a particular foreign country involved, but which one?

We all agreed it was too early in the investigation to be certain of anything. If Pollard was telling the truth about Lohbeck, the information he had passed on the Soviets was probably going to Pakistan, Afghanistan, or both. That seemed to make sense. The last country on anyone's mind was Israel.

On the horizon lay a lengthy and time-consuming investigation of Lohbeck. It was going to be hard to make this case stick. Without proof that the reporter was gathering classified intelligence for a specific foreign government, we had no espionage case.

Hard as it is to believe, that Wednesday evening Pollard slipped past the FBI surveillance ring one more time. Again he called Yagur, and again the phone just kept ringing. His handler had said to stall for seventy-two hours. The sandglass was quickly running its course, and it was beginning to dawn on Pollard that maybe he'd been abandoned. Though on the verge of panic, the analyst managed to keep his cool. Okay, so he would have to work this out himself. He was smarter than anyone; he could outfox the NIS and the FBI.

That same night, he and Anne decided that their only recourse was to get to the Israeli embassy. Under Israel's so-called law of return, Pollard, being a Jew, automatically qualified for Israeli citizenship. The embassy was sovereign territory, and once on its grounds, Pollard would be safe from arrest by U.S. authorities. The Israelis, he believed, would give him protection and immunity from prosecution until they could arrange his escape from the United States.

Some classified documents had not been recovered from the Pollards' apartment on Monday night, and they decided to shred all remaining evidence. The couple tore up every paper that could be used against them in court and threw all the scraps in the trash can in their apartment—not a wise move.

Pollard hadn't been lying about Anne's outpatient procedure scheduled for Thursday morning. Dr. Herbert A. Moskovitz, her internist, later wrote to the court that she had a motor abnormality of the stomach that caused delayed digestion and great discomfort, and that she needed an endosmotic procedure to correct the problem.

Pollard and Anne packed a suitcase Wednesday night, and this time it didn't contain classified documents. Instead, it had everything they needed to start a new life: pictures, credit cards, birth certificates, social security cards, their marriage certificate, and other important documents. They packed it up, along with a small red carrying bag, knowing that the outpatient procedure was a convenient excuse should the FBI stop and question them about having a suitcase in the car. They also planned to take their cat, Dusty. Transporting a feline to the hospital would be less easily explained, but then, Pollard had a proven track record of worming his way out of tangles. His plan was in place. All he had to do was call the embassy one more time and let them know in advance that he and his wife were coming. Escape was certain.

11-18-85
16:40:06

Chapter 19

A SPY LEFT OUT IN THE COLD

E arly Thursday morning, 21 November, Pollard left his apartment
and slipped past surveillance for the third time. FBI Agent Mike
Rolince told me later that no one knew how this had happened.
Perhaps the proximity of Pollard's apartment and Ronald Pelton's
girlfriend's caused some confusion, or perhaps there was a temporary
absence of eyes because the FBI field office had been stretched to the
limit. In addition to Pollard, they were surveilling Pelton and Larry Wu
Tai Chin. Whatever the cause of the foul-up, it must have given a boost
to Pollard's confidence in his ability to outmaneuver the authorities.

With no one trailing him, the analyst made his way to a pay phone,
dialed the Israeli embassy, and this time got a security officer on the other
end who spoke English. Again he explained his story and announced his
intent to seek asylum. The officer told Pollard to come to the embassy,
but only if he could shake surveillance. He should arrive at around ten
thirty or eleven that morning, at which point the security gate would be
open. Then the officer got a description of Pollard's car and hung up.

Pollard returned to his apartment and gave Anne the news. Free
at last! Elated, they gathered their suitcase, their cat, and the small red
carrying bag, piled into their 1980 Ford Mustang, and drove to the
Washington Hospital Center for Anne's procedure.

By now, whatever chinks there had been in the FBI's surveillance
were closed and a full team was shadowing Pollard. The analyst later
claimed he knew he was being watched, but the agents conducting
the surveillance, priding themselves on their ability to trail a suspect
invisibly, disagreed. At any rate, when the Pollards arrived at the
hospital, one agent followed them in, thinking Anne would be staying
overnight because of the suitcase in the Mustang. That proved not to be

the case. An hour or so later, when the procedure was over, the couple went down the elevator, returned to their car, and drove away.

Agent Rolince was in the lead surveillance vehicle, in front of the Pollards' Mustang. Following the Mustang was a vehicle carrying Agent Max Fratodei, another with Agent Phil McNally, and following him, several more cars transporting members of the FBI Special Surveillance Group. Rolince assumed the Pollards would be returning to their apartment. Instead, the analyst began driving in a different direction, going up Wisconsin Avenue Northwest and then making several turns that suggested he knew he was being followed and was trying to lose his pursuers. He drove in circles, down one street and then another, leading the FBI into an unfamiliar neighborhood. Presently, the suspect turned right onto Van Ness, then put on his blinker for another right turn. Now he was at the corner of Van Ness and International Drive. One agent cautioned his team not to arouse Pollard's suspicions. "Who cares if he's suspicious?" someone said over the radio.

What unfolded next was unorthodox by FBI standards. Normally, when the FBI is about to arrest a suspect for espionage, they have gradually built up their case with wiretaps and photographs and other evidence gleaned from deliberate investigative efforts. When the suspect is moving about, the surveillance team has a good idea where he or she is headed and stations agents at the destination point pending the arrest. In this case, however, they had only had their suspect under surveillance for three days. Nobody knew what country Pollard was working for, if any, or where his Mustang was going. Rolince later told me no one on the FBI team would have ever suspected their quarry was zeroing in on the Israeli embassy. Israel wasn't even on the FBI's criteria country list.

So yes, the surveillance team was supposed to be cautious and not arouse suspicion, but at the same time they were intent on preventing Pollard's escape.

At the time, I was working in my office at the Washington Navy Yard, out of touch with what was unfolding, but my agents from the NIS, Rich Cloonan and Veronica "Ronnie" McCarthy, were in the operations center at the FBI field office. The surveillance team was communicating Pollard's progress by FBI radio, and Cloonan and McCarthy were listening in. When Cloonan heard the agents mention the corner of Van Ness and International Drive, it occurred to him that the only place of

Aerial view of Israeli Embassy, Washington, D.C. —NIS/FBI PHOTO

importance in that area was the Israeli embassy. Because he had worked out the protective detail for Defense Minister Rabin just a few weeks earlier, he knew the neighborhood like the back of his hand. But this was just a fleeting thought, and Cloonan didn't act upon it. No one had any idea that Pollard was working for the Israelis.

According to Rolince, what followed next happened so fast it was hard to keep track of events. At approximately 10:20 AM, Pollard turned onto the 3500 block of International Drive. In response, Rolince executed a U-turn halfway down the block and pulled off to the side, then watched as Pollard entered a compound where a secret service car was parked. Agent Fratodei, not familiar with the location, got on the radio and announced that the Mustang was heading into some kind of mission. As soon as the car pulled through the gate, it closed, cutting off Pollard's pursuers. Then the Mustang proceeded down a driveway and came to a stop under an overhang.

According to several later reports, an embassy deputy drove through the gate ahead of the Mustang. Rolince told me that while this was possible, he didn't recall seeing any other car.

Israeli Embassy driveway, Washington, D.C. in 2005 —RON OLIVE

Though the FBI agents still couldn't identify the compound, it didn't take them long to grasp what was happening. This was obviously some sort of official residence, and Pollard was trying to seek asylum.

As the G-men piled out of their cars, the FBI radio erupted with the news: "Pollard just turned into the Israeli embassy!"

Back in the operations center, Cloonan's hunch was confirmed. That was it—Pollard had been spying for Israel. Phones began ringing off the hook and people flew into action. McCarthy dashed upstairs to an office where the FBI special agent in charge was holding a meeting with his assistants and the NIS special agent in charge, John D'Avanzo.

"You'll have to interrupt the meeting," McCarthy told the secretary breathlessly. "Something important has broken in the Pollard case."

"They can't be interrupted," she responded, whereupon McCarthy blew by her, burst through the door, and said, "I'm sorry to barge in, but I thought you needed to know. Jonathan Pollard just entered the Israeli embassy."[1] That got their attention.

Meanwhile, the street outside the embassy was beginning to look like a parking lot for a Redskins football game, except the cars were all FBI. The bureau had the entire compound surrounded. The surveillance teams radioed headquarters and told their supervisors what was going on, setting off a flurry of flash phone calls to VIPs that didn't die down for twenty minutes. The FBI was in a legal gray zone. Because they couldn't make an arrest unless a violent felony crime was committed in their presence, a grand jury handed down an indictment for an arrest, or the attorney general authorized one, they had to await word from the Department of Justice.

What ensued is not entirely clear. Evidently, two men were at the embassy gate, a guard and a uniformed secret service officer. One FBI agent also saw a man standing in a window looking down on the proceedings. After Pollard's Mustang stopped under the overhang, the person in the window disappeared. Someone emerged from the embassy and began talking to Pollard under the overhang.

According to Rolince, who spoke to the secret service officer afterwards, it was this officer who was instrumental in keeping Pollard outside the embassy building. Evidently, the officer, whose name Rolince didn't recall, told the Israeli conferring with Pollard that because this case involved espionage it came under the FBI's jurisdiction, and that he couldn't let Pollard remain on the embassy grounds. A discussion ensued, and at last Pollard was told that he could come into the embassy but only after parking his Mustang on the road.

Pollard's account is somewhat different. According to him, an Israeli vehicle followed his Mustang down the driveway. Pollard stopped and he and Anne got out, whereupon the man in the other vehicle climbed out and came over and embraced him. A second man, a security guard, emerged from the embassy and greeted him. Pollard recognized the man's voice as the same he had heard on the phone earlier. The security guard walked back to the gate and talked to an FBI agent standing on the other side. Then, Pollard claims, he talked to someone else, probably the uniformed secret service officer. Finally, the guard returned to Pollard and said, "I hate to tell you this—you have to leave."

"Do you know who I am?" Pollard replied, incredulous. "Do you know how important it is for me to get to Israel? Can't I claim the right of return?"

Pollard's red Mustang. —NIS EVIDENCE PHOTO

"It isn't permitted," the guard said. "You can leave now or I'll have to let them in."[2]

Pollard believes that had it not been for the presence of so many FBI agents and vehicles, which put psychological pressure on the Israelis, he would have been allowed to stay.

Soon afterward the Department of Justice sent word to the FBI: The bureau could arrest Pollard if he left the embassy grounds and was passed on to the agents on the scene. However, they did not have authorization to arrest Anne.

By now, Anne was crying hysterically and Pollard, having badly miscalculated his moves, was dismayed and confused. Reluctantly, the couple climbed into their car and the Mustang inched up the embassy driveway. As soon as the two front tires touched the blacktop of International Drive, Agent Rolince reached through the window, grabbed Pollard by the arm, and ordered him to turn off the engine. He arrested Pollard and seized his Mustang with all of its contents.

It appears the suspect couldn't wait for a game of one-upmanship. Much to Rolince's surprise, no sooner had he packed Pollard into the back seat of his FBI vehicle than the analyst leaned forward and began chattering away. "You botched it!" he cried. "You thought this was a Soviet bloc operation, didn't you?"[3]

Anne, free to go, told the FBI agents she wasn't feeling well and they drove her and her cat back to the apartment.

D'Avanzo called me from the FBI field office and informed me of Pollard's arrest. The FBI wanted me to come over and interview the suspect again with Special Agent Jechorek. I made a beeline for the field office, on the way over visualizing Pollard handcuffed in the interview room, shoulders sagging, thinking his whole world had collapsed. The person I would be talking to this time would be vastly different from the man who just yesterday, with evident pride, had produced a handwritten statement detailing his sundry crimes. This new man, the wind taken out of his sails, would be frightened and meek. I couldn't have been more mistaken.

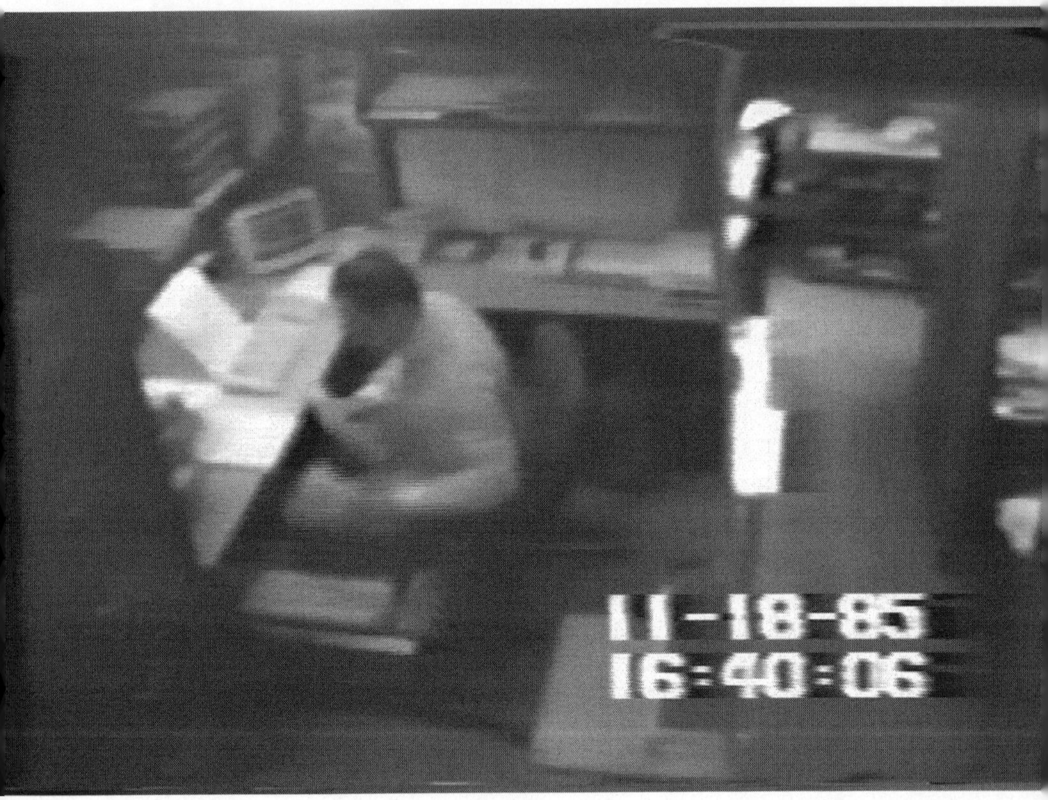
11-18-85
16:40:06

Chapter 20

UNREPENTANT

As soon as I arrived at the FBI field office, Lydia Jechorek and I joined Pollard in a room in the reception area. We sat down facing him, read him his Miranda rights, and again used the NIS Civilian Suspect's Acknowledgment and Waiver of Rights form to inform him that he was under arrest and suspected of the unlawful solicitation, acquisition, and disclosure of classified defense information to an unauthorized person and/or a foreign government. Pollard read and initialed each waiver.

Before signing the waiver of rights form, Pollard said he was willing to talk to us but would not answer questions in certain areas until he could consult with a lawyer. To clarify what he meant by this comment, and to ensure that he understood the waiver, we told him he could decline to answer any questions, he could consult with an attorney, or he could terminate the interview at any time for any reason.

"Now don't be stupid," Pollard said sarcastically. "Don't stop asking questions just because I won't answer a certain question. You just move on to the next question."

Pollard under arrest —AP/WWP

Ignoring his comment, we asked him one more time whether he wanted an attorney present and he said no. I'm sure Jechorek was thinking the same thing I was: Here was a guy who had admitted to espionage and just tried to gain asylum in the Israeli embassy, who was under arrest and in serious trouble, yet his reaction was one of overbearing cockiness. Pollard showed no remorse for anything. It was as if he were saying, I certainly fooled you, you idiots.

We zeroed in on Kurt Lohbeck right away, asking Pollard if in fact he had passed classified documents to the reporter, as he had told us twice before. Pollard admitted to giving only a few messages and maps to Lohbeck about a year and a half earlier; the highest classification was secret/no-foreign dissemination. He gave us the titles. These included some maps of Afghanistan, message traffic from the DIA concerning Soviet intentions in Pakistan, and a series of messages from the U.S. embassy in Kabul.

Jechorek and I started naming countries other than Israel, asking Pollard if he had ever passed information to them. He said no to each one. He was still lying to us about certain issues, but we wouldn't find that out for another six months. For instance, he denied there had been anyone else involved with him in espionage activity. He also denied passing classified information to any American citizen besides Lohbeck. Pollard claimed he had once driven Lohbeck to the Pakistani embassy in Washington with information concerning Soviet intentions in Pakistan. According to the analyst, when Lohbeck returned to the car, he said he had shown the documents to Pakistan's defense attaché. I suspected it was Pollard who had given the information to Pakistan, not Lohbeck, and the reporter later denied ever disclosing secrets to Pakistan.

Richard Haver, in charge of the damage assessment, later told me that Pollard had, in fact, tried to close a deal with Pakistan by giving them compartmented intelligence he had tucked away on the Indian program. The Pakistanis were standoffish and couldn't get rid of him quickly enough. Pollard left the highly classified documents with them and didn't ask for any money, so they were probably in total confusion about this weird fellow. The relationship between Pollard and Pakistan while he was working for Israel did not bloom because they would not use him, task him, or play his game. In any event, Pollard was never charged with passing classified information to Pakistan.

Pollard's crimes involving Israel were so blatant and the evidence against him so overwhelming that it would be easier for the Justice Department to build a case against him based on his Israeli activity rather than probing what he might have given to other countries. From this point on, therefore, Jechorek and I kept the focus on Israel.

We concentrated our questions on Pollard's reasons for providing that nation with classified information. At one point I asked Pollard if he had given his handlers information partly because he felt the United States was being stingy with defense intelligence. He said that was right, that he had sat in on intelligence-exchange meetings and been unhappy with the U.S. government's tight-lipped policy. Were his earlier handwritten statements about materials he'd passed on and money he'd received false? No, he said, everything was true except the part about Lohbeck.

"You should know that I needed operational time to make plans," he said in a supercilious tone. "Lohbeck was my fall guy."

It was also true, he went on, that he had received $2,500 a month for passing classified material. When asked how he had collected the payments, he said "they" picked the drop sites and he picked up the money from those drop sites. How did he know to use the term drop sites?

"I'm not stupid; I read a lot," he snapped.

Pollard also confessed that "they" had paid for two trips overseas, a four-week vacation in November 1984 and another five-week one in July and August 1985. When asked if he had visited Israel on either trip, he said yes. Money, however, was not what motivated him to spy. He maintained that it was only for operational expenses.

According to the analyst, he had never passed information to a Communist country. When we asked if the information he provided had been handed indirectly to a Communist or criteria county, he said not to his knowledge.

"There's a book written in Spanish in my apartment that should have tipped you off," Pollard remarked at one point. "It deals with arms in Afghanistan and I have no business with it. That should have been obvious to you when you did your search."

Sensing that he was trying to belittle us as a defense mechanism to make himself feel better about his own egregious errors, I ignored the comment. Rather than engaging him in a fruitless confrontation that might result in more lies, I tried to disarm him by making him feel somewhat justified in what he had done, and more comfortable talking about it.

I related my experiences conducting a drug operation in Israel, telling him about a visit I had made to the northern border, marked off with barbed wire, and having lunch at a kibbutz where I had met many fine people. At the time, I didn't know Pollard was Jewish—in fact, no one involved in the investigation, not even his coworkers, knew—but I decided to find out. Did the constant threat of war hanging over Israel and his Jewish extraction partially explain why he had passed classified documents to that country? He smiled and nodded, appearing to believe that I was sincere.

So he was Jewish. Oddly enough, not once during the entire interview did he mention Israel by name. In fact, he studiously avoided the word.

When we asked him if there was still classified information somewhere in his possession, he replied we had it all—the contents of the suitcase dropped off at the neighbors and everything that was in his Mustang. By the way, he added, the Esfandiaris had no idea what was going on and were not involved in any way. They were just friends. He said the contents of the suitcase represented less than what he normally provided to his contact.

As for his method of delivering documents, he explained that he would usually drop them off on Friday and on Sunday pick up those that needed to be returned. "They" would keep everything else. The suitcase in our possession held documents he had picked up from his handlers and intended to return. Pollard described in detail how he would remove the documents, store them in his Mustang, and then, when he made his way to a convenient place—Sam's Car Wash in Suitland, for example, or a secluded location at Bolling Air Force Base—transfer them into the suitcase in the back of his car. Two or three times a day, three times a week, he followed this same procedure. It became a habit with him. The only reason he had purchased the Mustang was for its fold-down backseat, behind which he hid the suitcase.

We asked him why he had gone to the Israeli embassy that morning. He said he had phoned the embassy twice trying to get help, that there was some sort of misunderstanding the first time—he wouldn't elaborate—but that during the second call they told him to come in if he could shake surveillance. Had he gone to the Israeli embassy to seek political asylum? Yes, he replied.

Under continued questioning, Pollard said he had seen his contact looking out the embassy window. Then he clarified the statement, adding that this person was not one of the contacts to whom he had passed classified information.

He was still carefully avoiding the word Israel. Trying to pin him down, I asked him to respond yes or no to the following question: "Did you pass classified U.S. national defense documents to the Israeli government?"

"Yes," Pollard responded.[1]

We had come far with Pollard during this interview, but we still had a long way to go. The suspect was doing what he liked best—talking—and if that made him feel as if he were in control of the interview, that was okay by me because we were gathering a lot of crucial information. As time went on, he became more and more talkative, and I felt confident that within three or four hours, total, we would have his whole story. But it wasn't meant to be.

A knock came at the door, and when I opened it, two FBI agents I didn't know were standing there. I left the room to see what they wanted, closing the door behind me, and they informed me they had to take Pollard in front of a federal magistrate for an arraignment. It was about two in the afternoon, and they only had until three to accomplish this.

"You've got to be kidding me!" I said.

"We're not."

"You want to arraign him now because the magistrate court closes at three? You're crazy. Pollard's talking; we can't stop now. He doesn't have to be arraigned if he's still talking!"

They had no choice, they said. It was FBI policy to arraign on the day of an arrest.

"I'm telling you you're wrong. No agent has to stop talking to someone who has waived his constitutional rights against self-incrimination and is confessing to espionage. We're in the middle of an interview with Pollard; we *have* to continue."

"Sorry, but we have to get him over there before three."

I kept trying to reason with them. They could take him to the jail that night and arraign him in the morning, I said. But it was useless, and because I was on their turf, I stopped arguing and turned back to the interview room in disgust.

As soon as I told Jechorek what had happened, she went and made arrangements to get an FBI mug shot of Pollard. Frustrated, I sat back down, mulling over the dilemma and not saying a word to Pollard.

He then broke the silence with an off-the-wall comment. "Ron, you know the government shouldn't give high clearances to Jewish people."

Startled, I looked up. "What are you talking about, Jay?"

"It's true," he said, and launched into a theory about there being three classes of Jews: those who travel to the holy land one or more times a year; those who don't or can't travel there but give Israel money and moral support; and, finally, "Jews like me," he said, "who can't afford to travel to Israel or give money. When asked to help, we're willing to do anything for the love of our country."

"That's ridiculous, Jay," was the only response I could frame to such an outlandish remark. Pollard must feel the Israelis have abandoned him, I thought. They've left him out in the cold, and while I had nothing but contempt for the crimes he'd confessed to, I couldn't blame him for being upset.

Jechorek returned, and as we waited for the FBI agents who would process Pollard before taking him to the metropolitan police department for arraignment, she asked him if he felt what he had done was illegal or immoral. "No," he replied.

After being photographed and fingerprinted, he was returned to the interview room for a couple more minutes. "Do you have any personal questions to ask me?" he said, ever ready to chat about himself.

Jechorek wanted to know why he had walked to his car several times a day carrying envelopes that could easily be recognized by coworkers as containing highly classified information.

I'll never forget his reply. "It had become so easy to remove documents, it just didn't make any difference."

Minutes later, the suspect was taken away in handcuffs. Unbeknownst to me, that was the last time I would ever speak to Jonathan Jay Pollard.

During Pollard's booking and processing at the Washington, D.C., Cen-tral Detention Facility at 1901 D Street SE, he had to provide information so that a representative of the pretrial services agency could determine conditions for possible pretrial release. In the health history section of Pollard's intake report, dated 21 November 1985, he admitted that three years earlier he had experienced emotional problems and received treatment. In the substance abuse section, the representative wrote, "Drug abuse indicated, no alcohol abuse indicated." Based on the information given to the agency, it recommended "that the defendant report for drug program placement at pretrial services agency."[2] No release bond was set.

At last our suspect was in jail and we didn't have to worry about him escaping. But there was little time to relax. The very next day a miscommunication between the U.S. Magistrate Court in Washington and the Department of Corrections almost resulted in a tragic mistake. Pollard was about to be released on bail, and Anne was doing everything in her power to make it happen.

11-18-85
16:41:18

Chapter 21

NO TIME TO LOSE

T ime was of the essence. Even before Pollard took his wife to the
doctor on Thursday morning, the U.S. attorney for the District
of Columbia, Joseph diGenova, was busy dealing with the
Department of Justice. Other attorneys were drawing up search warrants
for the suitcase Anne had left with her neighbors. Three assistant U.S.
attorneys were assigned to prosecute the case, and they needed to gather
the evidence required to connect Anne with the crime. Charles Leeper was
the lead attorney in the Pollard case, David Geneson the lead in Anne's
case, while Stephen Spivack and other attorneys would assist. Anne hadn't
been arrested and was obviously
trying to flee the country, which put a
lot of pressure on Geneson.

In the court records that later
emerged, Geneson gave a meticulous
description of events that unfolded
that day and the next.[1] Everyone at
the U.S. attorney's office was working
frantically to patch together sufficient
evidence to arrest Anne. They wanted
to establish that she had known of
her husband's activities and had
cooperated with him. After obtaining

Anne Pollard under arrest —AP/WWP

a search warrant from the Washington, D.C., magistrate, Geneson had
FBI agents search the contents of the suitcase on Thursday afternoon and
into the late evening. They couldn't just page through the evidence. Each
seized document had to be handled with gloves and packaged separately to
prevent contamination so that the crime lab could obtain fingerprints and

look for possible microdots, which had to be read using a microscope. With microdot technology, a page of instructions or documents could be photographed and reduced to a size less than one millimeter. It was quite sophisticated in its day and particularly popular with the Soviets, who used it to communicate detailed instructions to spies.

On Friday morning, with the clock ticking, several agents from the NIS and the FBI went to the U.S. attorney's office in Washington to obtain three search warrants: one for Pollard's Ford Mustang, another for his apartment, and the third for the small red bag and purse that Anne had carried with her to the Israeli embassy and that had been seized when she left. While the warrants were being prepared, Geneson interviewed NIS agent Lisa Redman and asked her to repeat what she had heard Pollard say the previous Monday when he called his wife and said "cactus." That afternoon the word *cactus* was discovered in a copy of a paper seized from the suitcase. It was apparent to the attorneys that Pollard had used it as a code word to alert Anne to remove the documents from their residence. This critical piece of evidence suggested that she knew full well that the documents in the suitcase were classified.[2]

Hoping for more evidence, Geneson hurriedly dispatched agents to reinterview the Esfandiaris to see if they could recall any further details of their conversation with Anne on the night she left them with the suitcase. But the neighbors weren't home, nor could they be found.

In the meantime, Anne, accompanied by her father-in-law, had dropped by the Central Detention Facility to try to bail her husband out. Because her purse had been seized at the embassy on Thursday, she had no identification to get through the door, much less to see Pollard. On the verge of panic, she spent the rest of the day making calls to the assistant U.S. attorney's office in an attempt to reclaim her identification, credit cards, and cash. She pleaded on the phone with them, saying she needed her identification immediately to make an out-of-town business trip that had been scheduled prior to Pollard's arrest. The very idea of a wife taking a business trip while her husband was sitting in jail on charges of suspected espionage was ludicrous, a clear signal that Anne intended to flee, and as a result the FBI tightened its surveillance knot. But her comment didn't amount to evidence.

When the affidavits for permission to search the Pollards' apartment were approved, NIS and FBI agents hustled over to Dupont Circle. During the ensuing search, they uncovered four documents classified confidential that we had missed on Monday night. Also recovered from the apartment were three large trash bags stuffed with hand-shredded papers. Later, working against the clock, the agents reconstructed some of these, including notes Anne had made on a notepad after reading the classified documents on the PRC. They also uncovered the note in which the ficti-

Anne Pollard's handwritten notes transcribed from documents pertaining to China — NIS UNCLASSIFIED EVIDENCE PHOTO

tious Uncle Joe Fisher informed Anne that he wouldn't be able to attend her wedding, and that he was sending her the diamond and sapphire engagement ring as a gift.

Ficticious letter from Uncle Joe Fisher —NIS EVIDENCE PHOTO

Just when it seemed as if the case against Anne had solidified, the U.S. attorney's office received an alarming phone call from one of the FBI agents surveilling her. He was at the jail, and had just been informed by a corrections officer that a bondsman was there at Anne's request. Pollard was about to be released on bond.

Pandemonium broke out at the U.S. attorney's office. How could this be? The court had a no-bond order for Pollard that was supposed to be in effect until the time of a preliminary hearing. Someone had dropped the ball.

In another flurry of phone calls, Geneson and his colleagues from the U.S. attorney's office communicated with the magistrate court and the Department of Corrections and discovered that word of the no-bond order had never been communicated to the jail. Just minutes before Pollard was to be released, the order went through and the analyst stayed put.

It was a bureaucratic blunder that took valuable time away from the effort to get an arrest warrant for Anne. Not until 6:15 PM was the search warrant for her purse and bag executed. From that point on, the investigation unfolded rapidly—so rapidly it was difficult for the U.S. attorney's office to keep track of what was going on. A search of Anne's personal effects revealed identification papers for both her and Pollard. Included were vaccination records for her cat, estimates of the value of her jewelry, pictures of family and friends, even a giant bottle of expensive perfume. All of these items, the government believed, pointed to Anne's desire to flee the country, taking with her what she valued and thought would be needed. By the time the agents finished going through her effects and all the trash, the government believed it had strong evidence that the Pollards had been attempting to make a clean getaway.

Sometime between 6:30 and 8:30 PM, while Anne was still at the jail, the Esfandiaris came home and underwent a second interview with NIS and FBI agents. They confirmed that on Monday evening, when Anne dropped off the suitcase, she had told them it contained classified documents, including some she had obtained for her presentation to the Chinese embassy.[3] This gave Anne no out if she later lied in court, claiming to have no knowledge of the contents.

As soon as the Esfandiari interview was done and the search of Anne's bag and purse documented, the FBI field office relayed the results to Geneson at the U.S. attorney's office. Geneson in turn contacted the Department of Justice, providing them with the accumulated evidence against Pollard's wife.

Losing no time, the attorney general's office ordered her arrest. On Friday night at about nine, as she and Dr. Morris Pollard were climbing into a taxi outside the jail to go to get something to eat, two FBI agents approached and placed Anne Henderson Pollard under arrest.

It had never been Anne's goal in life to achieve notoriety, but on 22 November 1985 she did just that. Her notoriety had less to do with her own crimes—committed for an engagement ring and the dubious promise of a more comfortable life, if not for love—than with the company she would join, for within the space of five short days, the FBI arrested Jonathan Pollard of the NIS, his neighbor Ronald Pelton of the NSA, and Larry Wu Tai Chin of the CIA.

While all this was going on, Minister of Defense Yitzhak Rabin was in New York continuing his lecture tour promoting Israeli bonds. Special Agent Al Zane, assistant special agent in charge of counterintelligence at the NIS's New York field office, had been called to Washington to work on the Pollard case. On Friday he called Special Agent Ernie Simon at the New York office to see how Rabin's protective service detail was going. Simon told him no one knew what was going on. The evening before, Rabin had been at Henry Kissinger's townhouse in New York City when he'd received a cascade of telephone calls. Rabin left early, asking Simon to return him to his hotel. En route the defense minister told Simon there had been a change of plans and he had to leave for Israel the next morning. Simon made arrangements for an early departure on Friday.

Rabin and his entourage flew off in a commercial plane from a semiprivate airport in Teterboro, New Jersey, owned by the Port Authority of New York and New Jersey. According to Simon, this was not the airport through which Rabin had entered the United States. Normally, the minister of defense flew on private Israeli aircraft. It wasn't until Simon found out about Pollard that he grasped the reason for Rabin's sudden departure.[4]

Chapter 22

OPERATION FOUL PLAY

O nce Pollard and Anne were in jail, the NIS and the FBI created a major task force to investigate the case. Dubbed Operation Foul Play—a reference to Israel's underhanded method of dealing with its closest ally and supporter—the unprecedented collaboration was the result of the efforts of two FBI supervisors, Nick Walsh and Joe Johnson. It was the first time in all my years with the NIS that the FBI worked directly with us as an equal in an investigation, and we formed a close professional relationship.

The Pollard investigation, to my knowledge, was the speediest international major espionage case ever worked, ending in two arrests after less than two weeks. Now the real work began. The job of the task force was to collect background information on Pollard, starting with his years in school, to gather evidence in preparation for trial, and to conduct interviews. Messages went out to NIS offices worldwide that leads on the case might be coming their way, and they should coordinate with local FBI offices.

Task force members from the NIS moved into a command center set up at the FBI field office. Toll-free hotlines were installed, and agents—many of them rookies from FBI counterintelligence divisions throughout the United States—took incoming calls from people offering information. Hundreds of leads resulted, and all the information was clearly documented and cross-checked, resulting in a chain reaction of other leads. All the spy indicators consistently overlooked throughout the years of Pollard's employment emerged and stared us right in the face. The truism I have always believed about the vast majority of spies was proven once again; namely, spies just can't keep a secret. Invariably, someone knew, saw, suspected, believed, or was told something. Only after an arrest is made will the floodgates of information open wide.

With the help of the U.S. attorney's office for the District of Columbia, procedures and policies were established for a smooth operation. To prevent redundant reporting, for example, the prosecutors agreed that, whenever possible, agents from the NIS and the FBI would conduct witness interviews jointly. The attorneys also advised us that all reports from the beginning of the investigation on would have to be declassified in preparation for trial, with the exception of the documents Pollard had removed, which would be evaluated for possible declassification. The assistant U.S. attorneys were to review all reports.

Though my duties as assistant special agent in charge of counterintelligence for the NIS's Washington field office kept me away from the task force's everyday work, I made several trips a week to the command post. The week following Pollard's arrest, Agent Jechorek and I sat down to write an FBI 302 report on the interview we'd conducted with him immediately following his apprehension. (We hadn't interviewed Anne because she requested legal counsel prior to talking.) On one of these trips I also had the opportunity to talk with Assistant U.S. Attorney Charles Leeper about the interview with Pollard that had been interrupted for his arraignment. Leeper verified my earlier claim that Jechorek and I could have continued talking to Pollard as long as he was willing.

The countless interviews conducted in preparation for trial laid bare Pollard's life—drug use, financial problems, attempts to recruit people, failed polygraph tests. The first matter on the agenda that needed to be resolved was Kurt Lohbeck's role.

In late November 1985 Lohbeck returned to Washington from New York, where he had been working on a story about the Soviets using napalm bombs in Afghanistan. His apartment was under surveillance, and no sooner had he put his suitcase down than the doorbell rang. Two agents—one FBI, the other NIS—were standing on his doorstep.

"Are you Kurt Lohbeck?"

"Yes."

"Do you know Jonathan Pollard?"

"Yes." Lohbeck thought they might be doing a background check on the analyst for a promotion.

"We just arrested Pollard for espionage," the agent said flat out.

The investigators had decided not to play games with Lohbeck; this interview was going to be straightforward, all the cards on the table.

They asked Lohbeck if Pollard had given him any classified information. Yes, he said, and went and got the material and gave it to them. Had he received any other classified information? Yes, he replied. The agents asked him what his plans were, and he replied that he was going immediately to CBS to tell them what had just happened. Then the agents took the classified material and left.

Two days later Lohbeck talked to the FBI with his attorney, Robert Barnett, present. Barnett asked the agency to obtain a letter from Attorney General Edwin Meese stating that Lohbeck wasn't a target of the espionage operation. The letter came a few days later, at which point the reporter began cooperating with the task force. Once the interviews were completed, the FBI didn't investigate Lohbeck further.[1] Although Lohbeck had received some secret maps of Afghanistan from Pollard and was shown several classified documents, the U.S. attorney's office wanted to focus all its efforts on Pollard and Israel. Furthermore, Lohbeck could come in handy as a witness in the trial phase. Last, there was no evidence Lohbeck had any knowledge of Pollard's espionage activities.

The CIA came forward, providing the task force with a report concerning Pollard's application for a job in 1978. It will be recalled that earlier, when Pollard was applying for a position with the NISC and the DIS was doing a background check, the CIA, in the mistaken belief that it had to protect Pollard's privacy, claimed to have no information on the man. As the report submitted to the task force now revealed, the CIA had in fact talked to thirteen individuals about the applicant, mostly Pollard's relatives and friends. One reference had said he was a fervent supporter of Israel, another relayed that he smoked marijuana. The report also disclosed that Pollard had committed the serious transgression of informing nine foreign nationals that he was applying for a job with the CIA.

In the media frenzy that broke out in the wake of Pollard's arrest, hundreds of newspaper articles, magazine stories, and TV specials exposed his years in college and the events leading up to his arrest, and old friends and acquaintances began emerging from the woodwork with stories about his behavior. Unnamed sources who "were not speaking out in spite" claimed they "saw Mr. Pollard and his wife freebase cocaine on several occasions," and that Jay's cocaine use was enough to cause "a personality swing."[2] In an interview with Pollard conducted during the JAG investigation, the suspect admitted that both he and Anne had previously used marijuana and cocaine.[3] To my knowledge no narcotics surfaced during any searches of Pollard's apartment or vehicle. Besides, the U.S. attorney's office wasn't interested in prosecuting the Pollards for drug use.

Former acquaintances from Stanford University claimed that Pollard had boasted about being on the payroll of Mossad, which was grooming him to be a mole in the U.S. government, that he had dual citizenship, was a colonel in the Israeli army, and belonged to the Golani Brigade, an elite infantry unit.[4] One day Pollard was observed waving a pistol in the air, declaring that everyone was out to get him and his life was in danger. When agents questioned him about working for Mossad, Pollard said the claim had been "an invention" on his part. As for the gun incident, it "was the result of delirium from a fever caused by mononucleosis and hallucinogenic mushrooms."[5]

The task force also interviewed Pollard's coworkers in the ATAC. A pall had fallen over the center, which completely shut down for about a week to do a complete inventory of classified information to determine what was missing. The men and women employed there felt deeply betrayed by the spy who had had the gall to conduct his crimes right under their noses. His arrogance had always been tolerated in the office. Whenever he made an outlandish boast, people would just brush it off, thinking, Oh, that's just Pollard. The devastation they experienced was tinged by guilt and humiliation. Even when dealing with their usual contacts within other agencies, ATAC personnel sensed they were being shunned by colleagues.

At the request of the prosecution team, the task force went to great lengths to prove that the Pollards had received money for spying and spent it lavishly. Unexplained funds would serve as both an indicator of and a motive for espionage. To this end, agents conducted interviews, served subpoenas, and conducted analytical studies, equipping prosecutors to demonstrate the point not just at trial but also during a possible sentencing phase.

The task force discovered that, after taxes, Pollard had been bringing home approximately $1,600 a month as an ATAC analyst at the GS-12 level, while Anne, employed with a trade association until July 1985, had been earning roughly $1,000. Their combined disposable income didn't even begin to cover routine living expenses such as rent, food, and clothing, much less the indulgent lifestyle they lived during the year before their arrest. For example, on their European trip in November 1984 the Pollards stayed at many five-star hotels as they traveled to Marseilles, Saint Tropez, Cannes, Nice, Monte Carlo, Pisa, Florence, Rome, Venice, Innsbruck, and Munich. No hotel charges and only a few meal charges appeared on their credit card bills and checking account records, making it apparent that they had paid for most of the vacation with cash.

Numerous other indicators of unexplained cash payments surfaced, including the purchase of a gold necklace, a bracelet, and earrings for $2,100 at a Georgetown store in March 1985, half of which were paid for by check. In July, after Anne quit work, the Pollards' legal monthly take-home pay dipped back to $1,600. During the weekend before Jay's arrest they ate out twice, once at Marrakesh, where they treated their unidentified guest to a bottle of Dom Perignon, and once at La Maree, where they hosted Sella and his wife. The cost of the two dinners totaled $448, a quarter of the Pollards' monthly income. The year prior to their arrest the couple expended through their checking accounts their entire combined salary of $29,000 for what appeared to be routine, although hardly paltry, living expenses. In the same period they spent some $30,000 in cash for what can only be described as extraordinary expenses.[6]

Both Jay and Anne insisted that their monthly espionage income didn't make much difference in their lifestyle, but neither the task force nor the prosecutors were buying it.

11-18-85
17:08:01

Chapter 23

ISRAEL CONFRONTED

■■

A s the case was making international headlines, tension between the United States and Israel flared. Israeli officials strongly denied any knowledge of Jonathan Pollard's espionage. They called it a rogue operation run by Rafael Eitan with the help of Yosef Yagur, the Israeli attaché in New York, Ilan Ravid, the scientific consular at the Israeli embassy in Washington, and Irit Erb, a secretary in the embassy. The name Aviem Sella wasn't mentioned, nor had it surfaced in Pollard's initial interviews. By 30 November 1985, the Israelis offered to return the documents Pollard had passed to the conspirators, but they wouldn't allow Yagur and Ravid to be questioned in Washington. An Israeli official told the *Washington Post* his country would "retain diplomatic immunity and that the principle of international diplomacy would not be surrendered under pressure from Washington."[1] The Israelis did promise, however, to undertake a separate investigation of their own.

Furious, U.S. Secretary of State George Shultz fired off a letter to Israeli Prime Minister Shimon Peres demanding to know whether Israel was conducting espionage operations in the United States, what documents had been sent to Israel, and what his country intended to do about the two recalled diplomats, Yagur and Ravid. Members of Congress also demanded answers.

Eventually, through diplomatic channels, the two countries decided that an American delegation headed by Abraham Sofaer, a retired judge acting as a legal adviser for the Department of State, would travel to Israel. There the delegation would retrieve the classified materials and interview Pollard's handlers.[2] The Justice Department agreed not to prosecute them if they were fully debriefed and filed court documents identifying them as unindicted coconspirators.

The delegation, put together by the Justice and State departments, included U. S. Attorney Joseph diGenova, two members of Pollard's prosecution team—Charles Leeper and Stephen Spivack—two people from the Department of Justice, and FBI representatives. No one from the navy was invited. This promised to be a grave mistake. The navy was cataloguing the materials Pollard had passed to the Israelis, which put it in the unique position of being able to grasp the scope of the damage he had inflicted on the defense intelligence community.[3] According to Jerry Agee, commander of the ATAC as well as Pollard's boss, the Department of Justice blamed the Israelis for the exclusion of navy personnel, claiming they had put a cap on the number of people allowed to enter Israel.

When the Justice Department informed Judge Sofaer that no one from the navy would be going, he was puzzled. He called up NIS headquarters and requested a representative from the navy, someone who knew about the classified information to which Pollard had access and who could give him a feel for the analyst and his background. Commander Agee being the obvious candidate, the NIS sent him to the State Department to meet with Sofaer. Agee impressed Sofaer, and the judge included him in his official State Department entourage.

In early December 1985 the delegation left for a ten-day stay in Israel. Agee traveled with Judge Sofaer and his assistant on a separate aircraft, apart from the Department of Justice group. When their plane arrived in Tel Aviv, it was mobbed by journalists waiting for them to deplane. While Sofaer was going through the fanfare of giving statements to the press, a reporter spotted Agee standing in the background. Suddenly, the media descended on him, shoving microphones in his face and taking pictures. One photographer walked right up and snapped a picture just inches from his face, then began taking additional shots from different angles. What the hell is he doing? Agee wondered, guessing the guy thought he was CIA. But no one asked him his identity, and he didn't offer it.

Shortly afterward, a limousine arrived to take them to their hotels. Agee was dropped off at the Jerusalem Hilton, where he would be staying with members of the delegation from the Department of Justice, while Judge Sofaer and his assistant were whisked off to the King David. Reporters were milling around the lobby, and when Agee walked up to the desk and produced his passport to show the clerk, they swarmed around him with their cameras clicking, evidently trying to get a close-up of the inside of his passport. When Agee saw what was happening, he promptly pocketed the passport and told the clerk he would provide it later.

Israeli security, eyeing the delegation warily and suspecting them of mischief at every turn, kept track of their comings and goings at all times. On one occasion, Agee walked into the hotel gift shop, bought a newspaper, and decided to look around outside. The shop had a second door leading to the street and Agee exited that way, not thinking twice about it, to do some sightseeing in the area. After walking two blocks he returned to a chaotic scene. The area outside the hotel was overrun with police cars and plainclothes security personnel—Mossad agents, Agee believed. What on earth is going on? he wondered. Out of the corner of his eye, he saw one officer elbow another and point at him. The second man, glaring at Agee, came up and barked, "Don't you ever do that again!" Nothing more was said.

On another occasion, FBI Special Agent Eugene Noltkamper, Agent Joe Johnson, and Commander Agee went into the gift shop in the hotel lobby, and when they finished, they exited through two different doors. Agee went his own way, not intending to confuse anyone. When Johnson and Noltkamper got up to their rooms a few minutes later, there was a knock on the latter's door. It was the same two security people who had been sitting in the lobby logging the delegation members' comings and goings. They said they wanted to make sure he had a fire exit sticker on the inside of his door. They both came in, and he believed they might have actually put another sticker over the one already on the door. He said it was obvious they were confused as to who went into which room and apparently were trying to account for everyone.[4] The Israelis didn't seem to understand they were dealing with U.S. counterintelligence experts who viewed their phony ploys as bordering on the ridiculous.

Agee didn't take part in interviewing the coconspirators, but from those who did he heard about the roadblocks thrown in their way. Every day the delegation was wakened long before dawn and driven from the hotel in Jerusalem to the U.S. embassy in Tel Aviv, about ninety minutes away. The interviews were arranged on Israeli terms. The first several days were spent doing nothing but working out ground rules—what the Americans could and could not ask the Israeli suspects.

The delegation would wait at the embassy all day before being herded onto a bus in which the shades had been drawn. They were then transferred to a van with darkened windows and later switched to yet another van. They were driven to an installation in the middle of nowhere that resembled, not a military base, but a civilian-run facility.

The interviews, according to Noltkamper, were all conducted late at night, in the basement, with the Americans sitting on one side of a big conference table and each coconspirator—one at a time, with his Israeli legal team—on the other.

Compounding the frustration of FBI Agent Noltkamper and the other Americans was the ritual that every time they asked a question, the Israelis would translate it into Hebrew, then the coconspirator would respond in Hebrew, and they would translate the answer back into English. The most annoying part was that the coconspirators spoke perfect English and everybody knew it. But rules were rules.

Needless to say, the delegation would arrive back at the hotel in the wee hours, exhausted, and fall into bed to catch a few short hours of sleep. It was obvious the Israelis had decided not to cooperate fully.

According to Noltkamper, when they interviewed Rafael Eitan, the leader of the spy ring, he immediately began to lie. The U.S. delegation got up and told the Israelis that the interview was over. After a day or two of negotiations, they resumed the interview and this time Eitan was much more straightforward.[5]

Commander Agee had with him a list of classified documents Pollard had passed to his handlers. It was just a preliminary list, for over the course of eighteen months the analyst had taken such a huge volume of material that it would take more than a year to compile a complete list. At first the Israelis handed over sixty-three documents to the Justice Department, saying that was all the analyst had provided. This was a blatant falsehood. The entire delegation knew Pollard had turned over thousands of documents and classified pages, a vast amount of them classified TS/SCI. They could prove this from a cursory check they had done before the trip, and back it up with Pollard's confessions.

When pressed for the return of all the classified material in their possession, including the TS/SCI documents, the Israelis insisted that was all they had. The Americans pushed the issue, showing them Agee's short list of classified information. After continued denials, the Israelis finally conceded and relinquished additional documents.

Fed up with the long travel hours, the Americans decided to move into a hotel in Tel Aviv to be closer to the interview site. When Judge Sofaer informed the Israelis of the planned switch, they said they didn't want the team to change hotels. Rather, they would arrange for future interviews to be conducted closer by, outside of Jerusalem. The Israelis never made good on their promise.

By now the lack of cooperation was so exasperating that Judge Sofaer called Prime Minister Peres and informed him that he was releasing a statement to the press and pulling his team out of Israel. The Israelis backed off somewhat, appeasing the delegation rather than fully cooperating. They still didn't mention Aviem Sella or his involvement in the operation, apparently relying on Pollard's silence.

One day at the Hilton, Agee called up from the lobby to Charlie Leeper's room, which happened to be to the right of Agee's. A stranger with an Israeli accent answered the phone. When Agee asked for Leeper, the person said, "He's in the conference room downstairs having a meeting." This struck Agee as odd. Thinking he might have dialed the wrong room, he took the elevator up to check the number on Leeper's door. Agee was correct—he had dialed the wrong room, the one to the left of his. Who, then, was in the room he had dialed—and how did that person know Leeper was in a meeting in the basement? It dawned on him then that all of their rooms might be bugged.

This was a strong possibility. The U.S. intelligence community knew that hotel rooms where State Department and high-ranking military officials stayed when visiting the U.S. embassy in Tel Aviv were routinely bugged. In fact, official travelers to the embassy received briefings warning them not to discuss classified information in their hotel rooms and not to leave classified documents unattended.

Alarmed, Agee hurried down to the conference room where the interview team was having a strategy session, scribbled a note on a pad, and handed it to Leeper: "Your meeting is being monitored."

The United States kept its agreement not to prosecute Pollard's connections, and despite all the obstacles thrown into the Americans' way, his coconspirators ultimately did for the most part reveal their involvement. But the delegation still knew nothing about Aviem Sella, and they left Israel with just a small fraction of the documents they had received from Pollard—about 163, none classified higher than secret. The FBI's Johnson and Noltkamper carried the recovered documents in two orange diplomatic bags. The two agents had to fly back first class and buy three seats, one for the two diplomatic bags, which they couldn't put in the cargo hold of a commercial plane.[6]

Before the delegation left, the Israelis decided to give them the machine they claimed had been used to copy the documents. It came, they said, from the surplus inventory of the Israeli consulate in New York. There was no way of telling because the serial number had been removed. The FBI later said that the machine was not one of those used to copy the documents.

Agee experienced one last glitch as he was leaving Israel. During his stay he had purchased gifts for his family and copies of several Israeli-English newspapers. Agee recalled that one newspaper featured a full front-page picture of his face with a question mark over it. As Agee was going through the tight airport security, a uniformed security guard asked him if he had enjoyed his stay. Agee replied that he did enjoy his stay "for the most part."

The guard, in a cold, hard voice, stated, "Good, because you will never be coming back here again."

Agee didn't say another word to the guard and moved on to his gate. When he arrived home in Virginia and opened his suitcase, Agee found that its contents had been ransacked: all his gifts were gone, and so were the newspapers he had purchased that told about the Pollard case.[7]

The Israelis must have thought they were being clever, withholding the most highly classified materials, along with Sella's name, from the U.S. delegation. If so, they badly miscalculated the disenchantment Jonathan Jay Pollard felt over being abandoned and left in such a fix.

Chapter 24

GUILTY

F ollowing Anne's arrest, her attorney, James F. Hibey, and his
assistant, Gordon Coffee, filed a motion with the court for her
release on bond pending adjudication of the case. The government
promptly submitted a motion in opposition. After the first hearing on 3
December 1985, the court gave her six days to come up with a proposal
for release of some type of collateral, such as the family home. All she
could produce was a single painting that belonged to her father-in-law
and had no sentimental value to its owner. The government stated, "The
loss of such a painting, even given its claimed monetary value, is unlikely
to deter further efforts by the defendant to evade prosecution."[1]

At the same time, Anne had her physician send letters to the court
attributing her acute abdominal pain to a biliary tract dysfunction. She
claimed she had not been permitted to receive proper medical treatment
in jail. The chief judge, Aubrey E. Robinson Jr., of the U.S. District Court
in Washington, finally ruled in her favor, and on 24 February 1986, Anne
was released from jail on a $23,500 cash bond on the condition that
she report to pretrial services once a week, call them daily, live in the
Washington metropolitan area, obtain employment, report any change of
address, and show up for court dates.

As for Pollard, he remained incarcerated in Washington, held without bond. The days were long, and he had plenty of time to mull over
his situation. Apparently, he felt he had no options. He had confessed
his espionage activities to the NIS and the FBI. The physical evidence
against him was overwhelming. And his Israeli coconspirators had been
cooperating with the government, telling them how he had been handled
and how much he had been paid. Except for family and a handful of
friends, everyone was against him. With his fate predetermined, a trial,

it seemed, would be a waste of time. His lawyer, Richard Hibey—the brother of Anne's attorney—probably advised him that he had no choice but to plead guilty and take his chances. If he cooperated, the prosecutors would most likely not charge Anne with being an accessory to his crimes or conspiring to commit espionage; they would file lesser charges.

After consulting with their attorneys, both Pollard and Anne decided to plea-bargain. They entered their pleas before Judge Robinson on 4 June 1986. That very morning the federal grand jury returned an indictment against both husband and wife.

Pollard pleaded guilty to conspiracy to commit espionage. Judge Robinson informed him of three options: he had the right to a trial if he wanted one; the government would have to convince a jury of his guilt beyond a reasonable doubt; and there would be no trial if he, the judge, accepted the plea. Did Pollard know the possible maximum sentence for the offense to which he wished to plead guilty? Yes, Pollard replied. A life sentence and a $250,000 penalty.

Judge Robinson wanted to make another point perfectly clear: "And do you understand further that what the judgment of the court would be is entirely at the discretion of the court?" Again, Pollard said he understood.

"Have any promises been made to you with respect to what the sentence of the court will be?" Judge Robinson went on.

"No," Pollard said.

The judge reiterated, "Any representations of any kind?"

"No, no sir," Pollard replied. [2]

Once it had been ascertained that Pollard and his attorney fully understood the potential consequences of pleading guilty, and the rights he would give up, Judge Robinson accepted his plea and remanded him to the U.S. marshals for continued incarceration until a sentencing date could be set.

Anne went through the same procedure, confirming that she understood the two charges against her: conspiracy to receive embezzled government property and accessory after the fact to possession of national defense documents. Having reaped monetary rewards from a foreign government involved in espionage against the United States; having most likely disclosed classified information to her supervisors at CommCore, the public relations firm for which she worked; and having presented a briefing to a senior minister at the Chinese embassy,

Anne was getting off easy. She wasn't prosecuted for any of these other allegations, and she remained out on bond until a sentencing date was set. It was Jonathan Jay Pollard the government had its sights set on.

The two plea agreements specified the conditions with which the Pollards would have to comply. These included:

- Submitting to more interviews and polygraph examinations and testifying before a grand jury.
- Responding to all questions put to them by federal law enforcement agents and other government representatives.
- Turning over to the government any property, documents, or information in their possession or control related to espionage activity.
- Testifying fully and truthfully during any grand jury, trial, or other proceeding in which their testimony was determined to be relevant.
- Submitting to a damage assessment by representatives of the military and intelligence communities.

If, after signing his plea agreement, Pollard failed in any way to fulfill these requirements, the agreement would be null and void, the government would prosecute him, if warranted, for espionage, perjury, false statement, obstruction of justice, and other charges, and Pollard would have to waive his right to a speedy trial. As for Anne, if before sentencing she failed to cooperate fully with these conditions, the government would be relieved of its obligation to her under that agreement.

In return for his cooperation in the investigation and damage assessment, when Pollard appeared before the court for sentencing, the government would bring to its attention—and, later, to the attention of the parole board—the extent of his readiness to comply. The government warned that it would recommend that the court impose a substantial sentence along with a monetary fine, and that it still had the discretion to impose the maximum sentence.

The final condition the government made in the plea agreement was that Pollard refrain from any unauthorized disclosure of classified information obtained while he was employed by the U.S. Navy. Should he write anything or "otherwise provide information for purposes of publication or dissemination," he would have to submit it to the director of naval intelligence for prepublication review. Furthermore, Pollard would have to give the government the profits or proceeds from any publication or information describing his employment by the navy, his espionage activities, or the circumstances leading to his arrest.[3]

I assigned NIS Agent Redman to work with FBI Agent Jechorek on coordinating interviews with Pollard and his wife. Because she was out on bond, Anne had debriefings at her attorney's office and the FBI field office, where Barry Colvert polygraphed her. Pollard's initial polygraphs, before and after he was transferred to the federal detention center in Petersburg, Virginia, were conducted at the courthouse in Washington. Every Tuesday, Wednesday, and Thursday morning, Redman and Jechorek would go to the detention center and pick him up, then drive him to a bungalow, or safe house, not far from the prison to be interviewed. Without fail, on each of these trips Pollard would say to the women agents sitting on either side of him, "How are my two bookends? I love my two bookends," or words to that effect.[4]

Various intelligence agencies debriefed Pollard, and he basked in all the attention. According to Redman, when Thursdays came around, marking the end of another round of interviews, he seemed to grow despondent.

Among his first revelations were the identity of his handler Aviem Sella and the $300,000 the Israelis had planned to put into a Swiss bank account for Pollard. Proof that the Israelis had dissembled in this matter angered the Department of Justice, and before long the story was all over the news, setting off another flurry of diplomatic recriminations and prompting the department to consider rescinding its promise not to prosecute Rafi Eitan and the other coconspirators. The question now was how far up the conspiracy reached and how much Prime Minister Peres's administration knew about it. The Americans also wanted to know why no disciplinary action had been taken against Eitan and Sella.

As the interviews continued, Redman gained insight into the dynamics of the relationship between Pollard and Anne. Pollard always asked how his wife was doing, while Anne would rarely mention her husband, much less ask about his welfare. She struck Redman as bitter, arrogant, and defiant. Polygraph examiner Colvert had the same impression. He said that, for the most part, Pollard was easy to interview and cooperative; his wife, on the other hand, was "tough."

"You had to work hard in an interview with Anne, who thought everything out before she would answer," Colvert recalled. She was cautious and didn't want to contradict anything her husband said, while Pollard would just "spit it out."[5]

For instance, during a pre-polygraph interview with Colvert, Anne told him about her sapphire ring and the subterfuge concerning Uncle Joe Fisher, but she wouldn't say what had become of the ring. When the government arrested Anne, she hadn't been wearing it and they couldn't find it. She adamantly clung to her story that the ring was lost.

Redman and Jechorek didn't buy it. When a woman has a ring priced at ten thousand dollars, it isn't easily misplaced. They gave Anne two choices: either she turned the ring over to the government or they were going to have Colvert hook her back up to the polygraph machine. That did it. Anne admitted to stashing the ring, and during her next debriefing she handed it over to the government. An appraisal of the ring valued it at $5,400—slightly less than what it had originally cost the Israelis.

Following a polygraph session in which she revealed what she knew about Pollard's operation and the Chinese documents, Anne asked her examiner if she was going to jail. Colvert looked her in the eyes and said, "If I were you, Anne, I'd pack my toothbrush." Surprisingly, she thanked him, explaining that he was the only person who had leveled with her about her future.[6]

Pollard spent much more time taking polygraphs than Anne did, and over the many days and hours of exams, Colvert earned his trust. Near the polygraph room in the courthouse there was a small coffee shop. On occasion, to establish a rapport with Pollard, Colvert invited him there for coffee and pastries. (Colvert had obtained permission from U.S. marshals to take Pollard there.) Pollard took him up on the offer, telling his examiner that he was the only person who treated him like a human being. Colvert's talents won over both Pollards.

During his interviews with Colvert, Pollard admitted to passing classified information to countries besides Israel and to individuals other than Israelis, but still the government preferred not to prosecute Pollard for those offenses.

It was Colvert's conviction that Pollard committed espionage not so much for greed or ideology, but rather for recognition. Although he described Pollard as intellectually arrogant and cocky, he had a desperate, childlike craving for recognition. Giving secrets to the Israelis, Pollard confessed, made him dream of being a hero in "the lead tank in a parade going into Jerusalem." That is what the Israelis did for him—they treated him like a hero.

According to Redman, Pollard repeatedly claimed to have been an "Israeli soldier left in the field alone," who was paid only because all Israeli soldiers are paid. He said he took classified documents for ideological reasons, to help Israel, and not for money. Pollard also revealed that following his trip to Israel, he had seriously considered changing jobs. He maintained he had cultivated an attaché at the Saudi embassy and that the Saudis might hire him as an analyst. Saudi Arabia would be a "cleaner" espionage target than the United States. Pollard believed that if he could establish himself with the Saudis, the Israelis might turn him over to Mossad for future operational use. He didn't believe his activities with the Israelis constituted disloyalty to the United States, but he did consider them "dishonest," and the fact he was "living a lie twenty-four hours a day was causing him to burn out."[7]

When the FBI and NIS agents finished their initial debriefings, all the other intelligence agencies had a crack at Pollard, including the DIA, the CIA, the NIC, and the NSA. Gradually, it became clear that the analyst didn't know much about the contents of the majority of the documents he had taken. Not even a man of Pollard's prodigious intelligence could come close to remembering the titles and contents of such a huge volume of material. "If I could see it and touch it, you can assume I got it," Pollard told his interviewers. "My only limitation was what I couldn't physically carry."[8]

Right up until the day Judge Robinson handed his sentence down, memorandums in aid of sentencing went flying back and forth between the defense and the prosecution. In Pollard's memorandums to the court, he made excuses for what he had done and denied some statements made earlier to investigators during debriefings.

In an unusual sixty-one-page motion prepared in August 1986—

but not submitted to the prosecution until early March 1987, just prior to sentencing—Pollard relayed a personal story explaining why he had spied, what Israel had learned as a result of his spying, the pernicious effects of being paid for espionage, his remorse, and his personal plans to mitigate whatever damage people perceived he might have caused to the special relationship between the United States and Israel. His story, which began in the 1940s with the plight of the Jews during the Holocaust and included his analysis of the reasons Israel found itself embroiled in continuing conflicts, was passionate, yet bombastic.

His reason for spying, he claimed, was to save Israel and to hurt the Soviet Union. He also said he was motivated by anti-Semitism in his office. The purpose of every statement in the motion was to exonerate himself and to enlist the aid of the Jewish community. The government took exception to his arguments, claiming that in his attempt to cast his actions in a positive light as being for the good of Israel, he was trying to craft a "political solution" to criminal proceedings. Prosecutors reminded the court that in a statement Pollard made to the FBI, he had said that "he would commit espionage for Israel again if given the chance."[9]

Pollard's insistence that he didn't commit espionage for financial gain spurred prosecutors to resolve the issue. FBI agent Colvert polygraphed Pollard again, asking him two questions: whether he had spied for Israel solely for personal financial gain, and whether he had intentionally lied about his true reason for spying. After he had said no to both questions, the polygraph indicated that his responses were deceptive. Pollard insisted he had started spying for ideological reasons, then admitted he was quickly corrupted by the remuneration. He told Colvert he developed an "addiction to money."[10] Among other points, prosecutors showed that in interviews he had admitted his motives were mixed.

On 15 February 1987, three weeks before Pollard's sentencing, Wolf Blitzer came out with an article in the *Washington Post* that caused an uproar in Washington: "Pollard: Not a Bumbler but Israel's Master Spy."[11] At the time Blitzer was a correspondent for the *Jerusalem Post,* and a similar article appeared in that newspaper, along with a cartoon depicting an Israeli soldier sprawled on the ground, being abandoned by four other soldiers walking away with an empty stretcher. *Pollard* was written next to the abandoned soldier.

Based on his interview with the incarcerated spy, Blitzer revealed what

Pollard claimed to have provided the Israelis, including reconnaissance satellite photographs of Palestinian Liberation Organization (PLO) head-quarters in Tunisia, specific capabilities of Libya's air defense system, and movements of American, Soviet, and French ships in the Mediterranean, all of which, according to Blitzer, had allowed the Israeli air force to evade detection and bomb the PLO headquarters on 1 October 1985. Moreover, the author wrote, sources informed him that Pollard had also passed on intelligence about Iraqi and Syrian chemical-warfare-production capabilities; Soviet arms shipments to Syria and other Arab states, including specifics on SS-21 ground-to-ground and SA-5 antiaircraft missiles; and Pakistan's nuclear weapons program, along with satellite photographs of its facility outside Islamabad.

"In general," Blitzer went on, "Pollard gave Israel the pick of U.S. intelligence about Arab and Islamic conventional and unconventional military activity, from Morocco to Pakistan and every country in between. This included both 'friendly' and 'unfriendly' Arab countries."

The government was stunned by the disclosures. Clearly, Pollard was a loose cannon. If ever released from prison, he would be a much larger risk than they had ever imagined.

By allowing a reporter to interview him without a representative from the DNI's office present—indeed, without any authorization at all from the DNI—Pollard had violated his plea agreement. The prisoner claimed he had obtained permission; the government denied it.

During a subsequent interview Pollard blamed the revelations on Blitzer, claiming he had only been confirming information the journalist asked him about. According to Colvert, when Pollard was asked about this in yet another polygraph test, he "blew" it.[12]   Soon thereafter, Pollard admitted he had been lying, that it was he who disclosed the information to Blitzer and not the other way around. In the end, the U.S. attorney's office decided not to file papers with the court indicating that Pollard had broken the plea agreement.

As if the Blitzer article weren't alarming enough, Pollard apparently convinced his wife to submit to an interview on CBS's *60 Minutes*. On Sunday evening, 1 March 1987, three days before her sentencing and still out on bond, Anne appeared in front of investigative reporter Mike Wallace before a nationwide audience. The Pollards must have believed that if Anne could explain their rationale for giving secrets to Israel, the American public—or at least Jewish Americans—would demand a more lenient sentence.

If that was their thinking, they were badly mistaken. One has to wonder where Anne's lawyer was. What she failed to realize when she agreed to go on *60 Minutes* was that she would be subjected to questions from a seasoned interviewer who knew how to get information out of anybody. Prior to the interview, many of us involved in the case felt Anne would get probation based on her first-time offense and the relatively minor charges against her. Her chance withered as soon as she admitted to Wallace that she had known exactly what her husband was getting into and that she had gone along with it from the beginning. Angry at Israel for not helping her and her husband after all he had done for them, Anne also blamed Rafael Eitan for not allowing the Israeli embassy to give them asylum.

Wallace quoted aloud from a court document: "[T]he breadth and volume of the U.S. classified information sold by defendant Pollard to Israel was enormous, as great as any reported case involving espionage on behalf of any foreign nation."

"Let's look at that, I mean, any person can logically look at that and say, this is absurd," Anne remarked. "Number one, he was not spying against the United States. Number two, he was not spying on behalf of our worst and bitter enemy, the Soviet Union."

The interviewer cut her off. "So what you're saying is that citizens who believe that they know better than their own government what should be given . . . to an ally should simply take the law into their own hands, Anne?"

"I'm not saying people should take the law into their own hands, but I am saying that when people have a moral belief and are adamant about it, they are expected to do what they can do to better and help those people. My husband felt that it was necessary to do this, no one else had done it." She went on to say that Pollard was paid because he was a "soldier in the field." When Wallace commented that Israeli soldiers were not paid $2,500 dollars a month, Anne agreed, saying, "The amount is determined by their handler."

Anne continued making excuses for herself and Pollard until, finally, Wallace said, "Listening to you, Anne, I get the impression that you feel that everyone else is wrong and you and your husband are right."

"I feel my husband and I did what we were expected to do," she replied, "what our moral obligation was as Jews, what our moral obligation was as human beings, and I have no regrets about that."[13]

Hearing Anne's statement, I recalled what Pollard had said to me about how Jews should not be given high clearances because they would do anything for the love of Israel. It seems as though both husband and wife believed their moral obligation as Jews was to spy against their own country. It was an insult to the American Jewish community. In just three days, she would stand before a judge asking for leniency. Her lack of remorse would come back to haunt her.

In another turn of events, two days after the *60 Minutes* broadcast, the U.S. government indicted Aviem Sella on three counts of espionage, each carrying a life sentence and hefty fines. Israel wouldn't let Sella be interviewed unless the United States gave him immunity, as it had for the other coconspirators, but in light of Israel's earlier lack of cooperation, the government didn't agree to this condition.

Following the indictment, Sella was promoted to brigadier general and put in charge of one of Israel's largest air bases. Moreover, Israel awarded Rafael Eitan with a high-level position as head of Israel Chemical, a large government-owned company.[14] It was a sharp slap in the face, and Congress reacted by threatening to discontinue aid to Israel amounting to billions of dollars. Eitan was given a job to oversee the Cuban water treatment system, and Sella stepped down from his new prestigious position. Because Israel will not extradite citizens wanted for crimes committed in the United States, to this day Aviem Sella is still under federal indictment for espionage against the United States, a criminal fugitive from justice.[15]

Chapter 25

THE DAMAGE

O n 19 January 1987, before Pollard was sentenced, Secretary of Defense Casper Weinberger submitted a forty-six-page classified memorandum to Judge Robinson detailing the havoc Pollard had wrought with U.S. intelligence. "Declaration of the Secretary of Defense"—commonly known as the Weinberger memorandum—carried a TS/SCI classification, and to this day most of its contents remain under wraps. The memorandum presented nineteen items illustrating the different types of TS/SCI material Pollard had passed on. These were selected out of hundreds of thousands of classified messages and documents gathered by Richard Haver's damage assessment team at the Department of Defense.

Because the Weinberger memorandum is classified, I cannot address its contents other than to say that the damage Pollard inflicted was colossal. The government estimated how much material he took based both on signature cards and on the signatures he wrote when requesting classified material from libraries, archives, and message centers throughout Washington, D.C., Maryland, and Virginia. Had Pollard gone to trial, the prosecutors would have been able to prove in court that in terms of sheer volume, the classified documents he removed measured at least 360 cubic feet—one million-plus pages delivered over the short period of eighteen months. Add to this the material he removed without a signature, and the total figure, though unknown, would be even more staggering.[1] When presented with these findings, Pollard agreed they were probably accurate.

To put it into perspective, one has to remember that the Pollard case arrived on the heels of the Walker family spy case. Navy radioman John Walker had provided codes to the Soviets for intercepting and

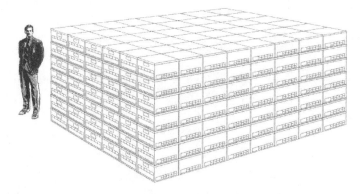

Bankers boxes—visual representation of the sheer volume of classified documents—measured at least 360 cubic feet, one million-plus pages—Pollard provided to Israel over the short period of eighteen months —PETER BURCHERT

deciphering military transmissions. In the Department of the Navy's damage assessment report to the presiding judge in the Walker trial, Rear Admiral William O. Studeman, the DNI at the time, wrote that "the harm caused by John Anthony Walker is of the gravest nature," pointing out that during his eighteen years of spying he had enabled the Soviet Union to decipher more than one million messages.

Mr. M. Spike Bowman, a well-respected military attorney who worked with the team assessing damage done by Pollard, told me that this case, breaking so soon after Walker's, overwhelmed the Department of Defense. Among the documents compromised were detailed analytical studies containing technical calculations, graphs, and satellite photographs. Many of those studies were hundreds of pages long, including analyses of Soviet missile systems disclosing how the United States collected information. From these documents a reasonably competent intelligence analyst could infer the identity of human intelligence sources. Moreover, some analyses carried the author's name. Disclosure of such specific information to a foreign power, even an ally of the United States, could have exposed American agents and analysts "to potential intelligence targeting."[2]

According to Bowman, when the scope of the damage Pollard had inflicted became clear, Secretary of Defense Weinberger was beside himself. Before submitting his memo to Judge Robinson, he sent it back to the damage assessment team six times asking for harsher words to describe how gravely Pollard had compromised U.S. national security.

Pollard's and Anne's attorneys, Richard and James Hibey, were given access to the Weinberger memorandum—Anne, not being prosecuted for espionage, wasn't allowed to see it—but first they had to sign a memorandum of understanding informing them of the sensitive nature of the documents and ordering them never to reveal their contents to anyone unless authorized.[3] The defense team also had to read and sign a nondisclosure agreement and a security briefing acknowledgment, as well as to undergo special background checks.

In the unclassified portions of the document, Weinberger laid out how damaging it can be to the United States when classified information is disclosed to friendly powers without authorization. The harm can be as great as giving classified information to hostile powers because "once information is removed from secure control systems, there is no enforceable requirement . . . to provide effective controls for its safekeeping. . . . Moreover, it is more probable than not that the information will be used for unintended purposes. . . . [S]uch disclosures will tend to expose a larger picture of U.S. capabilities . . . than would be in the U.S. interest to reveal to another power, even to a friendly one."[4]

Weinberger pointed out that the United States shares intelligence with friendly countries under exchange agreements made by high-level officials after carefully evaluating "the costs of disclosure to our national security versus the benefits expected to be obtained if disclosure is approved." Pollard, he went on, personally confessed to and identified from memory more than "eight hundred classified publications and more than one thousand . . . classified messages and cables which he sold to Israel." According to Weinberger, not one of the publications Pollard provided was authorized for official release to Israel, not even in redacted form.[5]

Those parts of the memorandum addressing the significance of Pollard's disclosures and his compromised sources and methods were almost entirely censored. In a section on the risk to American personnel, Weinberger warned the court, "U.S. combat forces, wherever they are deployed in the world, could be unacceptably endangered through successful exploitation of this data."[6]

When Wolf Blitzer came out with his article in the *Washington Post* describing some of the intelligence Pollard had passed to Israel, it prompted Weinberger, on the eve of the sentencing, to submit another memorandum to the court. In this second memorandum, unclassified, he strongly aired his personal and professional feelings.

> It is difficult for me, even in the so-called year of the spy, to conceive of a greater harm to national security than that caused by the defendant in view of the breadth, the critical importance to the United States, and the high sensitivity of the information he sold to Israel. That information was intentionally reserved by the United States for its own use, because to disclose it, to anyone or any nation, would cause the greatest harm to our national security. Our decisions to withhold and preserve certain intelligence information, and the sources and methods of its acquisition, either in total or in part, are taken with great care, as part of a plan for national defense and foreign policy which has been consistently applied throughout many administrations. The defendant took it upon himself unilaterally to reverse those policies and national assets, which have taken many years, great effort, and enormous national resources to secure.[7]

Pollard had betrayed the public trust and the security of the United States for money. Weinberger went on to say that any citizen, particularly a trusted government official, who sells secrets to any foreign nation, be it friendly or hostile, should be punished not as a common criminal but in a way that reflects "the perfidy of the individual's actions, the magnitude of the treason committed, and the needs of national security."

The defendant had both likened himself to an Israeli pilot shot down behind enemy lines and expressed the hope of emigrating to Israel. "Whatever else his analogy suggests," the defense secretary commented, "it clearly indicates that his loyalty to Israel transcends his loyalty to the United States."[8] Weinberger mentioned the *Washington Post* article without confirming or denying the information Pollard had released to Blitzer: "I have no way of knowing whether he provided additional information not published in that article, but I believe that there can be no doubt that he can, and will, continue to disclose U.S. secrets without regard to the impact it may have on U.S. national defense or foreign policy. Only a period of incarceration commensurate with the enduring quality of the national defense information he can yet impart will provide a measure of protection against further damage to the national security."[9]

In the end, much to Blitzer's relief, an expert analysis of the content of his article revealed that the context was broad and the information not classified. During the sentencing phase, it appeared that Judge Robinson decided to ignore the article and concentrate strictly on the revelations offered by Weinberger in his first, classified memorandum.

Having never read the uncensored copy of that memorandum, and knowing I will never be allowed to, I asked Rich Haver to comment in a general way on the severity of Pollard's crimes. When someone like Pollard takes "the keys to the kingdom," Haver told me, the harm is incalculable and possibly unstoppable. Such information gives a foreign nation not only a step-by-step blueprint of America's intelligence-collection capabilities, sources, and methods, but also the ability to analyze those capabilities and to identify vulnerabilities. It tells a country, in essence, how to test American security systems and avoid detection. When the United States loses its ability to protect its citizens, they stand to lose their freedom.

At one point, Haver said, Pollard was out of the office sick and it disrupted his daily routine of gathering secrets. When the Israelis found out that their gofer had not retrieved messages during that time, they were extremely upset with him. Government officials who participated in the damage assessment suspect that Israel was testing some of the SCI manuals Pollard had turned over to them, conducting clandestine operations to gauge American vulnerabilities. According to Haver, in a larger attempt to override U.S. intelligence-gathering capabilities, Israel wanted to see if the United States was able to pick up communications on its secret training operations.

Pollard also damaged U.S. relations with Middle Eastern countries. At a time when the United States was trying to establish a working relationship with Tunisia, he provided the Israelis with highly classified satellite photographs indicating the location of the PLO headquarters there. In October 1985 a U.S. delegation was meeting with the Tunisians in Tunis to lay the groundwork for establishing a relationship when the Israelis led a bombing mission on the PLO headquarters. Infuriated, the

Tunisians accused the United States of giving away the location to Israel and knowing about the attack. After all, Israel was the United States' closest ally in the Middle East, they reasoned. Nothing the delegates said could convince their hosts otherwise, and the Tunisians promptly asked them to pack their bags and leave.

The U.S. government didn't discover the truth about the satellite photographs until after Pollard was arrested. Pollard's hubris was evident in his taking full credit for the raid. The incident wiped out several years of negotiations with Tunisia and severely hampered U.S. attempts to gain the trust of other Middle Eastern countries, of critical importance in bolstering American foreign policy.[10]

In its memorandum in aid of sentencing, the government emphasized that "the widely published reports of defendant's espionage activities on behalf of Israel have led to speculation within other countries in the Middle East, with which the United States also has enjoyed friendly relations, that defendant's unauthorized disclosures to Israel may have adversely affected the national security of these other Middle Eastern countries." Moreover, allies of the United States "have expressed serious concern that a government employee with such far-ranging access to sensitive information has breached his . . . duty to protect that information." In arguing for a stiff sentence, the government made the point that "if a less severe sentence were ruled out because the foreign nation involved is a U.S. ally, a potentially damaging signal would . . . be communicated to . . . foreign countries contemplating espionage activities in the United States."[11]

In addition to damaging relations with the Middle East, Pollard's activities could have weakened the hand of the United States in its dealings with the Soviet Union. In his book *The Samson Option,* Seymour Hersh alleges that Israel passed some of Pollard's top secret information to the Soviet Union in exchange for Russian Jewish prisoners. Although this has never been proven, it is a fact that a significant portion of the thousands of documents Pollard took from the DIA had nothing to do with the Middle East. According to Stephen Green in an article that appeared in the May 1989 issue of the *Christian Science Monitor,* many such documents contained details about both U.S. and Soviet communications and military capabilities, suggesting that they could have been of use to only one country, the Soviet Union. "This concern was heightened," Green writes, "when, during the Pollard investigation, a Soviet defector in U.S. hands revealed in addition to the two Israeli spies serving prison terms in Israel for spying for the Soviets, Shabtai Kalmanovitch and Marcus Klingberg, there was a third person Israel had not yet caught. . . . This person was well placed in the [Israeli] Defense Ministry and still active."[12]

Colonel Shimon Levinson was another convicted Israeli spy. During an assignment in Bangkok in 1983, Levinson offered his services to the KGB. Two years later, during Pollard's ascent, the colonel was appointed security chief for the Israeli prime minister's office. (Rafael Eitan served as a special intelligence adviser in this same office.) Israel later accused Levinson of passing highly classified nuclear and military intelligence to the KGB, and he was arrested in May 1991.[13] Was Levinson the unknown third spy? And if so, did the Soviet Union receive through him at least some of the information that Pollard delivered into the hands of the Israelis?

The American public will probably never know the true extent of the devastation Pollard visited on the national security of the United States. The lion's share of the information he sold was coded TS/SCI, and that sort of material is rarely declassified. One thing is certain: in terms of volume of classified material that Pollard removed, the U.S. agency hardest hit was the DIA. The loss was so devastating that it prompted officials there to strengthen their counterintelligence awareness program. In 1989, when I served as division chief of counterintelligence investigations at NIS headquarters, the DIA approached me about helping them coordinate interviews for their training film on this subject for their employees. The result, *Jonathan Pollard: A Portrayal*, addressed the damage the spy had done to national security and illustrated the ease with which he managed to commit his crimes. Eventually, the film would be shown to every DIA employee around the world and in many navy commands, making the name Pollard synonymous with treason.

Pollard in prison —AP/WWP

Chapter 26

THE SENTENCING

P ollard had been in jail for fifteen months when at last it arrived: 4
March 1987—sentencing day.* I reached the U.S. District Court
a little before the scheduled start, accompanied by Lydia Jechorek
and Lisa Redman. The weather seemed to cooperate with the media. It
was a sunny day, and television trucks owned by networks from around
the world stretched for blocks. We entered through a side door that was
reserved for attorneys, judges, and law enforcement officers.

The courtroom was packed with bodies, and seats were in short
supply. Lucky for us, some agents had reserved a place for us not far
from the bench. Jerry Agee was there, as were other agents involved
in the case, including some of Pollard's coworkers from the ATAC. I
didn't see the Henderson or Pollard families in the courtroom, though
they did attend. While waiting for the hearing to begin, I briefly thought
about Jay's and Anne's parents, how they were victims of their children's
misguided decisions. What they were about to hear would make this
one of the hardest days of their lives. My heart truly went out to them.

The courtroom buzzed with a low undertone of anticipation, but
when Judge Aubrey Robinson made his entrance, the voices quickly died.
After ordering the defendants to come forward with their attorneys,
Robinson read the charges. Defense lawyer Richard Hibey wanted to
make sure the court understood that Pollard was pleading guilty to a
single count of conspiracy to commit espionage for the benefit of Israel.

---

*All quotations regarding the Pollard sentencing are excerpted from the transcript of
the hearing. The full transcript can be found by the following citation: *U.S. v. Jonathan
Jay Pollard and Anne Henderson Pollard*, Criminal Action Nos. 86-207 & 86-208, 1–65
(U.S. District Court for the District of Columbia, 1987).

There was no evidence of any intent on Pollard's part to injure the United States, Hibey emphasized. He also reminded Robinson that in the plea bargain the prosecution had agreed not to ask for a life sentence.

These preliminaries dispensed with, the defense team began its arguments for lenient sentences. With the courtroom hanging on his every word, Hibey spoke first on behalf of Pollard, admitting that his client was "undeniably guilty of the charge to which he pled guilty," but adding that money had corrupted Pollard. His motivation to help Israel was irreparably soiled, Hibey argued, by the addictive effect of accepting money for his work. Pollard's conduct violated the trust put in him as a keeper of the nation's secrets, and when found out he lied long enough to allow his handlers to flee the United States. Nonetheless, the classified information did not end up in the hands of an enemy of the United States, and as a result, Hibey argued, "the facts call out for . . . leniency, for the damage to our national security is, I submit, minimal."

Robinson listened intently without interrupting as Hibey asked him to take into account Pollard's warm, loving family. His aim was to request not that Pollard be put on probation—that would be "a fantasy"—but rather that he be confined in a place where he could receive visitors.

When it came time for Anne's attorney, James Hibey, to speak, he pointed out that the government's case against Jonathan Jay Pollard was vastly different from that against his wife. Anne Henderson Pollard hadn't spied for Israel or China, hadn't participated in operational activities, hadn't obtained, copied, or delivered any classified information to anyone. "Contrary to the government's shrill mischaracterizations of Mrs. Pollard as a mercenary driven by need and greed," she was, in fact, "a wife, albeit a knowing wife, who was motivated by love for her husband."

For instance, he continued, on the night she had tried to dispose of the suitcase and called Aviem Sella, the call was intended to help her husband, not one of his handlers. He mentioned her suffering, particularly under the "cruel conditions" to which she had been subjected in jail. Threats were made against her for being a spy, and she'd had to be placed in protective custody. "Effectively, she was locked down for twenty-four hours a day in a windowless cell, without exercise, without sometimes any communication from any of the other inmates."

And then there was her medical condition, biliary dyskinesia, a rare gastrointestinal disease requiring constant care. Anne, he contended, had not received adequate medication in jail, and what medication was given to her didn't arrive in a timely fashion. As a result, she couldn't eat the food served in jail and had lost forty pounds. Were she to go to prison, she wouldn't receive the frequent medical care she needed.

Hibey denied an accusation made by the prosecution that Anne had tried to recruit a friend of Pollard's, denied that the Pollards' spending habits were lavish—most of their restaurant bills, he told the court, didn't exceed seventy-five dollars—and stressed that his client had never known the contents of the documents her husband gave to Israel. "Mrs. Pollard took no notes on the intelligence information contained in the People's Republic of China documents. She essentially ignored the intelligence information contained in those documents and did not relate any of that . . . to her colleagues at CommCore or to anyone at the PRC embassy."

He asked the court to impose a lenient sentence rather than leaving it up to the parole board, and closed by saying: "We submit that it would be unfair and inappropriate, considering all of the facts and circumstances of her case, to sentence Mrs. Pollard to further incarceration. Probation will serve the ends of justice and will provide her with an opportunity to be a contributing and law-abiding citizen. She has the intelligence and the promise to lead such a life. She should be given that opportunity."

Now it was the defendants' turn to speak on their own behalf. Pollard went first. When he told the judge he would be as brief as possible, I smiled, knowing from experience that if you gave him an inch, he would take a mile. "I have as much time as is necessary," Judge Robinson remarked patiently.

Pollard began by proclaiming that, while in jail, he had had ample time to reflect on his motives and the impact of his actions on behalf of Israel. While his motives "may have been well meaning, they cannot, under any stretch of the imagination, excuse or justify the violation of the law, particularly one that involves the trust of government, and no higher trust than those in the intelligence community. . . . I broke trust, ruined and brought disgrace to my family." Nothing that he might have done to benefit Israel could excuse or justify his breaking the law. "I must admit wholly and unequivocally my criminal culpability before the court. In spite of the fact that I neither intended nor wanted to take monetary compensation for my actions on behalf of the Israelis, I did."

He went on to say that in addition to violating the trust of the nation, he had violated the trust of his wife. Several times he repeated that he had broken the law, but still he tried to defend giving Israel secrets and appeared to have little remorse for doing that.

After a lengthy digression about other courses of action he could have taken, he tried to get back on track. "[When] I am alone, . . . I can rationalize in my moments of desperation the possible good that might come of it, [but] it is cold comfort, because we are, I guess, at the bottom, your honor, a nation of laws."

"You guess?" Judge Robinson interrupted.

Pollard was taken aback. "We are a nation of laws, and not—"

"You aren't convinced of that, are you?"

"I am very convinced of that," Pollard responded smoothly, regaining his composure. "We are a nation of laws, not a collection of individuals that go off in twenty different directions, defining what they consider to be the national interest. . . . I took sectarianism to an illogical extreme. No rationalization, no justification, no explanation, no mitigation, for the breakage of a law."

Winding up, Pollard repeated that he had hurt his wife and broken the law. "And that is something I will have to live with long after this case is but a distant memory. Thank you," he said, and sat down.

Anne opened by saying she was speaking from the heart and not from the text she had prepared. After telling the judge that she loved her husband, wanted to be reunited with him and have children with him, she launched into a defense of his actions.

[H]e believed that at the time he was doing good for both the United States and Israel and he believed . . . that by strengthening Israel, a vital strategic ally, he was indirectly strengthening . . . the United States, considering the special relationship which both nations share.

My husband and I are vehemently anticommunist and . . . would never do anything to . . . hurt this country in any shape or form. We are dedicated and patriotic Americans and we are also loyal to Israel. We look at Israel as a, shall I say, as a . . . nation or state that represents the end of the systematic extermination of Jews or of mankind in general. . . . I cannot lie and say I was not aware that my husband was assisting Israel at the time, but I can say that my husband fully assured me that he was doing nothing in his power to hurt Israel—or rather, to hurt the United States in any shape.

She did finally say she was sorry for what happened, adding, "at the time I believed it to be correct."

At one point she touched on the subject of the code word *cactus*. Pollard, she said, had asked her "to remove certain items from the house should he ever use this word, and it came through in his call and I did it." For her own protection Anne should have stopped there, but like Pollard she had loose lips and couldn't seem to help herself. "And I can't say that I would never not help him again. However, I would look for different routes or different ways. . . . I cannot change history but I can say I am very sorry to have seen two nations come to this point, who share such a close relationship. . . . I am very, very sorry to have seen this happen."

Finally, after asking for leniency and mercy, especially for her husband, she sat down.

Not one time did Anne Pollard admit to breaking the laws of the United States or say she was sorry for doing so. Not one time did she show any remorse for the crime of espionage her husband had committed, and which at the time she knew he was committing. Her presentation to the court, coming on the heels of her interview with Mike Wallace on *60 Minutes*, convinced me that she didn't have a prayer of getting probation.

On the prosecution side, Assistant U.S. Attorney Charles Leeper was first to address the court. Leeper began by quoting a biblical reference Pollard had used in his memorandum in aid of sentencing about despair being the unforgivable sin. "As I was growing up," Leeper said, "I was taught that there are, in fact, two sins that are unforgivable, and they are arrogance and deception. . . . It is arrogance and deception which drove this defendant" to commit his criminal acts and that characterized "the way he has sought to defend and excuse the things that he has done." Leeper referred to a pleading he had received just the night before in which Pollard stated he hadn't injured the United States in any way. "This defendant," Leeper went on, is saying Jonathan Jay Pollard is right, but the Secretary of Defense in his sworn declaration to this court is wrong when he states that as a result of Jonathan Pollard's activities enormous damage has been wrought to the national security.

Jonathan Jay Pollard is right, but the president of the United States, when he issued Executive Order 12356, was wrong when he said that the disclosure, the unauthorized disclosure, of top secret information, to any nation, would cause or could be expected to cause exceptionally grave damage to the national security. Jonathan Jay Pollard is right and every administration since 1948, since the creation of the Israeli state, Republican and Democratic alike, have [sic] been wrong when they determined that the disclosure policies should not permit the disclosure to Israel of the kinds of secrets that this defendant sold.

He proceeded to tell the court about the staggering volume of documents Pollard had taken, posing a rhetorical question: Was the court to believe that the spy had personally studied each page to weigh the effect of its disclosure on U.S. foreign relations, assessing whether Israel could and would protect it? No, Pollard had decided from the beginning that it was Israel first, right or wrong, "and once he made that judgment, he was on automatic pilot. . . . He no more understands today how much damage he has done to the national security than he understood back then when he was cramming all that stuff in the suitcase. He didn't care then and he doesn't care now. In short, your honor, our view is that his argument that he caused no harm to . . . national security is equal parts of arrogance and deceit."

One area Leeper touched on was the blind contempt Pollard expressed in his memorandum for the U.S. military and intelligence community. "I came to the conclusion that the United States Navy, like many other naval establishments around the world, was the last refuge of the patrician bigot," Pollard had written. Elsewhere he had commented that he was motivated by "my ideological convictions and sense of outrage over terrorist incidents, which the world seemed to accept with equanimity, so long as the only casualties were Jews. The reaction in my office to the *Achille Lauro* incident, in which an elderly Jewish man, who also happened to be an American citizen, was brutally murdered, bordered on the comic." Pollard was referring to an incident on the night of 10 October 1985, in which terrorists had attacked a cruise ship, killed Leon Klinghoffer, and later made an escape by plane.

Pollard, Leeper remarked, had failed to mention that when the United States found out that the perpetrators were fleeing to freedom in Tunisia by an Egypt Air 737 commercial airliner, it took immediate action, launching navy fighters from an aircraft carrier in the middle of the night and intercepting the plane, which was forced to land in Sicily.

Leeper highlighted the fact that Pollard had signed numerous nondisclosure agreements and violated every one, including the nondisclosure clause in his plea agreement, signed in June 1986 and violated soon thereafter when he talked to a reporter—Leeper refrained from mentioning Wolf Blitzer by name—without authorization.

After touching on other aspects of the case, Leeper concluded by saying: "When it comes to protecting against further disclosure of U.S. secrets, Jonathan Jay Pollard is not a man of his word. And in combination with the breadth of this man's knowledge, the depth of his memory, and the complete lack of honor that he has demonstrated in these proceedings, I suggest to you, your honor, he is a very dangerous man."

When Leeper was done, Assistant U.S. Attorney David Geneson stepped forward to address the court about Anne. His demeanor was smooth, and his comments—well argued and concise—mesmerized the courtroom. After mentioning that Anne had paid $20,000 in cash to American Express between August 1984 and November 1985, the day the operation crashed, he said

> [T]here is no rationale, be it political, ideological, practical or personal, for the fact that she assisted Jonathan Jay Pollard in undermining this country's national security. Being knowledgeable of his conduct, from its inception, in detail, understanding its implications, accepting the fruits, the benefits, the monetary compensation, the two luxurious trips taken within an eight-month period, she also sought and obtained from her husband classified, secret PRC documents, used those documents, examined them, took notes on them, left her fingerprints on them, and then kept them along with other classified documents her

husband was storing in her apartment. . . .

Geneson gave a blow-by-blow account of Anne's actions triggered the night Pollard had called her and uttered the code word *cactus*. Next he launched into her *60 Minutes* interview with Mike Wallace the previous Sunday. When Wallace had asked whether she had understood what she was getting into, her response was, "Very much so." And when asked how everyone else could be wrong and she and her husband right, Anne replied, ". . . I did . . . expected to do . . . our moral obligation was as Jews . . . our moral obligation was as human beings, and I have no regrets about that." Geneson emphasized this comment.

"This defendant comes to this court with a mask of contrition and remorse," Geneson exclaimed. "She is terribly sorry, according to her counsel, according to herself, about what has happened. Your honor, the government suggests she is terribly sorry that she is caught. . . . [M] oreover, the government believes, based upon how she appeared, what she said, how she acted in a much less emotional environment this past Sunday night, if given the opportunity, she would do the same today as she did before."

Anne's characterization of her conduct as a political crime was misleading, he concluded. Rather, it was a criminal act, and should be paid for with "a sentence of incarceration reflective of her lack of remorse and . . . commensurate with the severity of the acts in which she was engaged."

The defense had the last word. Richard Hibey asked if his brother James could go first.

"Yes, age before beauty?" Robinson said, breaking the tension in the courtroom.

"That's one way of putting it, your honor," Richard replied.

Quiet laughter rose from the packed courtroom, then James began his attempt to diminish the harm Geneson had done to his client. He suggested that there was nothing sinister about Anne's motive, repeating that she had acted out of love for her husband. As for her comment on *60 Minutes* that she had no regrets about helping her husband, Wallace, he contended, had cut her off and asked another question before she could finish her answer. The comment had been taken out of context, he maintained.

"Did you know about it?" Robinson inquired.

"No, your honor, not until it was done."

"I didn't think so."

Hibey's attempts to salvage his defense argument were strained, and in light of what Anne had said on nationwide television, his conclusion struck me as especially so: "What I am suggesting to the court is she has been punished enough. She will continue to be punished simply by the very virtue of separation from her husband. We ask the court to consider it all, show some mercy, and place her on probation."

Without further delay Richard Hibey stepped forward, his last chance to speak on Pollard's behalf. After reiterating that Pollard wasn't denying guilt—he knew he was wrong and admitted it to the court—the attorney held that in providing documents to the Israelis, Pollard had done no real injury to the United States, and certainly not enough to warrant a maximum sentence.

Judge Robinson broke his silence. "That depends entirely upon what credence I give to what I have read, doesn't it?"

"That is correct, and that, in the final analysis, your honor, is what I have to rely on. Obviously, all of us, and understandably so, are restricted by the laws involving the discussion in open court of classified information. . . ."

Robinson and Hibey went back and forth about the extent of the damage Pollard had caused to national security, treading gingerly on account of the classified material used as evidence. "The point I am trying to make," Hibey reiterated, "is that the arguments, both under seal and in the redacted public record, . . . stand for the proposition that the damage here is not serious damage to the United States."

"Well, then, I would ask you to think and not articulate," Robinson said.

"Yes sir."

"But I would ask you to think about the secretary of defense's affidavit, as it related to only one thing, and I won't even pinpoint it, as it related to only one area with reference to one particular category of publication, and I fail to see how you can make that argument."

"Your honor," Hibey replied, "I must say, in all candor, my recollection of the secretary's affidavit is not so precise that I can be responsive to you, even in a generalized sense."

Robinson summoned the attorneys to the bench and a short conversation ensued, put under seal by the court. Afterwards, Hibey changed his strategy and started to mention the terrible conditions Pollard had lived under during his fifteen months in jail.

Robinson said, "Do you honestly think that this is going to make any difference? . . . Give me some credit."

Hibey went on to contend that what the government had first thought was classified information provided by Pollard to the media—again, he didn't mention Blitzer by name—had in fact not been, and that should enable Robinson to exercise his sentencing discretion in a "lenient and merciful manner."

"I wish you would focus on sentencing *judgment* and not discretion," Robinson responded. "I don't have unlimited discretion. . . . What I exercise is judgment in the context of everything I know about the case."

What Robinson was probably referring to was the fact that the U.S. Office of Probation and Parole and the U.S. Sentencing Commission provided guidelines and recommendations on what the prison sentence should be for federal crimes, and the recommendation given to Robinson in the case of Pollard was thirty years to life. He did, however, have the authority, as stated in the plea agreement, to make a final determination given all the facts of the case, regardless of what sort of sentence the prosecution requested.

The exchange continued between Robinson and Hibey, the latter claiming that Pollard's arrogance and deception would become candor and cooperation should Aviem Sella ever be taken into custody by the United States, since the evidence against Sella would rely solely on Pollard's testimony. In the end, Hibey suggested the government had not acknowledged Pollard's cooperation and asked the court for "a judgment tempered with mercy." Judge Robinson asked the prosecutors if they wanted to respond to Mr. Hibey's claim. Leeper replied that in the "Government's Classified Sentencing Memorandum," a pleading filed on 9 January 1987, Pollard's cooperation had indeed been acknowledged.

"Does that refresh your memory, Mr. Hibey?" Robinson asked.

"Yes sir."

At that point Robinson asked the defense attorneys if another recess was necessary. They said no, but after Pollard said something to his attorney, a five-minute recess was requested. Perhaps he wanted to say one last good-bye to Anne before the sentences came down.

When the court resumed, Judge Robinson summoned the attorneys and their clients to the bench. Anne's attorney stood behind her. As they moved forward, several federal marshals closed in behind the Pollards. Dead silence fell over the packed courtroom and people leaned forward in their seats. Pollard was breathing heavily and Anne had her arms crossed over her stomach as if in pain.

Abruptly Judge Robinson broke the silence. "I think I should state for the record," he began,

> that during my tenure in this court, I have never had more voluminous submissions in connection with the sentencing of a defendant than I have had in this case. And in addition to those voluminous submissions by each side, I have also received numerous communications directed to the court with respect to this procedure.
>
> I have read all of the material once, twice, thrice, if you will, and I have given careful consideration, not only to the submissions, but to argument of counsel, and I pronounce sentence as follows: With respect to the defendant Jonathan Jay Pollard, who is being sentenced for violation of Title 18, United States Code, section 794 c., I commit the defendant to the custody of the attorney general or his authorized representative for his life.

"No, no, no!" Anne screamed, and slumped forward. While she cried hysterically and gasped for breath, the guards to either side of her grabbed her under the arms and with great difficulty tried to keep her up.

The instant Robinson uttered the word *life,* Pollard looked at Anne collapsing into the guards' arms. His face paled and he seemed dazed and confused, like a beaten man with no energy left to respond. The guards to his rear immediately grabbed him by the arms and held him.

Anne was crouched over, still holding her stomach and crying uncontrollably. "With respect to the defendant Anne Henderson Pollard,"

Robinson continued, talking over her cries, "I commit [her] to the custody of the attorney general or his authorized representative on the first count of the information to a period of five years."

This prompted another screech from Anne, and more hysterical crying. Had it not been for the guards propping her up, she would have collapsed on the ground like a rag doll. Before the sentencing, she must have been convinced 100 percent that she would be released on parole.

By then the courtroom was in an uproar. Robinson pounded his gavel, trying to subdue the voices, but they were still buzzing when he continued. "With respect to the second count . . . , commit the defendant to a period of five years to run concurrent by the counts. In addition, as required by the comprehensive crime control act, I impose a fifty-dollar assessment on each count, which Pollard also received. There will be a special designation with respect to the place of incarceration."

James Hibey shouted over the chaotic noise and Anne's continued screams, "Your honor, could I request that she be allowed to remain on bond pending that commitment . . . and . . . to submit herself directly to the institution?"

"That request is denied," Robinson said emphatically, then rose from the bench and turned to the clerk. "Recess the court."

Pollard tried desperately to grab Anne and comfort her, and as he did, guards and U.S. marshals seemed to come out of the woodwork. They were swarming all over the place. Pollard finally got hold of his wife's arm, but for no more than a split second before he was bundled out of the room by marshals. Anne, now totally out of control, whipping her head back and forth and still wailing "No, no, no," had to be literally dragged out. Reporters scrambled for the doorway, knocking into benches in their rush to be the first to tell the story.

It was a little after five. In the frenzy I became separated from Agents Redman and Jechorek and ended up on the front steps of the courthouse, not far from where U.S. Attorney Joseph diGenova was being mobbed by reporters. I stopped to listen. When someone asked if Pollard would really have to spend his whole life in prison, diGenova responded, "It is likely he'll never see the light of day again."

During years of spinning tales from prison, Pollard has misled the public regarding his sentence. It is therefore important to stress this truth: the stipulation in the plea agreement was that the *government* wouldn't ask for a life sentence, and indeed the government did not. As laid out in the plea agreement, it was the judge who was responsible for determining the sentence. If, based on the federal sentencing guidelines he had been issued, Judge Robinson decided that the former analyst deserved the strictest sentence they allowed, so be it. Clearly, the judge believed that the damage Pollard had inflicted on the United States justified the punishment of a lifetime behind bars.

Immediately after sentencing, Anne went to the federal penitentiary in Lexington, Kentucky, while Pollard was transferred from the federal penitentiary in Petersburg, Virginia, to a federal penal institution and hospital in Springfield, Missouri, to undergo physical and some psychological testing. In January 1988, after it was determined that he was fit, Pollard was moved to the federal penitentiary in Marion, Illinois, a level-six prison that happened to be home to navy spy John Walker and many infamous, hard-core criminals. For his own protection, Pollard was put in a cell apart from potentially violent inmates. (Oddly, prisoners with a history of violence tend to hate spies.) His cell happened to be next to Walker's. One day Barry Colvert, the FBI polygraph examiner who had gained Pollard's trust during their interviews, dropped by the prison facility to visit Walker and noticed that Pollard occupied the adjacent cell. When he finished talking with Walker he knocked on Pollard's cell door and looked inside. The convict glanced at him and said, "I don't ever want to talk to you again without an attorney." Five years later Pollard was switched to a medium-security prison in Butner, North Carolina.

In June 1987 Richard Hibey filed a motion to reduce Pollard's sentence. The analyst's actions, he argued, had not compromised national security. Moreover, Pollard had cooperated fully with the government, which had failed to give him due credit for this, in breach of its promise in the plea agreement. The harsh sentence could have a deleterious effect on future cases when defendants pleaded guilty because, believing they would get nothing in return, they would have less incentive to cooperate. Then there was the problem of disparity in sentencing. Pollard, Hibey argued, had received a much harsher sentence than defendants in other espionage cases who had spied for allies, and some of them hadn't even cooperated with the government.[1]

In its response, the government contended that every reason cited by the defendant in the effort to reduce his sentence had already been considered and rejected in the court's original decision. The damage assessment provided in Weinberger's memorandum was accurate.[2] As for Pollard's cooperation with the government, during sentencing no specifics had been mentioned in the prosecution's address to the court because they were classified. Only the judge, the defendant, and his attorneys had seen the document that detailed the information Pollard had provided to the government.

In arguing against a reduction of sentence, the government asked the court to consider the fact that Pollard had lied to the court at his original sentencing when he expressed remorse for his actions. Indeed, after the sentencing, the *Jerusalem Post Foreign Service* had published a letter from Pollard in its op-ed page, "Reflections from a Jail Cell." The government attached this rambling missive, written on 17 March, to its motion. The letter read, in part,

> Needless to say, our experience at the sentencing was cruel beyond comprehension. Although I would have preferred to have gone down flying my "true colors," the attorney stressed the fact that I had to show remorse if Anne were to stand any chance at all of receiving probation.
>
> Accordingly, I agreed to say things which burned my soul with shame, hoping that by such contrived regret the court's apparent need for a moral victory over my convictions would be satisfied. In hindsight, this recantation, which fooled no one, was reprehensible and debased the memory of those Jews who had found the courage to endure such torment, unsullied by submission to either their persecutors or despair.[3]

Not only was Pollard not remorseful, the government held, but also he had leaked classified information and continued to do so. After the sentencing, the Federal Bureau of Prisons had begun reviewing his correspondence. "Perhaps not surprisingly," the government commented, ". . . on three occasions defendant included extensive classified information in letters to his wife, and more recently in a letter to an attorney/author, who has written critically of the sentence imposed by this court and from whom defendant has sought assistance on the public relations aspects of his case."[4]

As for other spies who had received lesser sentences, the government maintained that all sentences handed out in espionage cases had to be based on the merits of each separate case. It went on to say that the volume of TS/SCI materials Pollard compromised was enormous, as great as in any reported espionage case, and that because of the depth of the defendant's knowledge, his paramount loyalty to a foreign nation, and his refusal to comply with nondisclosure agreements contained in the plea agreement, the defendant, unlike other individuals who had spied for non-Communist countries, would remain a threat to U.S. national security for the foreseeable future.[5]

In its motion the government also noted that on 17 April 1987, the U.S. Sentencing Commission had promulgated more restrictive and uniform guidelines for espionage. Sentences were based on a point system reflecting the severity of the crime. The number of "gravity of crime" points dictating a mandatory life sentence for anyone gathering or transmitting top-secret defense information to aid a foreign nation, whether an ally or not, was forty-two. Pollard's number under these guidelines was forty-eight.[6] A sentence of life imprisonment in cases such as his was now required.

The court denied Pollard's motion to reduce his sentence, but from his cell he continued to argue that he was right for helping Israel.

Poster campaign on side of bus in Israel to win support in Pollard's bid for freedom —ELECTRONIC MED

Chapter 27

THE AFTERMATH

■ ■

For the past twenty-one years in a bid for freedom, Pollard has orchestrated a brilliant public relations campaign from his jail cell. Assisting in this effort is a list of attorneys that reads like a Who's Who of the legal profession. Since his arrest in 1985, the lawyers he has retained from both the United States and Israel number well over a dozen. Multitalented and high priced, they include Alan Dershowitz, defense attorney, prolific author, and professor at Harvard Law School, and Theodore Olson, the former forty-second solicitor general of the United States and a man who has argued thirty-four cases before the U.S. Supreme Court.

By twisting or omitting relevant facts and making unsubstantiated allegations of anti-Semitism, Pollard has garnered the support of many well-meaning people and organizations that might look at his case differently if they knew the whole truth. In May 2000, in an interview on CNN's *The World Today* with David Ensor, Richard Haver, who was in charge of damage assessment for the Pollard case, described him as a "confused person who loved the thrill of espionage and had security problems long before he worked for the Israelis. . . . Pollard . . . would've compromised the Israelis in a heartbeat, if it had struck him as something that he wanted to do. . . . He has now reinvented himself as a great Jewish patriot. . . ." Several analysts who worked with Pollard in the ATAC told me that at that time, they didn't even know he was Jewish. Indeed, he remarked to Richard Sullivan that he was High Church Episcopalian.

Kurt Lohbeck, the reporter to whom Pollard told investigators he had passed classified materials, would agree that the analyst reinvented himself. On page 136 of his book, *Holy War, Unholy Victory*, he writes:

"Jay's reason for selling government secrets to Israel . . . was not a deep personal commitment to Israel, but a personal commitment to his wife and to his pocketbook. Jay wanted to wine, dine, and travel first class and to bedeck Anne with jewelry. He never concealed that he was an intelligence analyst. In fact, he boasted about it, proudly displaying a courier card that allowed him to avoid customs and immigration checks at ports of entry, calling it his get-out-of-jail-free card."

Pollard started his campaign from jail by courting Jewish leaders and was initially rejected by much of the American Jewish community. After gaining the support of ardent Zionists, he used them to help him convince others that he was right and the government wrong. His support group started growing slowly while he was at the federal correctional facility in Marion, Illinois, and picked up speed in the 1990s. Today he has a huge network of supporters in Israel as well as a substantial following in the United States. More than sixty organizations have pushed for his release. From his jail cell he has even managed to pull the strings of the Israeli parliament, the Knesset, on issues that directly affect his bid for freedom. Thousands of news reports, numerous television programs, several books, and a personal web site have made Jonathan Jay Pollard a virtual household name.

It was 11 October 1988, and after lengthy negotiations among CBS, the Department of Justice, and the DNI, Mike Wallace of *60 Minutes* sat down at the federal prison in Marion for an interview with Pollard. Alan Dershowitz was also interviewed in this segment, along with U.S. Attorney Joseph diGenova, Jim Jones of the U.S. Bureau of Prisons, and the woman Wallace had interviewed once before, Anne Pollard.[1]

The DNI had stipulated that Pollard not be interviewed by anyone without an ONI representative present. In fact, two other people attended—an officer from the ONI and a special agent from the NIS. "I see the rats have come out of the woodwork," Pollard commented upon spotting the two men sitting behind him.

The prisoner made an opening statement in which he apologized for breaking the law. He had merely wanted to assist Israel, he said. Then he started talking about the Holocaust and how in the 1940s the United States had abandoned the Jewish people to their fate.

Wallace pointed out that John Walker had received life for spying for the Soviets for twenty years. Why, he asked diGenova, did Pollard receive the same sentence as someone who had spied for a hostile nation and for a drastically longer period? DiGenova replied that the Weinberger memorandum spelled out in detail how severely Pollard had compromised U.S. national security. If the American public were ever given access to what he had taken and sold, the attorney said, "there would be no question about the sentence."

Pollard continued to deny passing any information that would hurt the United States. When asked why he had signed the plea agreement, he replied that the government had been holding his wife hostage and he was told if he didn't sign, her medical care would be withheld. He neglected to mention that months before the plea agreement was finalized, his wife had been out on bond.

Even after he signed the agreement, he claimed, she wasn't given medical treatment because he wouldn't identify the man the media had dubbed Mr. X. (Mr. X was the shadowy U.S. official who the government suspected was still actively spying on behalf of the Israelis.) The suspicion arose from the fact that on several occasions his Israeli handlers had asked Pollard for specific TS/SCI materials, citing exact titles and in some cases document control numbers. The suspicion was never proven. Following his guilty plea, Pollard told Wallace, someone in the government had shown him a master list of Jews suspected of being Mr. X. Though pressed hard by Wallace, Pollard wouldn't say who showed him the list, on the grounds that agents changed their names every time he talked with them.

Then he changed his mind and said that diGenova had shown him the list. Wallace queried diGenova about this. The district attorney adamantly denied the existence of such a list, saying that what Pollard was alleging was an outrageous falsehood, an "example of the level and depth to which he had stooped in order to try and extricate himself from a situation that he, and he alone, was responsible for." Pollard retaliated by calling diGenova "a pathological liar, and an unethical and incompetent attorney."

When Wallace reminded Pollard that several of the U.S. attorneys on his case had been Jewish Americans, he looked agitated and responded, "Yes, and there were Capos also during the concentration camps."

Pollard ended his interview with a quote from Graham Greene's novel *The Quiet American,* saying, "I never met a man who had better motives for all the trouble he's caused."

Wallace spoke with Anne at the federal medical center in Rochester, Minnesota, where she had been moved to receive medical attention. Once again, she was holding her stomach as if in pain. In response to a question about her medical care, Anne compared her situation to "what it must've been like in Auschwitz forty-seven years ago in terms of medical treatment, in terms of abuse—it's terrible." She claimed that her problem had been diagnosed but not treated, and that prison officials had told her she needed to learn how to deal with the pain.

Jim Jones had a different story. He acknowledged to Wallace that Anne was ill and in pain but denied that proper medical treatment had been withheld. She had filed numerous motions to have her sentence reduced or commuted on the grounds that she needed to seek outside medical treatment. The prison doctor had seen Anne, and more than twenty physicians from the Mayo Clinic had examined her. Jones said she had been refusing treatment because, in his judgment, were she to accept treatment and get better, it would remove her excuse for trying to spring herself from jail.

Later in the segment, diGenova commented to Wallace, "What this case is all about is what the Pollards have done to themselves, from day one. This has never been about what anyone has done to the Pollards."

In January 1988 the Knesset had submitted a resolution to the U.S. Congressional Record in the form of a letter, and Congressman Norman Lent of New York forwarded it to President Ronald Reagan. It was read into the Congressional record on 19 October 1988. The letter read, in part, "We the undersigned, members of the Knesset, the parliament of Israel, ask you to grant executive pardon to Jonathan and Anne Pollard. We are fully cognizant of the complexities of the issue; however, we approach you on a humanitarian basis, assuming that after the Pollards are granted pardon they will immigrate to Israel. Humanitarian considerations especially require that generosity be applied to Anne Pollard, whose health requires utmost consideration of her needs."[2] The president took no action.

In August 1991, Pollard's attorney at the time argued before the U.S. Circuit Court of Appeals in Washington, D.C., that Pollard's sentence should be commuted on the following grounds: His plea had resulted in a miscarriage of justice, the government had breached its plea agreement, and Pollard's counsel had been denied access to important evidence. Theodore Olson wrote the brief. President George H. W. Bush followed the lead of his predecessor in the White House by refusing to commute the sentence.

Many years later, in March 2005, I attended a conference on counterintelligence sponsored by the Office of the National Counterintelligence Executive and the George Bush School of Government at Texas A&M University. CIA operations officer Brian Kelley and author and lecturer H. Keith Melton gave a presentation on the Robert Hanssen spy case. Former President George H. W. Bush attended, and after the presentation I had a chance to speak briefly with him. I shook his hand and said, "Mr. President, if you think the Hanssen case is interesting, you may want to read the book I'm writing on Jonathan Jay Pollard."

He looked me in the eyes and replied: "He belongs just where he is, in jail. You do know there are a lot of people trying to get him out. That really burns me up."

After serving three years and four months of her sentence, Anne was released on parole in March 1990. Four months later, her husband filed for divorce. Allegedly, Anne, in total disbelief, was served with divorce papers while in the hospital suffering from the stomach ailment that had plagued her for years.

Many conflicting stories circulated in the media about why Pollard decided to divorce Anne. According to one, he thought she was better off leaving him behind and getting on with her life. Other versions attributed the rift to rivalries flaring up between their parents over money and movie rights, and to a dispute over money owed to Anne from Pollard's fundraising efforts.[3] So many charges and countercharges were being bandied about—a situation exacerbated by the meddling of family and attorneys—that almost no one could decipher the truth.

Why the former analyst and the redheaded beauty with whom he had been so smitten divorced will probably never be known. Had Pollard rejected Anne—or was it the other way around? Anne's interviewers had remarked that she hadn't asked after Pollard's welfare when the two of them were in jail, before the sentencing. Whatever the case may be, it was a sordid ending to a sordid love story. Fortunately, their union had produced no children.

On 20 August 1990, the Immigration and Naturalization Service reported that one of the coconspirators in the Pollard case, Ilan Ravid, arrived at New York's Kennedy Airport with a tourist passport and a fourteen-day visa. He provided the address of 3514 International Drive, Washington, D.C. (the Israeli embassy). Although he was interviewed by the U.S. delegation in Israel in December 1985, he was less than forthcoming and did not reveal the names of the individuals in his residence that helped copy the classified documents Pollard provided. The government considered the possibility of asking him to submit to an interview. The NIS Investigative Summary Report indicated that it was unknown whether this interview ever came about.

Anne moved to Israel in 1991, looking to start a new life and bring closure to the Pollard espionage affair. She received her Israeli citizenship shortly after arriving.[4] In 1998, however, she moved back to the United States and settled in California. According to an article in the 23 May 2004 edition of the *Jerusalem Post*, Anne, with the help of a Toronto-based film company, was demanding five million dollars in damages from the Israeli government for what she called "a horrific nineteen years following her arrest," during which the Israelis abused and neglected her. She claimed that while she'd been living in Israel a watchdog of sorts was assigned to her, and that he demanded a monthly accounting of all her actions and expenses. The Israeli government was leaking lies about her and trying to make her leave, she complained. "I left Israel. I couldn't stand it."[5]

As for her ex-husband, when Pollard transferred to the federal penitentiary in Butner, North Carolina, in 1994, he married an ardent admirer and supporter of his from Canada, Ester Seitz. According to Ester, the two were married in a private ceremony during one of her visits to the penitentiary, though reporters could find no official records of the marriage.[6] Since that time, she has dedicated her entire heart and soul to setting him free.

Not long after President George H. W. Bush refused to commute Pollard's sentence, the Orthodox Union of Jewish Congregations of America, representing one thousand synagogues, wrote a letter to Attorney General William Barr strongly recommending commutation.[7] In a two-to-one decision, the U.S. Court of Appeals denied Pollard a new hearing, but in a radio broadcast in April 1992, the president-elect, William Clinton, said he would "reevaluate Pollard's life sentence and compare it to sentences handed out to other people under similar circumstances."[8]

While the Anti-Defamation League of B'nai Brith declared they believed anti-Semitism had not been the driving force behind Pollard's sentence, and the American Jewish Congress had not yet fully thrown its support behind him, more and more newspaper columns, mostly in the Israeli press, began to call for Pollard's release. On 30 November 1993, in a show of solidarity for Pollard in the Jewish religious community, a full-page advertisement showed up in the *New York Times*, "An Open Letter to President Clinton," signed by a thousand rabbis. The ad read in part: "We . . . wish to voice our plea for justice for Jonathan Pollard. We in no way condone acts of espionage or any violation of our country's laws. We nonetheless call upon you, Mr. President, to recognize that the lifetime sentence imposed upon Jonathan Pollard is unduly harsh and grossly inconsistent with the punishment given to other Americans convicted of similar and even worse crimes." A week later Leonard Garment, one of Pollard's attorneys, made the same plea in an op-ed piece in the *Washington Post*.

David Geneson, the former assistant U.S. attorney who had prosecuted the Pollards, broke his silence and spoke out publicly about the case in a letter to the *Washington Post*, arguing that Pollard had passed secrets to Israel for money, and that his giving them to an ally didn't lessen the crime. "What [Pollard] did illegally disclose, and thereby compromise, was a range of this country's most important secrets, much of which was pure intelligence unusable to the Israelis except as bargaining chips and leverage against the United States. . . ." Pollard's life sentence was "what he deserved. . . . If a president wants to grant Pollard clemency, so be it. . . . Along with others, I did my part to enforce the law. . . . But let those who press Pollard's position not minimize, modify or be less than truthful. Jonathan Pollard committed espionage, the effect of which was to inflict grave damage to the national security of the United States. . . ."[9]

Responding to Geneson in the *Washington Post*, Olson denounced a claim of his that the government hadn't broken the plea agreement. He cited three breaches of the plea agreement, stating that the government had "savagely" attacked "Pollard's motives and personality" and defamed him by saying he was motivated by money. "The government's emotional and hyperbolic arguments," he concluded, "succeeded in securing the harshest possible punishment of Jonathan Pollard—life imprisonment—even though the government had promised it would not seek such a sentence."[10] This is the central contention of countless books, articles, and motions to the court for resentencing.

Despite mounting pressure from a number of American Jewish leaders, an important political constituency of President Clinton's, he refused to commute Pollard's sentence.[11] Leaders of the American Zionist movement released a statement on 24 March 1994, expressing deep disappointment and vowing to continue pressing for Pollard's release on humanitarian grounds when he came up for parole.

Around August 1995, Pollard filed a petition with Israel's Supreme Court asking for citizenship. His sister, Carol Pollard, had formed an advocacy group called Citizens for Justice for Pollard that sent twenty-plus thousand signatures to the parole board asking for his release, and it was alleged in the press that she and other members of Pollard's family were opposed to his receiving Israeli citizenship because it would hurt his chances of getting parole (something Pollard had never asked for) and clemency. A rift set in between Pollard and his immediate family, and he cut off all ties with them. Later, in a letter Pollard released via electronic media to his sister, he threatened to sue her if she didn't cease speaking to the press about his case. He also wanted a full accounting of the money she had raised through her advocacy group. He was alleged to have told Seymour Reich, president of the American Zionist movement, and Ammo Dror of the Public Committee Office for Jonathan Pollard, to dissociate themselves from his case because of statements they had made to the Israeli press expressing hesitation about supporting his effort to obtain Israeli citizenship.[12]

On 22 November 1995, ten years and one day after he had been arrested outside the Israeli embassy, Pollard was granted full Israeli citizenship. In a ceremony held later at the federal penitentiary in Butner, he was presented with his citizenship papers. The following month Prime Minister Shimon Peres met with President Clinton and asked for clemency for Pollard. The president also received letters from former Israeli prime ministers, defense ministers, and Knesset members pleading for his release. Pollard was confident that his Israeli citizenship would be enough to sway the president to release him. On 26 July 1996, however, his ploy to achieve freedom through Israeli citizenship backfired when Clinton denied his request for clemency.

For twelve years Pollard had been aggressively claiming that his espionage wasn't a rogue operation, that it was sanctioned by the very top echelon of the Israeli government, and for twelve years the Israelis had denied it. Pollard had to find a way to force their hand.

In the spring of 1997, with the help of Ester and a stable of attorneys, Pollard filed an appeal with the High Court of Justice in Israel to prod the government into admitting that in fact he had been its agent.[13] Though the Israelis reportedly tried to ban publication of the appeal, newspapers got hold of the story.

Meanwhile, news leaked that the FBI was investigating the possibility that a top U.S. government official, the mysterious Mr. X, had been passing sensitive information to the Israelis. According to the story, Secretary of State Warren Christopher provided a letter to Palestinian leader Yasser Arafat after Arafat negotiated a withdrawal of Israeli forces from the West Bank with Prime Minister Benjamin Netanyahu. The letter spelled out U.S. guarantees for the withdrawals. No copy was sent to the Israelis. The NSA managed to tape a conversation between an Israeli intelligence officer in the United States and his supervisor in Tel Aviv in which they discussed how to obtain a copy. The Israeli intelligence officer proposed that they get it from "Mega," whereupon the supervisor was reported to have said, "This is not something we use Mega for."[14] The Israeli ambassador to the United States strongly denied the allegation.

In an article in the *Washington Post* dated 14 December 1997, Netanyahu released a letter he had sent to Pollard in prison. "I hope that our efforts on your behalf will help and that you will be a free man soon," he wrote. The following February Pollard published part of a letter he had written to Netanyahu in which he blamed Eliakim Rubinstein for his arrest and the bitter fate that followed. Rubinstein, who had been the senior official present at the Israeli embassy in Washington, D.C., at the time of Pollard's apprehension, was in charge of the ministerial Israeli committee trying to secure his release. Rubinstein resigned from this position.[15]

The Israeli government tried desperately to come up with a way to appease Pollard without embarrassing the State of Israel. They offered to give a statement to the United States conceding that he had been recruited by Israelis and had acted on behalf of Israel, but without the government's knowledge of the actual operation. Enraged, Pollard demanded that he be recognized as an agent who had been fully sanctioned by the Israelis. Apparently, he told his attorney in Israel to cease all negotiations with the government there.

The Israeli newspaper *Ha'aretz* was a thorn in Pollard's side because it published a series of articles critical of the former spy. In one, Ronen Bergman and Arye Dayan wrote of "Israel's official contention that he was working as part of a rogue operation that was not authorized from above. Every Israeli leader who has asked the U.S. to release Jonathan Pollard has held steadfastly to this position. Acceding to Pollard's request would make liars of four Israeli Prime Ministers (Peres, Shamir, Rabin, and Netanyahu) and two defense ministers (Herzog and Weisman), who would all be shown to have told untruths to three U.S. presidents (Reagan, Bush, and Clinton)."[16] In admitting that it had sanctioned Pollard, Israel would also be confessing that for thirteen years it had lied to the people of Israel and the United States, the U.S. Congress, and numerous Jewish religious organizations.

Nevertheless, on 11 May 1998, Israel issued a formal proclamation that Jonathan Pollard had "acted as an official Israeli agent, handled by those serving as high-ranking senior officials of the Israeli Bureau for Scientific Relations [LAKAM]."[17] In acknowledging its obligation to Pollard and its readiness to assume full responsibility, the State of Israel had succumbed to thirteen years of persistent demands. Pollard, it seemed, had won.

Two months later, the Israeli paper *Ma'ariv* ran a cover story on Pollard's spy handler Rafael "Rafi" Eitan, who during all the years since

Pollard's arrest had kept relatively quiet about the involvement of the Israeli government. At last he came clean, and all was soon forgiven between him and his former agent. Eitan vowed he would do everything in his power to promote Pollard's release.[18] Other than Alexander Feklisov, the Rosenberg's KGB handler, no other spy handler has spoken out publicly for the spy he managed. It was also the first time Eitan admitted the operation had been sanctioned from the beginning.

As time went on, I grew tired of counterintelligence work and wanted to get back to what I liked best, general crimes and homicides, particularly cold cases. When John McEleny, the deputy director of the NCIS, offered me a job as the division chief for death investigations policy and oversight, I jumped at the opportunity. In the fall of 1998, while I was sitting at my desk at NCIS headquarters, my phone started ringing off the hook. At the time, President Clinton was meeting with the Israelis and the Palestinians at the Wye River Plantation in Maryland to hammer out a peace accord. Apparently to induce the Israelis to sign, and urged on by Prime Minister Netanyahu, Clinton had informed him that he would release Pollard.

This was leaked to the media, igniting a firestorm of reports about Pollard's imminent release from prison and setting the entire American intelligence community back on its heels. The prison authorities told Pollard to pack his bags, he was going home to Israel. Unable to reach Lydia Jechorek at the FBI, I called another professional acquaintance there, Les Wiser, the agent who had led the Aldridge Ames spy case and was still in counterintelligence. What was going on? According to Wiser, as soon as George Tenet, director of the CIA, heard about the carrot Clinton had extended, he met with the president and informed him that he couldn't arbitrarily release Pollard, that there was more at stake than just releasing a spy and that the entire intelligence community had to be consulted before a decision about Pollard could be made. Furthermore, if the spy were set free, he would immediately tender his resignation as director of the CIA.

Whether such a conversation really took place was questioned for years, and it wasn't until 2004, when the former president released his autobiography, *My Life,* that the conversation with Tenet was verified. At any rate, Clinton reconsidered and informed Netanyahu that he would take a serious look at the Pollard case and make his decision by January 1999.[19] If not for the steadfast position of Tenet, Pollard might be free today.

The intelligence community was incredulous that Israel would dare use Pollard as a bargaining chip with the United States in such a sensitive and highly politicized peace process. Four former directors of naval intelligence—Admirals William Studeman, Sumner Shapiro, John Butts, and Thomas Brooks—submitted a letter to the *Washington Post* explaining why they did not believe Pollard deserved a pardon. "In terms of sheer volume of sensitive information betrayed," they emphasized,

> Jonathan Pollard rivals any of the traitors who have plagued this nation in recent times. Nobody is clamoring for the release of traitors like Aldrich Ames, John Walker, or Jerry Whitworth. . . .
>
> We who are painfully familiar with the case feel obligated to go on record with the facts regarding Pollard in order to dispel the myths that have arisen from this clever public relations campaign . . . aimed at transforming Pollard from greedy, arrogant betrayer of the American national trust into Pollard, committed Israeli patriot.
>
> Pollard pleaded guilty and therefore never was publicly tried. Thus, the American people never came to know that he offered classified information to three other countries before working for the Israelis and that he offered his services to a fourth country while he was spying for Israel. They also never came to understand that he was being very highly paid for his services. . . .
>
> Pollard and his apologists argue he turned over to the Israelis information they were being denied that was critical to their security. The fact was, however, Pollard had no way of knowing what the Israeli government was already receiving by way of official intelligence exchange agreements. . . . Some of the data he compromised had nothing to do with Israeli security or even with the Middle East. He betrayed worldwide intelligence data, including sources and methods developed at significant cost to the U.S. taxpayer. As a result of his perfidy, some of those sources are lost forever.

Another claim Pollard made is that the U.S. government reneged on its bargain not to seek the life sentence. What is not heard is that Pollard's part of this bargain was to cooperate fully in an assessment of the damage he had done and to refrain from talking to the press prior to the completion of his sentencing. He blatantly and contemptuously refused to live up to either part of the plea agreement. . . . It was this coupled with the magnitude and consequences of his criminal actions that resulted in the judge imposing a life sentence. . . . The appellate court subsequently upheld the life sentence.

If, as Pollard and his supporters claim, he has "suffered enough" for his crimes, he is free to apply for parole as the American judicial system provides. In his arrogance, he has refused to do so, but instead insists on being granted clemency or a pardon.

A presidential grant of clemency or pardon in this or any other espionage case—regardless of the foreign government involved or the ideological motivation—would be totally irresponsible from a national security standpoint. It would send a most damaging message to the loyal U.S. citizens entrusted with our national secrets, many of whom have emotional ties to other nations but nonetheless have taken seriously their oath to keep our national security information secret.

It would also say to foreign governments, "Your secrets are not safe with us." In today's multipolar world, where the threat of international terrorism and the proliferation of weapons of mass destruction are constant concerns, intelligence and security cooperation with friendly foreign nations is essential. Anything that causes our friends to be reluctant to share intelligence with us could severely damage our national security. . . .[20]

On 11 January 1999, the Senate Select Committee on Intelligence sent a letter to President Clinton urging him to deny Pollard's request for commutation. They stressed that releasing him would establish two disturbing precedents. First, it would implicitly condone spying against the United States by an ally. Second, it would undermine the United States' ability "to act as an honest broker throughout the world.

We maintain relationships with many nations that are not necessarily complementary to one another. Those relationships depend upon our assurances of confidentiality. If you release Pollard, it will convey a message to our partners that we view secrets kept from our friends less sacrosanct." Chairman Richard Shelby signed the letter along with fifty-nine other senators, including Diane Feinstein, John Kerry, Frank Lautenberg, Joseph Lieberman, and John McCain. In the end, President Clinton decided against granting Pollard clemency.

Pollard responded with vitriol, calling Israeli defense minister Yitzhak Mordechai a national disgrace for allegedly messing up the deal to release him and, in reference to Netanyahu, remarking, "You cannot sit with the Americans and pretend to be a guardian of Israel's security while you sit back and let one of your own agents rot in their hand."[21]

Pollard's attorneys from New York, Elliott Lauer and Jacques Semmelman, had been working relentlessly since 2000, presumably on a pro bono basis, filing motions and attending hearings on his behalf. A little over a year after the Senate committee sent its letter, they filed a motion with the Washington federal court to gain access to the highly classified Weinberger memorandum so they could properly defend Pollard in his quest for resentencing. On 29 November 2000, Congressman Anthony Weiner wrote a letter to the U.S. attorney for the District of Columbia requesting that he allow Pollard's attorneys full access to the sealed portion of the memo.[22] The following January, Chief Judge Norma Holloway Johnson denied the motion, upholding the government's claim that Pollard's attorneys had no need to know. His attorneys also filed a separate motion to "vacate Pollard's sentence," which the court also later denied. In August 2001 Judge Johnson dismissed Pollard's motion for resentencing.

Though Pollard was growing despondent, his support continued to gain ground in Israel. Netanyahu, now the former prime minister, met with him in the Butner correctional facility to reaffirm his support for release, and the Knesset sent a petition to President George W. Bush asking that he commute Pollard's sentence on humanitarian grounds. One hundred twelve of the Knesset's 120 members signed the petition.

Pollard's next step was to approach the federal court of appeals. A new chief judge, Thomas Hogan, was assigned to hear his motions. In September 2003 Pollard's attorneys argued their case for a new sentencing and access to the classified Weinberger memorandum. Pollard experienced yet another setback when Judge Hogan refused them access to the Weinberger memorandum—they hadn't proven a need to know—and denied him a hearing on resentencing. They immediately filed another motion with the court to hear their case for a "certificate of appealability," which, if successful, would permit the previous motions filed to be heard and ruled on again. Judge Johnson summarily rejected their appeal.

In June 2004 Pollard had his first major win when a two-judge panel ruled that his attorneys could argue an appeal of the lower court's decision not to reopen his case on sentencing and denying him access to classified information. The following March they presented oral arguments to a three-judge panel of the appeals court. The presiding judges were Judith Rogers, David Sentelle, and Karen Henderson, and Assistant U.S. Attorney Mary McCord presented the government's case. According to some reports, the judges appeared cool to Pollard's attorneys in their bid for a new sentencing and access to classified information. Whatever their feelings, the appellate court set no date for a final ruling.

On 8 May 2005, the Associated Press reported that Pollard had submitted a document to the Israeli Supreme Court in which he alleged that he had been tortured in jail. In one incident, he claimed, he had been stripped naked in a subzero cell and had ice water thrown on him. He was trying to force the Israeli government to declare him a "prisoner of Zion," a status that had been created for Jewish activists imprisoned in the Soviet Union in the 1970s and 1980s. Supposedly, Israel was legally bound to do everything in its power to get prisoners of Zion released from jail.

Ten days after the AP report appeared, First Lady Laura Bush was visiting the Western Wall in Jerusalem. In a moment of silence, protesters demonstrating for the release of Pollard began chanting, "Free Pollard! Free Pollard!" The Israeli police held them back as Secret Service agents surrounded the First Lady.

On 22 July, in a two-to-one decision, the U.S. Court of Appeals denied Pollard's appeal.

On 16 January 2006, the Supreme Court of Israel rejected Pollard's plea to be declared a "Prisoner of Zion."[23] Then, in February, Pollard's attorneys petitioned the United States Supreme Court to allow them access to former Secretary of Defense Casper Weinberger's TS/SCI damage assessment.[24] The attorneys contend that having access will prove that much of the "supposed repercussions" of his spying activities never really happened. They may try to prove that the classified information that Pollard gave to the Israelis was not damaging to the United States.

The week of 13 March 2006 Pollard's web site reported that: The Committee to Bring Jonathan Pollard Home had launched a massive media blitz throughout Israel, hanging up gigantic posters that featured Jonathan Pollard's picture and the text (in Hebrew), AYFOH HA'BOOSHA? (Where is the sense of shame?). Citizens were being encouraged to hang the posters and banners on their balconies and buildings that displayed a graphic icon of Pollard and the Hebrew text: ROTZIM ET POLLARD BABAYIT! (We want Pollard home!) The cost of launching this country-wide campaign and where the funds were coming from was not mentioned.

A week later, on 20 March 2006, the U.S. Supreme Court justices rejected Pollard's appeal to grant him access to classified documents in his sentencing file, among them the damage assessment memorandum by former Defense Secretary Casper Weinberger. Pollard hoped the documents would assist him in his pursuit of clemency from President Bush. The high court moved without comment to let stand a U.S. appeals court ruling that federal courts lack the jurisdiction to review claims of access to such materials in clemency petitions.[25]

On 28 March 2006 Rafael Eitan, leader of the Pensioners' Party, ran in the Israeli elections and won one of the seven seats his party captured in the parliament. It was reported that a small contingent of Pollard supporters charged into Eitan's headquarters and accused him of abandoning Pollard.[26]

It was the latest chapter in the dramatic, seemingly endless saga of Jonathan Jay Pollard's quest for freedom. Most spies, when jailed, fade into obscurity. Not Pollard. No convicted American spies—not even Ethel and Julius Rosenberg—have ever enjoyed as much support from the country they spied for as Pollard. And none has received as much publicity in his own country. Even when selling his nation's secrets—an activity that demands discretion above all—he drew attention to himself, and incarceration has done nothing to stop that. Today Jonathan Jay Pollard is right where he loves to be—not in jail, but in the spotlight.

Chapter 28

MORE SINNED AGAINST THAN SINNING?

T he arguments continue—was Jonathan Jay Pollard's life sentence just or unjust? The federal statute to which he pleaded guilty falls under the criminal espionage laws of the United States. According to Title 18, section (794) (c), a person is in violation of this statute if he or she,

> with intent or reason to believe that it is to be used to the injury of the United States or to the advantage of a foreign nation, communicates, delivers, or transmits, or attempts to communicate, deliver, or transmit, to any foreign government, or to any faction, or party or military or naval force within a foreign country, . . . or to any representative, officer, agent, employee, subject, or citizen thereof, either directly or indirectly, any document, writing, code book, signal book, sketch, photograph, photographic negative, blueprint, plan, map, model, note, instrument, appliance, or information relating to the national defense, shall be punished by death or by imprisonment for any term of years or for life. . . .

Note that the statute speaks of a foreign nation; nowhere does it provide an exception for an ally.

There was a time when the intelligence community and the Justice Department considered it more advantageous to plea-bargain with a spy and assess the extent of classified information compromised than to go to court and risk the disclosure of yet more secrets. In some cases charges were dropped altogether. In fact, between 1966 and 1975, the U.S. government undertook no espionage prosecutions at all. Then, during Gerald Ford's administration, Attorney General Griffin Bell permitted spies to be tried in court because he believed one could do so without compromising state secrets.

The rationale for Pollard's claim that his sentence is unjust is that, before and after his sentencing, others who spied for allies—and in some cases even for the Soviet Union—received lesser sentences. Because he spied for a close ally, he believes a lenient sentence is justified.

In a brief to the court in 1987, when he was filing a motion to reduce his sentence, Pollard mentioned certain spies who had received lighter sentences.[1] One was Samuel L. Morison, grandson of the renowned naval historian Samuel E. Morison. In 1984, when he was working as an intelligence analyst at the NISC, Morison mailed three satellite photographs to the British publication *Jane's Defence Weekly*. All three documents were classified secret and showed a nuclear-propelled Soviet aircraft carrier under construction. Morison cut off the classification designation from the photographs' borders before sending them. A search of his apartment in Crofton, Maryland, turned up several hundred other documents, both classified and unclassified. Morison was charged with espionage as a lesson to those who would leak classified information to the press. It was the first case of its kind tried under the 1917 Espionage Act, which prohibits anyone with access to U.S. military classified information from disclosing it to an unauthorized person. Morison was sentenced to a two-year prison term.

Another spy mentioned in Pollard's brief was William H. Bell, who worked for Hughes Aircraft Corporation and provided classified information to a Polish intelligence officer, Marian Zacharski, in 1981. The information, none of it classified higher than secret, dealt with "quiet radar," which enabled a tank to direct its radar without alerting the target. The FBI quietly arrested Bell and he cooperated in an effort to entrap his handler. Once the agency had accumulated enough evidence to arrest Zacharski, he was tried and convicted and received a life sentence. Bell, charged under lesser offenses, pleaded guilty and was sentenced to eight years in prison.

Stephen Baba, a navy ensign, was arrested for attempting to sell a document on electronic warfare and two microfilm indexes of key code words to the South African embassy in 1981. None of the material was classified higher than secret. In a strange twist of fate, the South African government returned the three unsolicited documents to American officials, along with a twelve-page letter Baba had written expressing how desperate he was for money. Baba was convicted by court-martial and sentenced to eight years in prison.

Sharon M. Scranage, an operations support assistant for the CIA, was stationed in Ghana, Africa. She and her boyfriend were charged in 1985 with turning over classified information, including the identities of CIA agents and informants, to Ghanaian intelligence officials. The information she provided was not classified higher than secret. She received five years, a sentence that was later reduced to two.

These cases differed from Pollard's in two critical respects. In none was the defendant charged under Title 18, section 794, for delivering national defense information to aid a foreign government, and in none were the charges such that sentencing guidelines mandated a life sentence.

In his brief Pollard also reviewed cases in which the spies had received more severe sentences, but they still could not be given a life sentence. In the mid-1980s Nicholay Ogorodnikova and his wife, Svetlana, both KGB agents, emigrated to the United States. Svetlana was recruited to work for the FBI as an informant on the Russian community in the Los Angeles area. An FBI agent became intimately involved with her. When he retired, Svetlana was turned over to FBI agent Richard Miller, who in turn had an affair with her. She recruited Miller to spy for the Soviets—a tangled web and an extremely embarrassing situation for the bureau. Only one document that Svetlana received from Miller was passed to the KGB. A long investigation resulted in the Soviet couple's arrest and conviction. Nicholay received eight years, Svetlana eighteen in a plea agreement in which she agreed to testify against Miller. After two trials Miller, the first FBI agent ever arrested for espionage, received a twenty-year sentence.

Then there was Ludwig Forbrich, who made an attempt to deliver classified information to the East German government during the Cold War. As often happens in the lives of would-be spies looking for quick money, Forbrich's luck ran out before his plan came to fruition. The FBI caught on to his scheme in 1984, and an undercover agent—posing as an East German intelligence officer—arranged a clandestine meeting with

Forbrich. No sooner had Forbrich turned over a single secret document to the agent than he was arrested. Charged with attempted espionage, he received fifteen years.

David H. Barnett, a CIA agent, betrayed the identities of thirty CIA agents and, for $92,000, sold to the KGB details of a CIA operation against the Soviets. Arrested in October 1980, he was sentenced to eighteen years.

These cases were also unlike Pollard's in several key respects. In none did the defendant alert coconspirators to the existence of an investigation, allowing them to escape. In none was classified information destroyed or federal investigators misled. In none did the information carry a TS or SCI designation.

Over the years, Pollard has cited still more cases in his effort to prove that his sentence was unjust. In 1986 Michael H. Allen, a retired navy chief petty officer who was working as a photocopy clerk at the Naval Air Station in Cubi Point, Philippines, was arrested by the NIS on suspicion of espionage. He admitted to providing classified information to unauthorized Philippine officials—a handful of documents, mostly confidential, none classified higher than secret. Secretary of the Navy John Lehman ordered Allen back to active duty and he was convicted by court-martial. He received a sentence of eight years, was fined $10,000, and had to forfeit his military retirement benefits.

Robert E. Cordrey was a private in the U.S. Marine Corps. In April 1984 he began to make phone calls to foreign embassies on the criteria-country list in an attempt to sell classified materials dealing with nuclear, chemical, and biological warfare. Cordrey finally made contact with an intelligence agent from Czechoslovakia. He showed the agent a list of the documents he could obtain, all unclassified, and was told he would be contacted later. The NIS and the FBI caught on to his scheme. After his arrest and conviction by court-martial, he received twelve years of hard labor for eighteen counts of failing to report contacts with citizens of Communist countries. Because of a pretrial plea agreement with the military, his sentence was reduced to two years.

Lieutenant Commander Michael Stephen Schwartz, USN, was charged with passing classified materials to Saudi naval officers between November 1992 and September 1994 while assigned to a military training mission in Riyadh during the Gulf War. Schwartz was responsible for ensuring the

Saudi government received both classified and unclassified intelligence, but not until after it had been cleared by the Department of Defense. He chose not to wait for clearance before supplying his counterparts with information designated confidential/no-foreign dissemination and secret/no-foreign dissemination. The documents included military intelligence digests, intelligence advisories, and tactical intelligence summaries. An NCIS investigation concluded that everything Schwartz turned over to the Saudis was releasable information, and the original four counts of espionage were dropped. Schwartz claimed he was trying to support Saudi Arabia in its effort to cooperate with the U.S. military. There is no indication he received money for the documents passed. For minor infractions such as "failure to follow orders," the military allowed him to plead guilty to administrative charges in 1995. He received an "other-than-honorable" discharge and forfeited his retirement pay and other military benefits.

In 1991 Albert Sombolay, a native of Zaire, attempted to spy for Iraq and Jordan while serving in the U.S. Army during Operation Desert Storm. Sombolay contacted the Iraqi and Jordanian embassies to volunteer his services. He passed information on troop readiness to the Jordanians and promised them more information on U.S. equipment and positions. He provided the Jordanians with chemical warfare clothing, boots, gloves, and decontamination equipment. He received $1,300 for his services. Sentenced by court-martial in Germany, he received thirty-four years of hard labor for espionage and aiding the enemy.

Again, in none of these cases—some of which involve severe sentences—did the crimes even come close to Pollard's in terms of both the quantity of intelligence and the level of classification compromised.

In the end, it is not for me or for the public or for the investigators, prosecutors, and defense attorneys to decide what is just or unjust in the case of Jonathan Jay Pollard. It is up to the U.S. Federal Court of Appeals or the Supreme Court to make a final determination.

In doing so, the question of whether Pollard was motivated by ideology or greed will be irrelevant. All governments pay for information to keep spies on the hook. Federal parole and sentencing guidelines do not consider a spy's motive, or whether the recipient of intelligence is an ally or not. The question of anti-Semitism, of which there is no evidence, is also irrelevant. The only consideration in determining a sentence for espionage today is whether top secret material was delivered to a foreign government. If so, sentencing guidelines call for a punishment of thirty-five years to life (or death, if a person aids or abets the enemy in time of war).

Pollard was charged not with intent to injure the national security of the United States, but with aiding a foreign government. It was the highly sensitive nature of the information he compromised, and the staggering volume of that information, that determined his sentence, along with the fact that he failed to live up to the conditions of his plea agreement by speaking to a reporter without first obtaining approval from the DNI. Another probable consideration in determining his sentence was the danger that he might release highly classified information in the future. Pollard could still compromise TS/SCI materials he accessed twenty-one years earlier. To this day, when he receives visitors in Butner, an agent from the NSA is present to listen to his conversations to ensure classified information isn't compromised.

A big issue is whether the government broke Pollard's plea agreement in giving him his life sentence. Joseph diGenova and the Department of Justice strongly deny this; in fact, there are no closing arguments or motions in the court records in which the prosecutors recommended a life sentence for Pollard. The life sentence was decided by Judge Aubrey Robinson.

Moreover—and this is something few people realize—it was stated at the time he was sentenced to life imprisonment that Pollard would be eligible for parole after serving eight years and six months. Not one time, however, has he gone before the board to ask for a hearing. Presumably, this is because he considers himself innocent, and obtaining parole implies that he is guilty but free on good behavior. He now claims that if he does try for parole, it will either be denied him or his hearing will be delayed for another fifteen years.

I had the opportunity to speak on the phone with one of the Justice Department attorneys handling the motions for a reduction of sentence. He informed me that when Pollard was sentenced in March 1987, just before the sentencing guidelines were changed, there was an obscure rule that applied to individuals like Pollard sentenced to life and eligible for parole. Under that rule, if a person has spent thirty years in prison and maintained a good record, he *must* be paroled. Thus, on 21 November 2015, Pollard will automatically be released from prison.

Ironically, Pollard, not interested in parole, will fight tooth and nail for a resentencing hearing. No attorney in the world could fight harder for anyone than those he has working for him. His attorneys firmly believe that they will win him a hearing, and that they have at least a chance of getting Pollard out of jail. His decisions in the past have only hurt his chance of gaining freedom. First and foremost was the decision to alienate himself from his family. If he had stuck with the supporters who knew him best and loved him—his father, mother, and sister—he might be out of prison today. Other mistakes were his insistence that he receive official Israeli citizenship while in jail; failing to show true remorse for his deeds; bragging about how he had single-handedly saved the State of Israel; and insisting that Israel declare him an agent.

If and when he is released, he stands to make a lot of money. It is alleged that Israel doubles the salary yearly for Israeli spies caught and incarcerated on foreign soil. If Pollard's spy salary of $2,500 dollars a month plus the promised $30,000 annual bonus were doubled, he would earn approximately $3.6 million over thirty years. To my knowledge, no other spy in history, in jail or released from it, has been so handsomely rewarded.

On the subject of Jonathan Jay Pollard's fate, one big question hangs in the air: Why is he so adamant about getting clemency or a presidential pardon? For the sake of argument, let me present two hypothetical scenarios.

In the first, Pollard's attorneys win a ruling from the Supreme Court and get a hearing in front of a new judge, who orders his life sentence reduced to thirty years. Pollard has already served nearly twenty-one years. The judge releases him on parole for the remaining nine years, or he goes before the parole board and wins his release. He receives permission to serve out his parole in Israel. Once in Israel, Pollard begins to talk about all the TS/SCI information he removed, detailing its contents on the lecture circuit and to any media outlet that will listen to him. The U.S. government revokes his parole, but the Israelis refuse to turn him over to the United States because Israel has no extradition treaty with the United States and Pollard is now an Israeli citizen. He receives double his back pay and bonuses and lives out the rest of his life in luxury.

In the second, if he holds out for a commutation of sentence or a pardon from the president, and it is granted, it will mean a major victory for Pollard. He will still get all his money from Israel, and at the same time his crime of passing highly classified defense information to a foreign government will be forgiven. Rather than a spy with a tarnished record, he'll emerge from his ordeal a man more sinned against than sinning.

Perhaps this is the reason Pollard is willing to wait for the current or a future president who, for whatever political reason, will say, "Enough, it's time for a pardon." When and if that time ever comes, it will send a loud message to the world: It's okay to disclose national security secrets of the United States as long as they are given to an ally.

The former convict would revel in that outcome. Why? Because it would imply that he, Jonathan Jay Pollard, was right and everybody else was wrong.

EPILOGUE

T he navy's decision not to fire Pollard in 1980 was a fatal lapse
that resulted in untold damage to U.S. security. But it was not
the only failure, and when viewed with the benefit of hindsight,
it is certainly not the most shocking

When Rear Admiral John Butts, USN (Ret.), told me that in
January 1982, as commander of the NIC, he most certainly did not
authorize or restore Pollard's TS/SCI clearance, I was floored. His
account contradicted the report of the JAG investigation. According
to Butts, he decided that Pollard could retain his *secret* clearance only.
His work would have to be monitored, and eventually, *if* he kept up
his work, he could be reinstated and briefed back into SCI programs.[1]

Hoping to get to the bottom of the matter, I went straight to Rear
Admiral William Horn, USN (Ret.), who from 1982 to 1986 was the
Department of the Navy's special security officer and Chief of the
Security Division in the Naval Intelligence Command. In a discussion
of SCI waivers, Admiral Horn informed me that the DNI and the
commander of NIC could give SCI waivers. During his tenure, however,
there had been no case of anyone gaining instant SCI access without a
prior background investigation—that is, no "blind" waivers. The late
Earl Fleischman, then in charge of the NIC's personnel security branch,
kept Pollard's security file containing the notes on this issue in a special
cabinet in the adjudications branch, not in the personnel folder at
Pollard's command. During the NIS and FBI investigation, Horn saw the
file. In it was paperwork stating that special security officer Captain Mike
McCutcheon, reacting to Pollard's intensifying threats to sue the navy,
strongly recommended against restoring his clearance. Horn also saw
correspondence from McCutcheon addressed to Pollard's command, in

response to repeated requests for a renewed clearance, stating that he wasn't eligible. Horn said this file was probably destroyed during an office move to centralize the navy's personnel security adjudications.[2]

According to Horn, after several personal appeals from the commanding officer of the NISC, Captain Chauncey Hoffman, Admiral Butts phoned Fleischman and directed him to restore Pollard's SCI access because Hoffman had promised to limit his access within the NISC to the merchant shipping branch, where he couldn't do any damage. The merchant shipping branch had no TS/SCI material. Pollard would be working with information classified no higher than secret, a clearance he already held.

Did Butts actually restore Pollard's SCI clearance? Perhaps the confusion over this question can be explained by the admiral's belief that Pollard's command wouldn't allow him to work with SCI material until he proved himself, at which point he could be "read in" to SCI programs. This meant he had to listen to a short briefing for each separate SCI program and sign a non-disclosure waiver. This mandatory procedure never transpired.

In any event, Fleischman passed the word to restore Pollard's SCI clearance to the Suitland Federal Complex Consolidated Security Office, but not before writing a memo for the record stating that he had been personally instructed by phone to do so.

In reviewing Pollard's file, Horn was surprised to learn that, although the analyst had regained his SCI access (at least on paper, in Fleischman's memo) and been given an access badge, he had never regained his TS clearance. A directive issued by the director of central intelligence authorizes certain high-level officials to give SCI clearances verbally, not for permanent access but only for short-term necessity, as in times of war or during special operations. Horn cited some U.S. Navy and Marine Corps personnel whose SCI clearances had been expedited quickly, but each of these individuals had already emerged intact from background investigations and possessed TS clearances, making them eligible to be read in to SCI. Regulations mandated that, with or without a waiver, a TS certificate *had* to be issued before someone could be authorized for SCI clearance, and the candidate had to pass a special background investigation before either clearance came through.[3]

According to the records, the matter of Pollard's TS/SCI clearance was closed when his temporary access to SCI was removed in August 1980. After this date, the analyst was not entered into the official navy records of people with SCI clearances. Nonetheless, and despite being told repeatedly by Captain Mike McCutcheon as well as special security officer Captain Earl DeWispelaere that he wasn't eligible for an SCI clearance, Pollard manipulated his way through the system and managed to obtain one. At the time there was a maxim that summed up the responsibility of the special security officer in authorizing SCI clearances: When in doubt, deny. In Pollard's case, the special security officers heeded this advice. It was the NIC commander who possibly ignored it, using his authority to overrule them.

Pollard's clearance came in January 1982, but again, it was on paper only. The stark fact is that from January 1982 until his arrest in November 1985, Pollard had still not passed a special background investigation, he had no TS or official SCI clearance, and he was not read back into SCI programs. The series of missteps boggles the mind. No other spy in history has been able to operate as freely as Jonathan Jay Pollard, who, like a child gone wild in a candy store, not only secretly removed page after page of his nation's most highly classified documents but also did so with flimsy—indeed, nonexistent—credentials. Through sheer persistence, Pollard managed to shatter the glass security wall erected to protect the nation, and in so doing, he caused more harm to national security than anyone else engaged in espionage in recent memory—even the infamous figures arrested during the decade of the spy.

This never-ending story of the notorious navy analyst should serve as a constant reminder to those entrusted with America's secrets of the danger of bending rather than following the rules. When in doubt, deny. Ultimately, the only safeguard the nation has against those bent on acquiring its secrets is the person who, through attentiveness, knowledge, education, and a firm grasp of the threat from within, knows to report suspicious behavior or security violations when "something just isn't right."

APPENDIX

THE NAVY SHORES UP SECURITY

E very time a new espionage case is uncovered there is a knee-jerk reaction, with various government agencies scrambling to implement changes to prevent a recurrence. This was certainly true of the Department of the Navy in the wake of the Jonathan Jay Pollard fiasco. Fortunately, this time the changes actually strengthened security.

No one could have been more upset and angry over the NIS's old system for storing information about double agents than Lanny McCullah, the assistant director for counterintelligence when Pollard was working at the ATAC. After Pollard's arrest, McCullah immediately ordered the NIS's file card system for former sources to be corrected. The changes were entered into the Department of Defense's computerized Defense Central Index of Investigations (DCII). From that time forward, whenever anyone conducted a background check on the DCII, the name in question popped up.

The DCII was the military equivalent of the FBI's National Crime Information Center, used by both federal and local law enforcement agencies to obtain information about arrests, convictions, and wanted persons. When a military agency checking the DCII received a hit on an individual involved in special operations, for example, the text response might read, "For further information, please contact the Naval Investigative Service, Code 22B." A subsequent contact with the NIS wouldn't provide detailed information, but it would indicate that the subject of the search had been involved in a counterintelligence matter. This new procedure was an immense improvement in screening against potential or actual spies. Had it been in place when Pollard applied for a job with the NIS, it would have snagged him.

Additional measures were taken to improve personnel screening. The day after Pollard's sentencing, navy commands received the report that Captain Laurence Schuetz wrote up after single-handedly conducting the JAG's administrative investigation, a monumental eighteen-month task that involved close to one hundred interviews. In the report, Schuetz submitted a list of recommendations and asked for comments from senior navy officers.

The first recommendation was that no disciplinary or administrative action be taken against most of the individuals identified in the JAG report. "No single error, omission, or lapse of judgment" on their part "allowed Mr. Pollard to commit espionage," Schuetz wrote. He pointed out that most personnel who had erred were fulfilling their responsibilities in a manner consistent at the time with tradition and usage. Schuetz recommended that only two officers and a civilian receive letters of censure, which wasn't approved by higher command. As a result, no one was held accountable for mistakes.

Schuetz also recommended that the director of the CIA be asked to "respond truthfully to interagency requests regarding personnel data of a derogatory nature."[1] The Department of the Navy addressed the problem with the CIA, which has agreed to share this type of information during background checks on personnel requiring a TS/SCI clearance.

Another recommendation was for the NIS to brief prospective commanding officers of all navy commands regarding past or present investigations, operations, or collection efforts that could affect those commands.[2] Schuetz pointed out that the NIS had provided a counterintelligence assessment of Pollard resulting in his loss of clearance, then four years later hired him to work in the ATAC with an SCI clearance. "A sustained, pragmatic effort is needed throughout the Department of the Navy to counteract the pervasive tendency toward information loss," Schuetz commented. "The turnover of both military and civilian personnel at most, if not all, navy commands ashore results in a short and often flawed corporate memory."[3] It was almost impossible to address the danger that a high turnover poses to intelligence security.

He also recommended that a "foundation of empirically sound research" be established to vet candidates for security clearances. The DIS had a terrible backlog of background checks, sometimes a year or more. In an effort to catch up, personnel doing the checks often missed or overlooked information, and the result was that many people who didn't have a need to know obtained TS/SCI clearances. Slowly but surely, Schuetz's recommendation was implemented.

He also suggested that the NIS open an investigation into TF 168 and their relationship with Pollard, the statements they made to investigators about this relationship, and whether they had adhered to Department of Defense directives regarding files on human intelligence sources. Schuetz came down hard on the task force, openly accusing them of withholding records and initially refusing to comply with his requests. He cited possible violations, including making false statements and destroying files without authorization. TF 168 denied they had withheld information. No investigation was opened; TF 168 was later disbanded.

Things changed quickly after 8 September 1987, when Admiral L. A. Edney, the vice chief of naval operations, sent a letter following up on Schuetz's recommendations. The navy was going to do everything it could to stop another Pollard from slipping through the cracks. In part, his letter stated that commands had to be briefed on all NIS operations, investigations, and collection operations involving any naval command. Authorizing security clearances became the responsibility of the Department of the Navy's newly established Central Adjudication Facility (DONCAF), and at the direction of the secretary of the navy, clearances were reduced by a third. When personnel lost their SCI access, the adjudication facility now had to be notified immediately.

Now a single organization, and not individual commands, was responsible for making decisions about security clearances. The only exceptions were the NIC, the DNI, and part of the Naval Security Group, which could grant access to personnel who needed to read SCI on a case-by-case basis. They still had to undergo a special background investigation for a top secret clearance first, and they still had to be indoctrinated into SCI programs by briefings and nondisclosure agreements. Authority to revoke SCI clearances, however, rested solely with the DONCAF. The facility established consistent standards that were applied throughout the Department of the Navy.[4]

In the immediate aftermath of the Pollard case, the ATAC implemented the following security steps:

- SCI materials were moved from individual analysts' files into a central repository.
- Courier cards were held by the watch and inventoried at each shift change. Unnecessary cards were revoked.
- Non–watch standers could work in the ATAC from six in the morning to six in the evening on weekdays. Variations of the schedule and overtime on weekends or holidays required management approval.
- ATAC personnel were required to submit to periodic and random counterintelligence polygraph examinations.
- Random "baggage" inspections were instituted for personnel entering and leaving the NIC-1 building. These were later made universal.

The Department of the Navy directed that new security manuals be written and new security procedures be put into place. An espionage hotline was launched, and a separate hotline was put in place for the chief of naval operations so that questions about security issues could be answered immediately. In the naval intelligence and cryptology communities, a "passive listening post" program was implemented whereby employees watched suspected security violators, but it was later abolished because of privacy act concerns.

Among the other factors that led to the breakdown of the security system, which assisted Pollard in his espionage activities, were:

- Providing a set of NIS credentials
- Permanent certification of his clearances to DIA, CIA, and NSA
- Allowing him to carry his ONI courier card at all times

- Unchallenged access to intelligence libraries and librarians (NISC and DIA)
- Analyst sharing attitudes
- Availability of unfettered access to copy machines in secure locations
- Failure to challenge, verify, and enforce the need-to-know rule
- Portal security personnel were lax, with or without a courier card
- Failure to report suspicious activity

Although in the wake of Jonathan Jay Pollard's arrest the Navy Department's reforms helped to bolster security, it should be noted that in reacting to intelligence violations a bureaucracy can go overboard. The last thing the government needs is a hundred additional procedures and directives to observe every time a spy is flushed out of hiding. The problem of enforcing security should be addressed not by adding more layers of bureaucracy to an overloaded system, but by motivating personnel to follow those practices already in place, and monitoring them. The biggest danger to security is a complacency and a failure to report on the part of those who observe colleagues nonchalantly committing major security violations or engaging in suspicious activity.

ACKNOWLEDGMENTS

Nearly five years ago I started writing the story of Jonathan Pollard's capture. As I talked about the project to people in different walks of life outside of government, I was surprised to find them fascinated by the crime of espionage, whether they knew much about the topic or not.

So began the slow, on and off—and at times aggravating and frustrating—process of writing this book. My family and friends supported my effort to tell this story. First and foremost among them is my best friend and loving wife, Gail. Her unwavering support and encouragement kept me moving forward. Making this book a reality would never have happened if not for her efforts, helping me tirelessly every step of the way.

When this book was nothing more than a lengthy essay about Pollard's arrest, I showed our good friend April Lane a draft copy. I can't thank her enough for helping me at that stage. Her comments and suggestions on the manuscript and her belief that this is an intriguing story worth telling were both valuable and encouraging. I also want to thank freelance editor Magon Kinzie, who took what had grown to be a voluminous draft manuscript and whittled away at it until it was ready for a publisher to review.

Gail then e-mailed a query letter to a handful of various publishers, and to my amazement, four of them were extremely interested. When Mark Gatlin, the editorial director of the Naval Institute Press, received that letter, he personally phoned me to say he had waited twenty years for someone to tell the real story about Pollard. Mark became my strongest professional advocate in making this book a reality, and for that I am extremely grateful. Mark and the staff of NIP—Press Director

Patricia Pascale, Managing Editor Linda O'Doughda, Creative Director Chris Onrubia, Marketing Director Inger Forland, Publicity Manager Susan Artigiani, and Editorial and Production Coordinator Jessica Schultheis—were all very supportive.

After NIP accepted the manuscript, they hired freelance editor Connie Buchanan to fine-tune it. She is one of the most professional and outstanding editors in the country. A modern-day Michaelangelo, she chiseled away at the hard stone pages to form the words into a smooth work of art called a book. I cannot thank her enough for her efforts.

I also want to thank the special agent corps and the support staff of the former Naval Investigative Service, known since 1992 as the Naval Criminal Investigative Service. With a mission of worldwide law enforcement, counterterrorism, and counterintelligence for the Department of the Navy, they are second to none, and I was proud to be a part of that agency. To the individuals mentioned in the book who gave me their time and input, I am deeply grateful. The deaths of NIS agent Lanny McCullah and FBI agent Nick Walsh saddened me, not least because they won't see on these pages an acknowledgment of the part they played in this investigation.

I have special thanks to give to my immediate family. To my son, James Matthew, and my daughter, Shannon Rae, for their love and support. To my stepchildren, Stephanie Mariotti and Thomas Corda, for their encouragement. To my sisters, Loraine Grix, Dolores Netzela, and Marian Dobyns, and their husbands, Art, Bill, and Tony, respectively, who passed before their time. To my sister Shirley and her husband, Bob Eckardt, especially, for reading a draft manuscript and offering sound advice. To my parents-in-law, Thomas and Eunice Howard, and sister-in-law, Glenda Burton, who steadily supported my efforts.

I also want to express my gratitude to those who gave me suggestions as I polished the manuscript. Many thanks to my sister-in-law and brother-in-law Rhonda and Fred Wagner, who have always provided encouragement and moral support; Nancy Morgan, an avid reader and Gail's close friend; and attorney David Geneson, the former assistant U.S. attorney who prosecuted the Pollards.

To my good friend Peter Burchert I owe many thanks for helping me to beef-up a presentation with graphics and photographs, or to fix my computer. He was always there for me at the eleventh hour when needed.

Finally, I thank God for my wonderful parents. Even though they passed on long ago, they are forever in my heart and my thoughts. They taught me moral values, respect for my elders and others, to do my best wherever life took me, and to be thankful for what we have. I learned from them never to take for granted America's freedom, because freedom isn't free; it comes with great personal sacrifice. I'll never forget when my father refused to sign the papers for me to join the U.S. Marine Corps until I finished high school. He also taught me to do the hard chores first and then tackle the easy ones. Because of my sensitive job, neither of my parents really knew what I did for the NIS, but I knew they were always proud of me. If not for their unconditional love, support, and sacrifices, I would not be who I am today.

NOTES

CHAPTER ONE. A DREAM COME TRUE

1. Freedom of Information Act (FOIA), Pollard's post-guilty plea NIS debriefing report, 23 July 1986, 90.
2. Government's Memorandum in Aid of Sentencing, date unreadable but believed filed in January 1987, 3–4. (SCI is principally data about sophisticated technical systems for collecting intelligence, as well as the intelligence product collected by the systems. Conventional intelligence activities employ human sources; SCI intelligence collection primarily employs technical systems. Because of the extremely fragile nature of SCI, compromise of a technical collection system is much like the loss of a network of agents.)
3. Pollard's post-guilty plea NIS debriefing report, 23 July 1986, 90.
4. Ibid.
5. Ibid.

CHAPTER TWO. POLLARD LAUNCHES HIS CAREER

1. Unclassified portion of the Navy Draft Damage Assessment, 5 May 1988, no longer available for review by author. It is referenced in an unclassified report of consistent theme in Pollard's Campaign for Commendation dated 14 July 1993, 40 prepared by the intelligence community.
2. FOIA request from the office of the Judge Advocate General (JAG). U.S. Navy JAG manual administrative investigation, 5 March 1987, 7, ¶ 4.
3. U.S. Navy JAG manual administrative investigation, 5 March 1987. Fourth endorsement to Captain Schuetz investigation, from Vice Chief of Naval Operations, Rear Admiral L. A. Edney, USN (Ret.), 6 April 1990, 44, ¶ 7.
4. Rear Admiral Thomas A. Brooks, USN (Ret.), interview by author, 26 August 2004.
5. Richard Haver, who led the damage assessment in the Pollard spy case, interviews by author, February 2001, June 2001, and September 2004; e-mail correspondence to author, 29 May 2001 and 29 September 2004.
6. U.S. Navy JAG manual administrative investigation, 5 March 1987, 7–8, ¶¶ 6–7.
7. Ibid., ¶ 10.
8. FOIA NIS results of interview debriefing report following Pollard's plea agreement, 24 July 1986, 36–37.
9. 1988 NIS Unclassified Briefing Report; former NCIS Assistant Director for Counterintelligence Special Agent (SA) Lanny McCullah (Ret.), interview by author, 5 July 2001.

10. Rear Admiral Sumner Shapiro, USN (Ret.), interview by author, 19 June 2001; e-mail message to author, 13 July 2004.
11. U.S. Navy JAG manual administrative investigation, 5 March 1987, 8, ¶ 11.
12. Shapiro, interview by author, 19 June 2001; e-mail correspondence to author, 13 July 2004.
13. U.S. Navy JAG manual administrative investigation, 5 March 1987, 8, ¶ 11.
14. Admiral Shapiro, interview by author, 19 June 2001; e-mail correspondence to author, 13 July 2004.
15. U.S. Navy JAG manual administrative investigation, 5 March 1987, 8, ¶ 12.
16. Ibid., 8–9, ¶¶ 13–15, and encl. 10.

CHAPTER THREE. THE DOUBLE-AGENT RUSE

1. U.S. Navy JAG manual administrative investigation, 5 March 1987, 9, ¶ 18.
2. Ibid., ¶ 20.
3. NIS SA Kenneth Anthony (Ret.), interview by author, 29 August 2003.
4. NIS SA Sherman Bliss (Ret.), e-mail correspondence to author, 30 September 2003.
5. U.S. Navy JAG manual administrative investigation, 5 March 1987, 10, ¶ 22.
6. Ibid., encl. 11; a Declaration of Cooperation volunteering to participate in a double agent operation, dated 23 July 1980, signed by Jonathan Jay Pollard.
7. NIS SA Milt Addison (Ret.), interview by author over the events of Pollard's polygraph, 30 August 2003.
8. Taken from Milt Addison's copy of his old counterintelligence security test question structure.
9. U.S. Navy JAG manual administrative investigation, 5 March 1987, 11, ¶ 29.
10. Addison, interview by author, 30 August 2003.
11. Rear Admiral Cathal "Irish" Flynn, USN (Ret.), telephone interview by author, 22 May 2002.
12. Dr. Neil Hibler, interview by author, 26 September 2001; e-mail correspondence to author, 1 September 2004.
13. U.S. Navy JAG manual administrative investigation, 5 March 1987, 11, ¶ 29.
14. Ibid., 11–12, ¶ 30.
15. Ibid., 11, ¶ 27; NIS SA Mike Barrett, telephone interview by author, March 2004.
16. Ibid., 12, ¶ 31, encl. 12.
17. Ibid., ¶ 33.

CHAPTER FOUR. POLLARD'S BATTLE WITH THE NAVY

1. Mark Shaw, *Miscarriage of Justice: The Jonathan Pollard Story* (New York: Paragon House, 2001), 76.
2. U.S. Navy JAG manual administrative investigation, 5 March 1987, 13, ¶ 42, encl. 15.
3. Ibid.
4. Ibid., ¶ 43, encl. 19. Memo from Commander, Naval Intelligence Command, to Pollard. Subject: "Employee Grievance," date stamped 16 March 1981.
5. U.S. Navy JAG manual administrative investigation, 5 March 1987, 26, ¶¶ 7–8.
6. Ibid., 15, encl. 21.

7. Ibid., ¶ 49, encl. 22. The abbreviations contained in the memo identify specific SCI code word programs. An individual must be briefed into these programs and sign an acknowledgment statement regarding non-disclosure to unauthorized personnel.
8. Ibid., 16, ¶ 51, encl. 24.
9. Ibid., 12, ¶ 36.
10. Ibid., 16, ¶ 53.
11. Ibid., ¶ 54, encl. 26.
12. Ibid., ¶ 56.
13. Ibid., ¶ 57, encl. 27.
14. Ibid., 17, ¶ 60.
15. Ibid., encl. 29.
16. Ibid., encl. 30; Shapiro, interview by author, 19 June 2001.
17. U.S. Navy JAG manual administrative investigation, 5 March 1987, 17, encl. 31.
18. Ibid., 18, ¶ 68.
19. Ibid., ¶ 69, encl. 32.
20. Ibid., ¶ 70, encl. 33.

CHAPTER FIVE. RED FLAGS

1. Commander David G. Muller Jr., USN (Ret.), telephone interview by author, 14 January 2005.
2. Captain Laurence Schuetz, USN (Ret.), interview of Pollard while Pollard was incarcerated awaiting sentencing, 7 November 1986; Schuetz, telephone conversation with author, 7 September 2004.
3. U.S. Navy JAG manual administrative investigation, 5 March 1987, briefly mentioned Pollard's money problems throughout the investigation. Following Pollard's arrest, criminal investigations and interviews of coworkers also contributed to learning of Pollard's financial problems. This information was also discovered based on post-arrest investigative interviews of the Borger Management Company rental supervisor who rented Pollard the apartment.
4. Uncovered during post-arrest criminal investigation; Muller, interview by author, 14 January 2005.
5. U.S. Navy JAG manual administrative investigation, 5 March 1987, 19, ¶ 82.
6. Ibid., 20, ¶ 84.
7. NIS SA Richard Sullivan (Ret.), interview by author, 12 March 2002.
8. U.S. Navy JAG manual administrative investigation, 5 March 1987, 20, ¶ 86.
9. Ibid., ¶ 87.

CHAPTER SIX. THE ISRAELI CONNECTION

1. Pollard identifies an Australian navy officer in his Second Memorandum in Aid of Sentencing, submitted on 2 March 1987, 31–32, two days before he was sentenced. Pollard's debriefing report dated 29 July 1986, 51.
2. Government's Memorandum in Aid of Sentencing Introduction, following Pollard's guilty plea, motion date unreadable but believed filed in January 1987, 39, 40.
3. Wolf Blitzer, *Territory of Lies* (New York: Harper & Row, 1989), 9. Wolf Blitzer, who apparently had access to Israeli intelligence files, was the chief Washington correspondent for the *Jerusalem Post*.

4. In an interview with Richard Haver, I asked him what his take was on Pollard's claim that he had actually attended an official U.S. government exchange with Israel about highly classified intelligence information. Haver informed me that Pollard was not high enough in the chain of command to be involved in such an exchange. Shapiro, the former DNI, also verified Haver's statement and explained the process, which involved only high-level government civilians and high-ranking military officers.

5. NIS debriefing report of Pollard following his guilty plea, 23 July 1986, 89, ¶ 11.

6. Ibid., 90.

7. Blitzer, 3, 7.

8. NIS debriefing report on Pollard, 23 July 1986, 86, ¶ 2.

9. Ibid.

10. Ibid., ¶ 3.

11. Government's Memorandum in Aid of Sentencing, introduction for Anne Pollard, filed 7 January 1987, 4, 5.

12. Government's Reply Memorandum in Aid of Sentencing, ref. Anne Pollard, filed 3 March 1987, 5.

13. Government's Memorandum in Aid of Sentencing, introduction for Anne Pollard, filed 7 January 1987, 5.

14. Anne Henderson Pollard's Memorandum in Aid of Sentencing, filed 26 February 1987, 34–39.

15. Government's Reply Memorandum in Aid of Sentencing, ref. Anne Pollard, filed 3 March 1987, 3–5.

CHAPTER SEVEN. THE POINT OF NO RETURN

1. Pollard's post-guilty plea NIS debriefing report, 23 July 1986, 91, ¶ 13.

2. Ibid.

3. Ibid.

4. Ibid.

5. Ibid., 92, ¶ 17.

6. Ibid., 92–93, ¶¶ 18–19.

7. Pollard's post-guilty plea NIS debriefing report, 29 July 1986, 40. The date was confirmed by credit card receipts during the post-arrest investigation.

8. Ibid.

9. U.S. Navy JAG manual administrative investigation, 5 March 1987, 20–21, ¶¶ 89–92, encl. 34, with sub-enclosures.

10. Ibid.

11. Ibid. Having a TS/SCI code word clearance is not a right given to government employees. It is a privilege extended only to those who need to know in order to perform their duties. To retain that privilege, a certain set of personal standards must be maintained. These standards are specifically addressed in a Director of Central Intelligence Directive (DCID) 6/4 on "Personal Security Standards and Procedures Governing Eligibility for access to SCI." It covers a wide range of issues from temporary access to SCI information to mandatory investigations whenever adverse or derogatory information is discovered or inconsistencies arise that could impact an individual's security status for SCI access. Thirteen separate guidelines are set forth from allegiance to the United States, drug

involvement, and financial considerations, to emotional, mental, and personality disorders, to security violations and misuse of technology systems.

12. Ibid., 21, ¶ 92.
13. Ibid., ¶ 105; Schuetz interview of Pollard, 7 November 1986.
14. U.S. Navy JAG manual administrative investigation, 5 March 1987, 22, ¶ 106.

CHAPTER EIGHT. A THIEF IN THE NIGHT

1. Pollard's post-guilty plea NIS debriefing report, 23 July 1986, 93, ¶ 21.
2. Ibid.
3. Government's Reply Memorandum in Aid of Sentencing for Anne Henderson Pollard, 3 March 1987, 12.
4. Pollard's post-guilty plea NIS debriefing report, 23 July 1986, 94, ¶ 21.
5. Ibid., ¶ 22.
6. Ibid., 94–95, ¶ 22. The RASIN manual is mentioned in many electronic sites; Seymour M. Hersh, "Annals of Espionage—The Traitor," *New Yorker*, 18 January 1999, 26.
7. Pollard's post-guilty plea NIS debriefing report, 24 July 1986, 30.
8. Ibid.
9. Ibid., 31.
10. Ibid., 32.
11. Ibid.
12. Ibid., 34.
13. Ibid., 32, 33.
14. Ibid., 33.
15. Post-arrest FBI and NIS inquiry on Van Ness apartment property tax documents. The Department of Justice conducted no investigation and did not bring any charges against the Israeli attorney.
16. Government Factual Proffer filed 4 January 1986, 6.
17. Government's Memorandum in Aid of Sentencing, 41, date unreadable but believed filed in January 1987.
18. Pollard's post-guilty plea NIS debriefing report, 24 July 1986, 34.

CHAPTER NINE. THE FALL GUY

1. This chapter is based on personal interviews with Kurt Lohbeck and what he recalled of his relationship with Pollard. The Taliban killed Abdul Haq in an ambush during the U.S. war against the Taliban and al-Qaeda following the terrorist attacks on September 11, 2001. To this day, Lohbeck considers Haq like a brother and has never gotten over his death.
2. Lohbeck, interviews by author, 8 and 11 December 2002. This incident was also reported in the book by Kurt Lohbeck, *Holy War, Unholy Victory* (Washington, D.C.: Regnery Gateway, 1993), 132.
3. Taken from the Lohbeck interviews by author, 8 and 11 December 2002, regarding the conversation Lohbeck had with his CBS boss as he recalled it. Lohbeck also mentions several other incidents in speaking with the author, which are in his book.
4. Lohbeck, 133; Lohbeck, interviews by author, 8 and 11 December 2002.
5. Pollard's post-guilty plea NIS debriefing report, 5 August 1986, 60.
6. Pollard's post-guilty plea debriefing report, 29 July 1986, 50.

7. Ibid.
8. Kurt Lohbeck, interviews by author, 8 and 11 December 2002, regarding his personal observations of Pollard's drug use. Pollard later admitted to drug use.
9. No charges were ever brought against Pollard for these unauthorized contacts in commercial arm sale ventures while he was employed with the U.S. Navy. It is unknown whether Pollard disclosed classified information to these embassies to win their favor, and, to my knowledge, the FBI pursued no investigation. Neither Pollard nor Anne were indicted, charged, or prosecuted for any crime involving these contacts. They were also never charged with any drug violations, nor were any drugs found, to my knowledge, based on later searches in their apartment. Lohbeck cooperated with the government via CBS attorney, and no indictment or charges were brought against Lohbeck.

CHAPTER TEN. THE TEN-YEAR PLAN
1. Pollard's post-guilty plea NIS debriefing report, 29 July 1986, 41.
2. Government's Memorandum in Aid of Sentencing, date unreadable but believed to have been filed in January 1987, 31.
3. Pollard's post-guilty plea NIS debriefing report, 29 July 1986, 41.
4. Ibid., 42.
5. Ibid., 43.
6. Ibid.
7. Ibid., 44.
8. Ibid.; during Pollard's arrest, NIS and FBI agents seized numerous pictures of Anne and Pollard. Some were taken while on their Israeli trip, and, if necessary, would be used in the trial. Copies of the unclassified photographs seized from the Pollards were used in briefing the espionage case.
9. Ibid.
10. Ibid., 45.
11. Government's Memorandum in Aid of Sentencing, date unreadable but believed filed in January 1987, 32.

CHAPTER ELEVEN. TALL TALES
1. McCullah, interview by author, 5 July 2001.
2. Flynn telephone interview by author, 22 May 2002.
3. Sullivan, interview by author, 12 March 2002; e-mail correspondence to author, 12 October 2005.

CHAPTER TWELVE. A SECRET TIP
1. Jerry Agee, interview by author, 17 June 2001; e-mail correspondence to author, 20 August 2001 and 18 September 2004; telephone interview of Pollard's coworker by author, August 2001 (interview was conducted in confidentiality, and the name of the interviewee is withheld by mutual agreement).
2. McCullah, interview by author, 5 July 2001.

CHAPTER THIRTEEN. THE WHEEL BEGINS TO TURN
1. Due to numerous years passing since 1985 and there being no written report on the meeting, McCullah and others have differing opinions about, or don't recall, everyone actually present at the meeting.

2. McCullah, interview by author, 5 July 2001.
3. NCIS SA Robert Cathcart (Ret.), e-mail correspondence to author, 30 September and 21 October 2003.
4. FOIA surveillance tape of Pollard's actions on 15 November 1985.

CHAPTER FOURTEEN. THE BEGINNING OF THE END

1. NCIS SA Lance Arnold (Ret.), mail correspondence to author, 10 February 2002; FOIA video surveillance tape.
2. FOIA surveillance tape of Pollard's actions on the afternoon of 18 November 1985.
3. Government's Reply Memorandum in Aid of Sentencing, ref. Anne Pollard, 3 March 1987, 8.

CHAPTER FIFTEEN. A TWIST OF FATE

1. Government's Memorandum in Aid of Sentencing, ref. Anne Pollard, 7 January 1987, 10.
2. Ibid., 11.
3. Ibid., 12.
4. Ibid.
5. Ibid., 13.
6. Double-agent operation "Sackett Land" was declassified by CIA and NIS in 2002. Renowned, true-story espionage author David Wise wrote a short article on this operation in *Gentlemen's Quarterly (GQ)* magazine in the November 2000 "Men of the Year" issue titled "Spy on a Tightrope," 314.
7. Government's Memorandum in Aid of Sentencing, ref. Anne Pollard, 7 January 1987, 13; like comments made in front of author and Pollard.
8. Grand jury testimony of FBI Agent Eugene Noltkamper, 27 November 1985, 21. The author personally recalls counting thirteen TS/SCI documents but does not remember the exact number of secret documents. Court records show somewhere around fifty-seven.

CHAPTER SEVENTEEN. THE CONFESSION

1. Author's recollection of events that took place on 19 November 1985. Rights form taken from a copy of the FOIA interview and interrogation form used to advise Pollard of his Miranda warning.
2. FBI SA Lydia Jechorek and author remain friends and keep in touch from time to time. She retired in 2003 only to find she just couldn't stay away from the street and "the chase." She returned to the FBI as a retired annuitant in 2004.
3. FOIA unclassified written statement and confession of Jonathan Jay Pollard, 19 November 1985.

CHAPTER EIGHTEEN. A FATAL BLUNDER

1. NCIS SA Richard Cloonan, e-mail correspondence with author, 12 March 2001.
2. FOIA interview statement from Pollard, 20 November 1985.
3. NIS SA John D'Avanzo (Ret.), interview by author, 21 August 2001.

CHAPTER NINETEEN. A SPY LEFT OUT IN THE COLD

1. NCIS SA Veronica "Ronnie" McCarthy, interview by author, 29 August 2003.
2. Pollard's post-guilty plea NIS debrief report, 24 July 1986, 36.
3. Michael Rolince, special agent in charge of counterterrorism at the FBI's Washington Field Office, interview by author, 17 June 2003. This interview referred to the events that occurred 21 November 1985.

CHAPTER TWENTY. UNREPENTANT

1. Information taken from interview of Pollard by the author and SA Jechorek, previous notes and recollection of events that transpired during the interview and in public court documents; Government's Memorandum in Aid of Sentencing for Pollard, January 1987, 13–14.
2. Retrieved from federal public court records in the case file of Jonathan Jay Pollard, 86-0207, District of Columbia pretrial services agency, 21 November 1985.

CHAPTER TWENTY-ONE. NO TIME TO LOSE

1. Memorandum in Support of Government's Motion for Pretrial Detention, 2 December 1985, 8–12.
2. Ibid., 10.
3. Ibid., 11.
4. NCIS SA Al Zane, e-mail correspondence with author, 5 October 2003; NCIS SA Ernie Simon, e-mail correspondence with author, 10 December 2003.

CHAPTER TWENTY-TWO. OPERATION FOUL PLAY

1. Lohbeck, interviews by author, 8 and 11 December 2002; Lohbeck, *Holy War, Unholy Victory*, 134.
2. John McCaslin, "Friends of accused spy for Israel remember 'brilliant' cocaine user," *Washington Times*, 27 November 1985.
3. U.S. Navy JAG manual administrative investigation, 5 March 1987, 18, ¶ 71, reference "Z" indicated interview conducted with Pollard by Schuetz on 7 November 1986; Captain Schuetz, telephone interview with author to discuss this interview with Pollard, 7 September 2004. Pollard's pretrial services agency interview at the D.C. jail showed Pollard indicated his drug use and emotional problems, 21 November 1985.
4. House Permanent Select Committee on Intelligence (HPSCI) Report 100-5, "United States Counterintelligence and Security Concerns—1986," 7; Ruth Marcus, "Exaggerations Marked Stories of Spy Suspect," *Washington Post*, 30 November 1985.
5. Pollards post-guilty plea NIS debriefing report, 23 July 1986, 92, ¶ 16.
6. Government's Memorandum in Aid of Sentencing for Pollard, date unreadable but believed to have been filed in January 1987, 17–21.

CHAPTER TWENTY-THREE. ISRAEL CONFRONTED

1. William Claiborne, "Israel Offers to Return Documents," *Washington Post*, 30 November 1985.
2. "Israel OKs questioning by U.S. in Pollard Case," *Washington Times*, 3 December 1985.
3. Agee, interview by author into what was going on behind the scenes during the trip to Israel, including the personal experiences and frustrations he went through during his trip, 17 June 2001.

4. FBI Agent Eugene Noltkamper (Ret.), telephone interview with author concerning his recollections of the events that transpired, 17 September 2004.
5. Ibid.
6. FBI Agent Joe Johnson (Ret.), telephone interview with author, 10 September 2004.
7. Agee, interview by author, 17 June 2001.

CHAPTER TWENTY-FOUR. GUILTY

1. Government's Opposition to Application for Review of Magistrate's Order Denying Bail, 6 December 1985, 7.
2. Court transcript of Pollard pleading guilty before the Honorable Aubrey E. Robinson Jr., Chief Judge, United States District Court, Courtroom 9, 4 June 1986, 7.
3. Letter from U.S. Attorney's office to Richard Hibey, 23 May 1986, 3. The entire letter speaks specifically to the actual plea agreement requirements of Pollard and the government; Government's Memorandum in Aid of Sentencing for Pollard, date unreadable but believed to have been filed in January 1987, 22–23.
4. Former NIS SA Elizabeth "Lisa" Redman, interview by author, 19 June 2001.
5. FBI SA Barry Colvert (Ret.), interview by author, 18 September 2001. Colvert was the Pollards' FBI polygraph examiner.
6. Ibid.; Jechorek, interview by author, 17 June 2003.
7. Pollard's post-guilty plea NIS debriefing report, 6 August 1986, 65.
8. Redman, interview by author in reference to the debriefing of Pollard, 19 June 2001.
9. Governments Reply to Defendant's Sentencing Memorandum of Jonathan Pollard delivered to defense 3 March 1987, filed with the court 25 March 1987, 24.
10. Ibid., 13, 14.
11. Wolf Blitzer, "Pollard: Not a Bumbler but Israel's Master Spy," *Washington Post*, 15 February 1987.
12. Colvert, interview by author, 18 September 2001.
13. CBS television news program *60 Minutes* aired on 1 March 1987, interview of Anne Henderson Pollard by world-renowned news commentary and investigative reporter Mike Wallace.
14. Joe Pichirallo, "Israelis May Lose Immunity," *Washington Post*, 11 June 1986.
15. Department of Justice attorney, John J. Dion, chief counterespionage section, telephone interview with author, 22 March 2006.

CHAPTER TWENTY-FIVE. THE DAMAGE

1. Haver, interview by author, February 2001.
2. Government's Memorandum in Aid of Sentencing, date unreadable but believed to have been filed in January 1987, 48–49.
3. Court Protective Order for Pollard's Defense Attorney, filed 24 October 1986, with attachments.
4. Redacted copy of the Declaration of the Secretary of Defense, which details the TS/SCI damage assessment, 19 January 2001, 4. Pages six through twenty-one of part one were deleted from the court documents along with numerous other pages.
5. Ibid., part two, Damage to the National Security, 28–29.
6. Ibid., part three, 44.

7. Supplemental Declaration of Casper W. Weinberger, Secretary of Defense, executed 3 March 1987.
8. Ibid.
9. Ibid.
10. Haver, interview by author, June 2001.
11. Government's Memorandum in Aid of Sentencing, date unreadable but believed to have been filed in January 1987, 48–49.
12. Steven Green, "Israel's 40-Year History of Espionage Against the United States," *Christian Science Monitor*, 22 May 1989 (also obtained via electronic sources).
13. Norman Polmar and Thomas B. Allen, *Spy Book: The Encyclopedia of Espionage* (New York: Random House, 1998), 333. The authors released a new edition early in 2005 (also obtained via electronic sources).

CHAPTER TWENTY-SIX. THE SENTENCING

1. Reply Memorandum in Support of Motion to Reduce Sentence, by defendant, 29 July 1987, introduction.
2. Government's Opposition to Motion to Reduce sentence, 13 July 1987, introduction.
3. Ibid., 9, with attachment; *Jerusalem Post Foreign Service* published a letter written by Pollard in the op-ed section. The letter was sent to a Dr. Julian Ungar-Sargon, a physician in Brookline, Massachusetts, who inquired about Pollard's health. The title of Pollard's article is "Reflections from a Jail Cell," written on 17 March 1987.
4. Government's Opposition to Motion to Reduce Sentence, 13 July 1987, 15.
5. Ibid., 13.
6. Ibid., 14.

CHAPTER TWENTY-SEVEN. THE AFTERMATH

1. Quotes taken from *60 Minutes* interview with correspondent Mike Wallace on 11 October 1988.
2. Congressional record submitted on 27 January 1988 and was entered into the Congressional Record on 19 October 1988.
3. Electronic media.
4. Jacob Wirtschafter, "Anne Pollard Receives Israeli Citizenship," *Jerusalem Post*, 17 September 1991.
5. Tia Goldenberg, "Anne Pollard demands $5M damages," *Jerusalem Post*, 23 May 2004.
6. Jim Wilkes, "Metro Woman Weds Spy in Secret Prison Ceremony," *Toronto Star*, 9 June 1994.
7. Letter dated 20 February 1992, addressed to the Honorable William Barr, Attorney General of U.S., written by Sheldon Rudoff (electronic media).
8. Reported by the *Jewish Press,* 3 April 1992 (also obtained via electronic media).
9. David Geneson, "Pollard Deserves to be in Prison," *Washington Post*, 13 December 1993.
10. Theodore B. Olson, "Clemency for Pollard," *Washington Post*, 20 December 1993.
11. Ruth Marcus, "Clinton Denies Clemency to Israeli Spy Pollard," *Washington Post*, 24 March 1994.

12. Shawn Cohen, "New Pollard Strategy Mystifies Family, Key Supporters," *Washington Jewish Week*, 25 August 1995 (also obtained via electronic sources). During this period of time in 1995, numerous newspapers in Israel, the United States, and other countries reported on the progress of Pollard's application for Israeli citizenship.

13. Gwen Ackerman, "Pollard Appeals to Israeli Court," *Jerusalem Post*, 30 April 1997 (also obtained via electronic media).

14. Douglas Waller, "Hunt for a Mole," *Time*, 19 May 1997.

15. Associated Press, "Israeli attorney resigns from 'Free Pollard' committee," 11 February 1998 (also obtained via electronic media).

16. Ronen Bergman and Arye Dayan, "I want to be your spy," *Ha'Aretz*, 24 April 1998. This article was translated into English from an unclassified Tel Aviv embassy quotation from the magazine and guide supplement.

17. Reuters, "Israelis concede: Pollard's our spy," *Washington Times*, 12 May 1998. Several papers all over the world reported this admission by the Israelis.

18. Ben Caspit, "Rafi Eitan Vows to Bring Pollard Home," *Ma'ariv*, 6 July 1998, electronic media.

19. *Arabic News.com,* "Wye Plantation Israeli demand threatened finished agreement," 23 October 1998.

20. Editorial, *Washington Post,* 12 December 1998.

21. Reuters, "Israeli Spy Blasts Netanyahu, Says He Riots in Jail," Washington Times, 25 October 1998.

22. Congressman Anthony Weiner, letter to U.S. Attorney Wilma Lewis, dated 29 November 2000, filed in U.S. District Court 12 December 2000.

23. Arutz Sheva, *Israeli National News.com* quoted *Jewish World*, "Supreme Court Rejects Pollard's Plea to be Prisoner of Zion," 16 January 2006 by Hillel Fendel.

24. Matthew E. Berger, "Pollard Appeals to High Court," *JTA Wire Service, National News*, 14 February 2006.

25. Guy Taylor, "Pollard Denied Access to Papers," *Washington Times*, 21 March 2006.

26. Brianna Ames, "Pensioners' Party Greets Unlikely Success with Retiring Humility," *Jerusalem Post*, 26 March 2006.

CHAPTER TWENTY-EIGHT. MORE SINNED AGAINST THAN SINNING?

1. The spies identified are taken from unclassified files and court records of the government's Opposition to Motion to Reduce the Sentence, filed 1 July 1987; the Department of Defense Security Service; the Defense Personnel Security Research Center; the Office of the National Counterintelligence Executive; public source documents of the Naval Criminal Investigative Service; Polmar and Allen; and public media and other unclassified research sources.

EPILOGUE

1. Rear Admiral John Butts, USN (Ret.), telephone interview with author, 26 August 2004.

2. Rear Admiral William Horn, USN (Ret.), e-mail correspondence with author, 10 August 2003, and 9 and 10 September 2004.

3. Ibid.

APPENDIX

1. U.S. Navy JAG manual administrative investigation, 5 March 1987, 28.

2. Ibid., 29.

3. Ibid., encl. 43.

4. Ibid.

INDEX

Note: *Italicized* page numbers indicate illustrations or photos. Page numbers followed by *n* refer to end notes.

ABOUT THE AUTHOR

Born and raised in St. Louis, Missouri, Ronald Olive spent thirty years in law enforcement, the last twenty-two with the Naval Criminal Investigative Service (NCIS).

As a special agent, he worked criminal and CI investigations, counter-espionage special operations, and terrorist issues overseas and in the United States; he also held senior management positions in the Washington, D.C. area. Mr. Olive was the primary architect of the first felony crimes major case response team, and he planned and implemented the first Systems Technology Protection Program for the Department of the Navy. During Desert Storm, he led a team of special agents into Italy and Crete on a Counter-Terrorist Surveillance Detection operation against threats posed by Saddam Hussein on Navy installations and personnel.

For these and many more accomplishments, Mr. Olive became the first recipient of the NCIS Counterintelligence Career Achievement Award. He holds a master's degree in Administration of Justice and now runs his own Consulting and Confidential Investigations Company near Phoenix, Arizona. Mr. Olive teaches for the Department of Energy Counterintelligence Training Academy and works with the National Center for Missing and Exploited Children, Team Adam—Missing Child Rapid Response System.